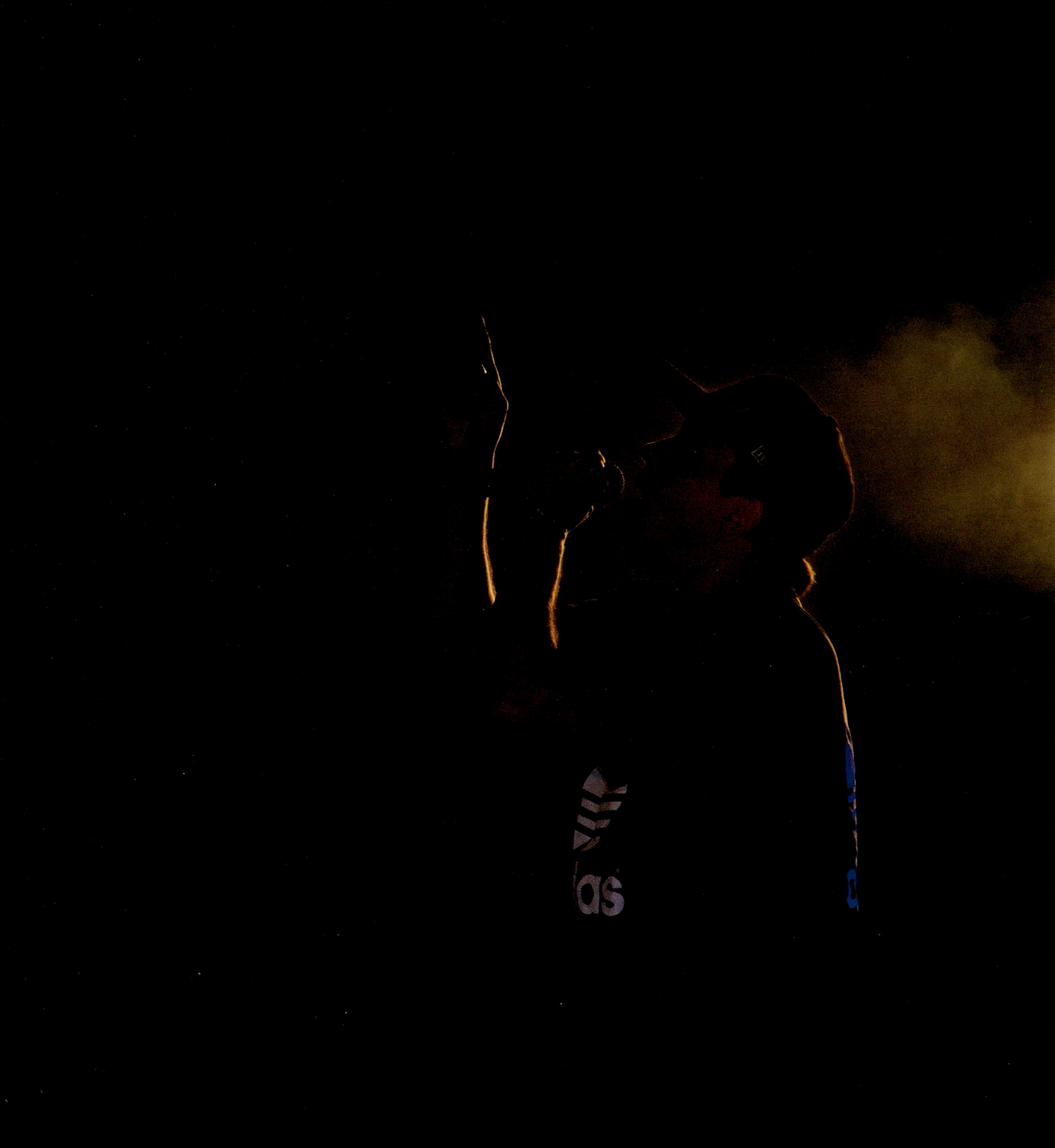

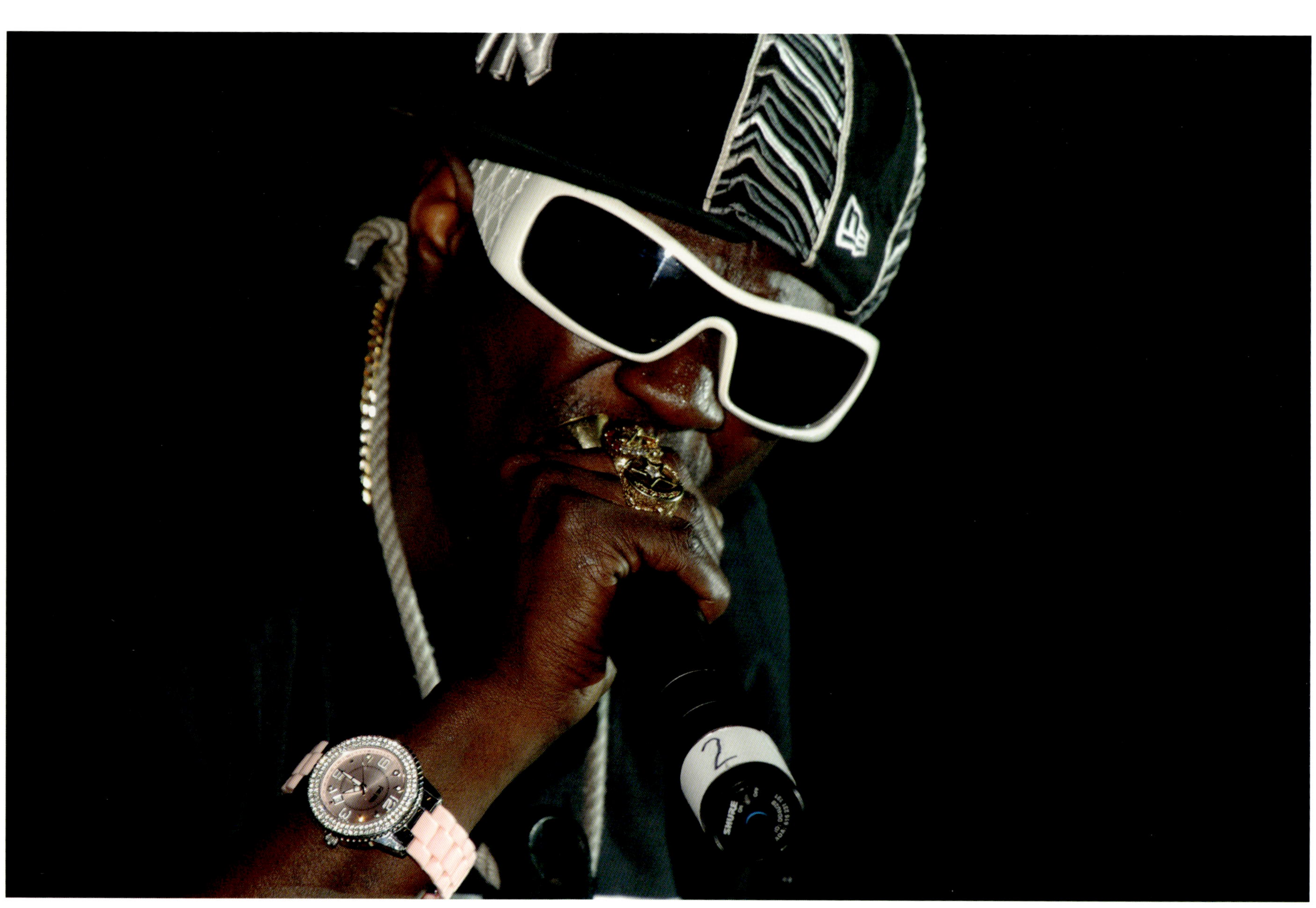

Portraits of an Urban Hymn

HIP HOP

PHOTOGRAPHS

DAVID SCHEINBAUM

WORDS

MICHAEL ERIC DYSON

FRANK H. GOODYEAR III

BRIAN HARDGROOVE

GAYE THERESA JOHNSON

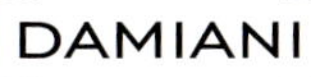

Life is precious, make every day count. If you have dreams, ambitions, goals, or wishes, do them. This book is dedicated to my family, Jon and Andra Russek and Zac Scheinbaum, who have enhanced my existence in *most* every way. And to Janet Russek, my partner in all my endeavors who has enhanced my existence in *every* way.

CONTENTS

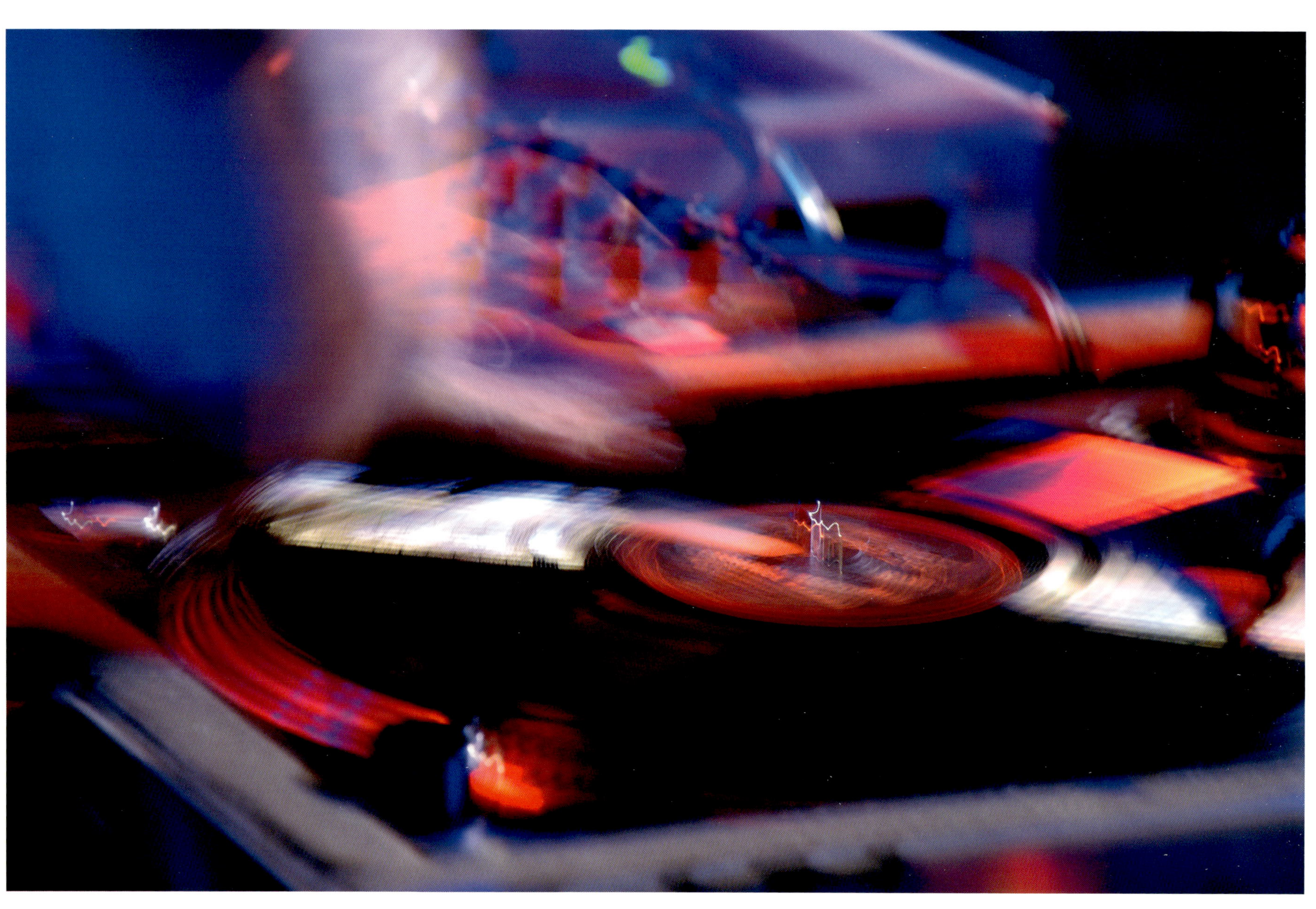

 Z-TRIP, 2007

It has inspired every generation since its birth

It unites the youth of enemy nations

It has the cultural impact likened to the world's most powerful religions

It is Hip Hop.

FOREWORD

As a witness to hip hop's early incarnations in the legendary music town of Hollis, NY, I was awed by the rise of this beautiful art form born of that ever-reliable mother called necessity. As a member of one of hip hop's most respected groups, I am equally in awe of the passion that artists from various disciplines have for this art form.

David Scheinbaum is one such artist. *Hip Hop: Portraits of an Urban Hymn* is the result of David's fourteen-year observation of the hip-hop phenomenon through the eyes of both history and the camera. The work compiled for this book is meant to help illustrate the positivity and political consciousness embodied in the work of the great majority of hip-hop artists, in addition to serving as a counterweight to the often-fearful misinformation that is sometimes attached to hip-hop culture via mainstream media.

Inspired by Roy DeCarava's work of Jazz photographs, *The Sound I Saw,* David's approach to the collected works in this book is of a collaborative nature. There are no celebrity photos here. These moments are captured with the permission and blessings of the subjects. As a performing artist, I know that every image committed to this book is a gift offered directly to you through the expert lens of David Scheinbaum.

—BRIAN HARDGROOVE

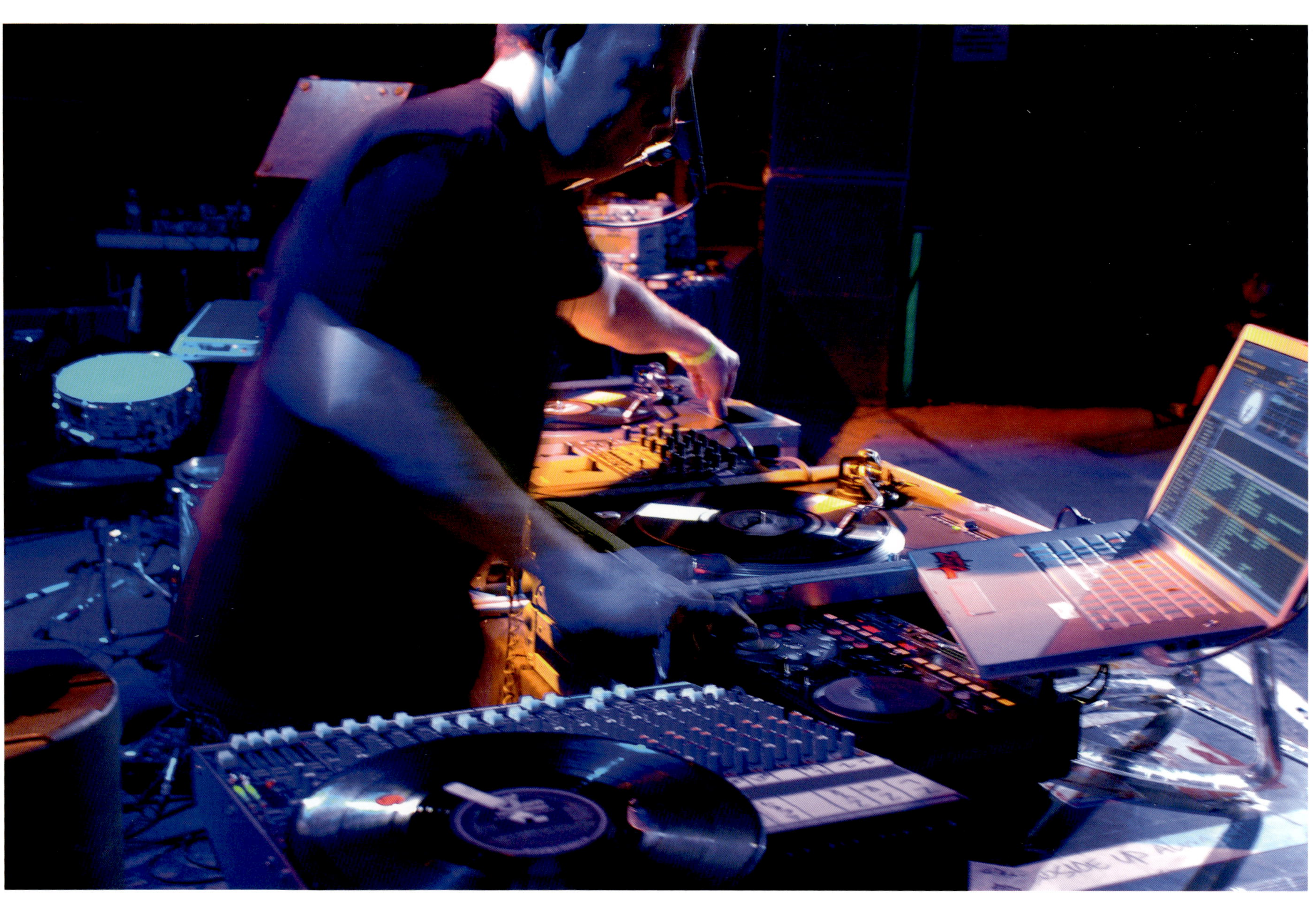

 Z-TRIP, 2007

WORD, WORDS, THE WORD

BY MICHAEL ERIC DYSON

Hip hop didn't invent the word, although one of its earliest benedictions radiates literary aspiration: Word. Some linguists argue that language burst on the human scene a hundred thousand years ago through a single chance mutation in one individual that spread like a verbal prairie fire to others in the breeding circle. Other linguists say that language evolved over long stretches of time and circumstance and emerged in Homo sapiens less than two hundred thousand years ago. If you believe biblical scribes, The Word stretches all the way back to God and the beginning of time and space and the universe. In the beginning was the word. In religious genealogy, then, grammar begets gravity, so to speak. Literally.

Neither did hip hop invent the beat; if it doesn't quite have the celestial bragging rights of speech, rhythm's origins are hardly less primitive, tucked inside our bodies where our hearts measure our existence one beat at a time. Blending word and beat as part of hip hop's own creation myth means that an art form that dates back just to the seventies connects to the creation myth of the universe itself.

Depending on how you view hip-hop culture, such a belief is heady, arrogant, or delusional, or a brazen remix of all three. From the start hip hop has been unwilling to settle for anything less than cosmic significance and global influence, even when it could barely make it from its Bronx bedroom to a train stop in Brooklyn, much less travel from Long Island to London. Hip hop's reach often exceeded its grasp, or else what's a cipher for? All of its bombast and outsize boasts seem to flow in the traffic between hood saviors and their divine inspiration in project flats that doubled as modern birthplaces for artistic gods.

If that comparison seems far too self-important and spiked with hyperbole, then consider this equally ambitious parallel: At least one holy book declares that God got his start on earth as the son of a single mother who got knocked up by someone out of the picture, leaving a brave man to step in and love the mother and raise the boy who would be delivered in harsh circumstances among the poor because the establishment barred them from comfortable birth.

Jesus meet Jay-Hova. Nazareth meet New York. Manger meet Marcy. Mother Mary meet Afeni Shakur. Swaddling clothes meet Underoos. Scripture meet scribbling in notepads. Missing years between adolescence and adulthood learning to bear the weight of the world as the messiah meet missing years between high school and rap career spent pushing weight before saving hip hop. Overturned tables in the temple meet the temple of hip hop and its turntables. Forty days in the wilderness meet no church in the wild. The list of such similarities could literally go on, if not ad infinitum, then at least ad nauseam.

Like sacred texts and the spiritual figures they reveal, the speech, rhythms, and representatives of hip hop battled mighty opposition to forge artistic triumph and commercial dominance. Hip hop has endured significant ridicule because the primary makers of its talk and beats are black. Black art has been relentlessly mocked as a hodgepodge of inferior form and puerile content. Thomas Jefferson savaged the artistic pedigree of black music; before him David Hume denied the existence of black arts at all. Black art was widely viewed as a black mark on what little humanity and intelligence black folk were said to possess.

The initial thorns in hip hop's flesh grew from the same bush-league criticism that has always dressed down black culture while its opposition is dressed up as highfalutin' theory or scientific analysis. It is chilling to recall, for instance, that the same society that in the name of science sponsored the Tuskegee experiment and allowed disease to spread in three hundred black men without treatment is the same society that tried to convince us that Tupac's meditations on black manhood were morally diseased. The Tuskegee experiment ended in 1972; 'Pac's life began in 1971. There is no relation between the two dates, except the relation forced on random events in history by human beings out to do harm or to relieve suffering through their words and actions. In a world where the Tuskegee experiment could exist to hurt black men, their sometime noble artistic defender Tupac had to be born.

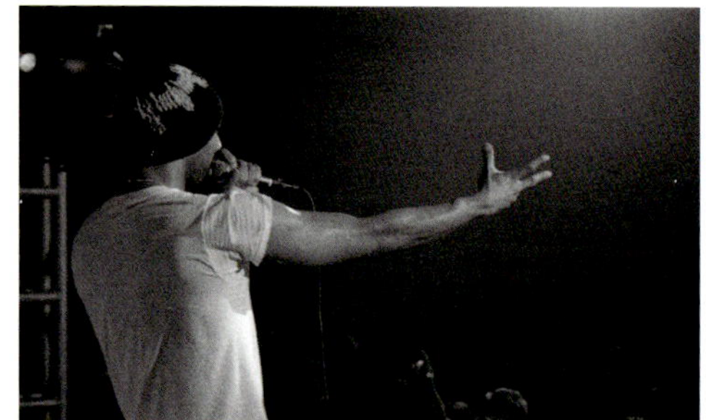

COMMON, 2003

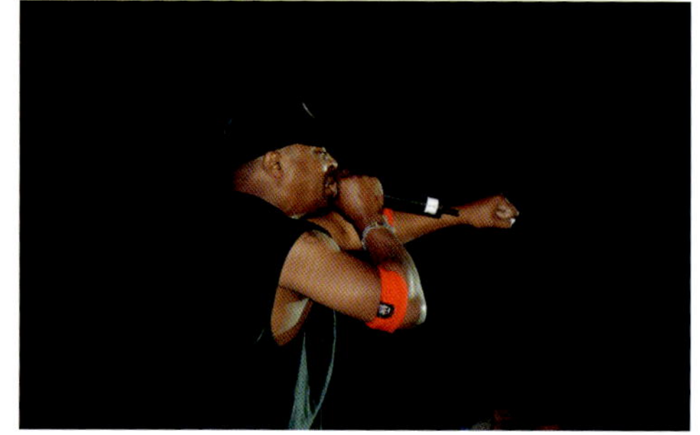

CHUCK D, PUBLIC ENEMY, 2007

That may be putting the proverbial sociological cart before the artistic horse. Hip hop has rarely had the freedom to just be, as Common allusively suggests in the title of one of his greatest albums, because it got dragged so quickly into political arguments about its right to exist, and because hip hop is widely viewed as the soundtrack to black pathology. Perhaps the condition of its emergence had something to do with how the shadow of politics has cloaked the roots and rise of hip-hop culture. The messiah in a manger metaphor aside, hip hop's birth is no less miraculous for taking place in crushing social, political, and racial conditions.

Hip hop got its start less than a decade after a defining and cataclysmic event: The death of Martin Luther King, Jr. King's death rocked our culture like few deaths ever have—Lincoln's death shook the nation, of course, and so did the death of the Kennedy brothers, but all of them were presidents or politicians who had the blessing of the state and the resources of government at their call. King magnetized the needle of America's moral compass as a private citizen and quite literally as a minster without portfolio. King challenged America's musty racial views through vibrant social struggle, and, like the hip hoppers who came after him, he moved the crowd through the power of his melodic speech.

King's death cast a pall of deep grief on black America and led many folk to question whether the nation was willing to genuinely support ideals of fairness and equality that it paid lip service to but steadily undercut. The racial miasma that triggered King's assassination briefly gave way to fleeting black empathy before hardening into white backlash. As the civil rights movement sputtered, the black power movement picked up steam to proclaim the beauty of blackness and the need for more aggressive resistance. On the cultural front the Black Arts Movement (BAM), sparked by the tragic death in 1965 of another seminal black leader, Malcolm X, had already begun to fight the power of white superiority by painting the canvas of history and aesthetics in bold black strokes.

By the time BAM reached its end in the mid-seventies, the battle against white resentment and, later, the fight over affirmative action would reenergize the civil rights movement. Together the waning black power movement and the revived civil rights movement flooded the ballot boxes of northern cities to elect black mayors in Newark and Detroit in the early seventies after successfully electing mayors in Cleveland and Gary, Indiana, in the year of King's death. The South and West got on board with black mayors in Atlanta and Los Angeles. At the same time black folk flexed their electoral muscles at the polls to sweep into office many more black members of congress.

If black folk gained on the political front, they continued to knock down barriers in television, film and radio, and in sports and entertainment as well. Bill Cosby and Diahann Carroll integrated the small screen while Sidney Poitier continued lighting up the big screen. And the original Foxy Brown—Pam Grier—torched the local Cineplex with her erotic charisma before Blaxploitation symbolically burned it down. The expansion of FM in the seventies garnered a bigger audience for black radio and its corps of spirited DJs. The ranks of major league baseball swelled with black players less than a quarter century after Jackie Robinson ended apartheid on the diamond. And black basketball players eclipsed white athletes in the NBA in the mid-seventies, but not before the New York Knickerbockers were derided as the New York "Niggerbockers." The NFL got a lot more color, too, paving the way for a league that today is nearly 70 percent black.

Motown and Philadelphia International Records bestrode the culture as recording colossuses, and R&B artists began to break free of commercial ghettos and cultural constraints. Marvin Gaye brought conscience to black pop with the groundbreaking *What's Going On?* a theme album meditating on war, spirituality, the ecology, God, and the salvation of children. Disco stars Donna Summer and Sylvester gave urgent voice to an art form that unapologetically traded on raucous female energy and gay bravura. Aretha Franklin amplified her sixties cries for respect at home and in society and returned to her spiritual roots with the landmark *Amazing Grace*. Stevie Wonder pled for universal love, cosmic enlightenment, social justice, and black equality on the monumental *Songs in the Key of Life*. And Michael Jackson released *Off the Wall* in 1979, a sonic harbinger of the eclecticism that made him the dominant musical artist of the 1980s and the greatest entertainer in the world.

In the same year, on September 16, a single dropped that forever changed the musical landscape: The Sugarhill Gang's "Rapper's Delight," the first hip-hop recording to popularize an art form that later won international acclaim. In the meantime, "rap"—the talking part of hip-hop culture—was largely viewed as a temporary musical trend that would eventually disappear like dolphin earrings and K-Swiss sneakers. But the music and the culture that supported it struck a nerve with youth in New York City and then around the country. For better and worse, males created hip hop and it is still a *testosterocentric* affair often booming with patriarchal ambitions. Hip-hop culture can therefore be heard and seen through four metonyms that relate the artist to the accoutrements used to craft his art: Man and mat, man and machine, man and marker, and man and microphone.

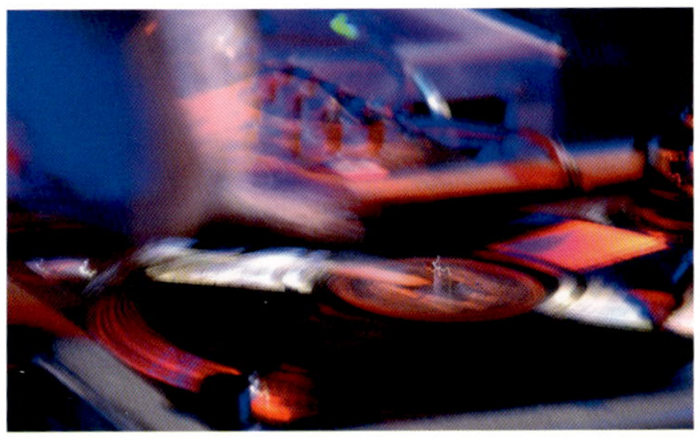

Z-TRIP, 2007

Man and mat—referring to the *break-dancer*—conjures the cardboard mats used by break-dancers on the streets to cushion their acrobatic moves as they spin on shoulders or heads in sync with the break beats isolated and looped on sound recordings. Man and machine—referring to the *DJ* and then the *producer*—summons images of the DJ's turntables that were central in the early sound of hip hop and, later, the machines used by hip hop's sonic architects to produce and perfect sound. Among the recent favorites are the Auto-Tune voice processor preferred by T-Pain and Lil Wayne and famously bashed by Jay Z on "D.O.A. (Death of Auto-Tune)." Of earlier vintage is the Roland TR-808 drum machine which, along with Auto-Tune, is used by Kanye West on his fourth studio album and even cited in the title of that searing reflection on love, loss, and loneliness, *808s & Heartbreak*—a seething musical stew of electronica, synthpop, R&B, electropop, and hip hop. Man and marker—referring to the *graffiti* artist—pictures the magic markers and other utensils employed by graffiti artists to scar the tissue of public space while inscribing their existence. And man and microphone—referring to the *rapper* or *MC*—symbolizes the sole possession necessary to project the voice and amplify the lyrical ambition of the rap artist to the world, as Nas immortally proclaimed in his classic "One Mic."

The MC is the heart of hip hop, the centripetal force that draws the varied elements of the culture to its rhetorical center. The MC's story is hip hop's story, and vice versa, since they came up together in the same hoods and either floundered or prospered under the same racial and economic forces. The MC has carried the symbolic weight of hip hop in his voice from the start as the art form rode the golden throats and silver tongues of its greatest artists all the way to platinum success. That success, however, is not the greatest measure of hip hop's achievement. The honor belongs to the genre's most gifted creators who obsess over the complicated lyrical content and complex rhythmic flows of hip hop at its best.

A few of hip hop's best MCs may sport gold teeth, but the bulk of rap's most talented artists surely weren't born with a silver spoon in their mouths. Their lives often tracked the evolution of the genre itself, which matured in the 1980s as budding MCs faced the cruel consequences of Ronald Reagan's voodoo economics, the alleged benefits of which never trickled down to working and poor people as advertised. Hip hop's original MCs often grappled with the low economic growth of the seventies and a vicious recession in the early eighties, high inflation and interest rates, energy crises, unforgivably high unemployment rates for black males, and the bottoming out of the manufacturing sector in an economy that brutally transitioned to a service industry where the high end excluded poor and undereducated people of color. The public school system was equally abysmal: Talented black students were steered toward vocational tracks while their white peers were overprepped for college. To make matters worse, budgets for visual art and musical training were ruthlessly slashed, hampering the musical and artistic prospects of black and brown youth for generations to come.

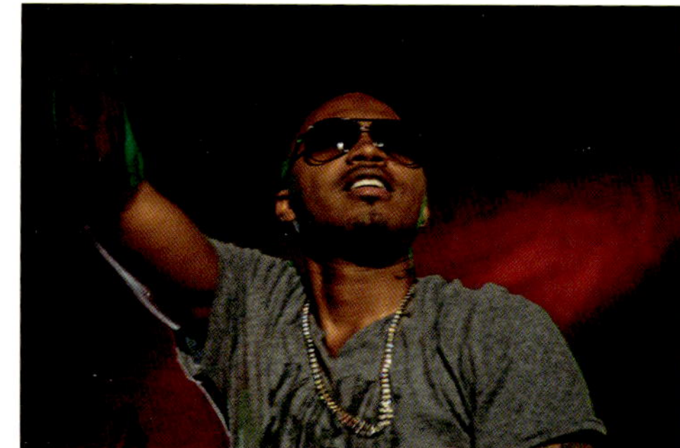

NAS, 2010

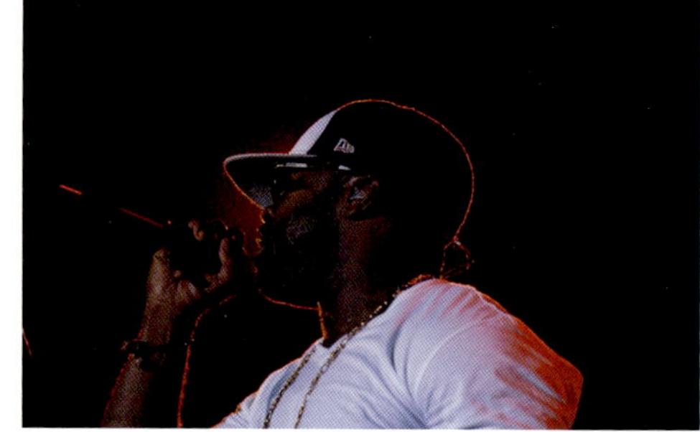

BLACK THOUGHT, THE ROOTS, 2008

It is no small wonder that black youth experimented with technology and literacy in creating an art form that has reclaimed poetry for common folk and opened the ears of the world to beautifully chaotic meters, spectacular cadences, and snaking rhythms. The argument about whether hip hop was even music raged for a spell, until the spell of hip hop became the rage of the world. The children of white snobs and black moralizers often made their parents' objections to hip hop obsolete with their discerning consumption and sophisticated analysis of rap music and the culture in which it was spawned.

The MC is the lightning rod and arbiter of hip hop's meaning in a world where lyrics matter so much that their creators are sometimes dragged before congressional committees and made to account for their menace to youth. MCs aren't alone in such ventures. Perhaps there's a fifth element, another metonym, that's gone unrecognized but which is crucial to hip hop's fortunes: Man and Mac—that is, the journalist, writer, and intellectual who uses his or her computer or notepad to critically engage a seminal art form. (Knowledge already unofficially exists as hip hop's fifth element alongside graffiti, break-dancing, DJing, and rapping, and can easily be absorbed in my proposed fifth metonym).

My own pilgrimage is an example, though my journey as a critic, scholar, journalist, and writer on hip hop surely isn't unique. My experience as a curious intellectual grappling with rap music is not unlike the struggle of many thinkers to define, defend, and deconstruct an artistic juggernaut that often barrels into the social and political arena. I began writing about rap music as a graduate student at Princeton University in the mid-eighties, publishing articles in magazines and journals that explored the history, politics, ethics, and aesthetics of rap. My first book, published in 1993, included several essays on hip-hop culture, and I've returned to the subject in my subsequent work, especially my critical estimation of the life and legacy of Tupac Shakur, my interview reflections on various elements of the culture, and my edited treatment of Nas's classic debut album, *Illmatic*. I've also taught college courses on hip-hop culture since the mid-nineties at the University of North Carolina at Chapel Hill, Columbia University, DePaul University, the University of Pennsylvania, and now at Georgetown University, where my course on Jay-Z drew national media interest and ire.

I've written about rap for the *New York Times*, discussed hip hop on countless television shows, including the *MacNeil/Lehrer NewsHour* on PBS and on HBO's *Real Time with Bill Maher*, and talked about rap on nearly every major radio show in the country. I've debated hip hop in lecture halls across America and, indeed, around the globe, most recently in London, where I was the advocate for hip hop in an international debate on the genre's virtues and vices that was broadcast on Google. And I've appeared before congress on three separate occasions to debate rap: Before the U.S. Senate in 1994 and again in 2000, and before the U.S. House of Representatives in 2007.

My senate testimony and vigorous exchange with Senator John McCain in 2000 was published in my book *Debating Race*. But my unpublished maiden voyage in congressional hearings before the senate in 1994 at the invitation of Senator Carol Moseley-Braun captures the stormy debate about hip hop at the height of the cultural resistance and political revulsion to rap music. The hearing took place before the Senate Subcommittee on Juvenile Justice, with the purpose, it was stated, of examining "the effects of violent and demeaning imagery in popular music on American youth."

I was called on to offer my analysis of rap music, along with figures like political activist C. Delores Tucker, who would gain her greatest fame for taking on the misogyny and obscenity in rap, and legendary entertainer Dionne Warwick, who, like Tucker, was appalled at the vicious portrayals of women in rap music. While I was respectful of Tucker and Warwick, I attempted to place hip-hop culture in its broader historical and political context without dismissing its troubling aspects, especially the gangsta rap of figures like Snoop Dogg, who had in particular sparked the outrage of Tucker and Warwick. I submitted a formal testimony, but my words that day flowed extemporaneously from my heart and head, and I ended by saying:

What we must not forget is that gangsta rappers represent a population that is among the most politically invisible, politically underrepresented, culturally maligned populations in American culture—young black males. How dare we [not] remember that . . . a culture that not a century and a half ago put black men on an auction block to sell them by describing them in the most crass, materialistic, consumerist . . . [fashion] . . . driven by an American desire to dominate black men's lives—[is] now hypocritically, less than a century and a half later . . . decry[ing] them for the very same . . . beliefs that it held . . . as precious principles of American culture. How dare we do that. We have to be more sensitive. We have to. . .[understand] that we cannot simply stigmatize the victims. We have to speak for them.

I might add, if we really want to get to the source of demonizing black women: Young black men don't have the power. This is why Senator Moseley-Braun ran for the senate, because it was a white-dominated male senate that had castigated black women's lives and made sure that the glass ceiling that was on their lives would turn into cement. This is the real enemy in American culture. Black bourgeois institutions, white male culture, and certain forms of gangsta rap all have certain things in common.

So as we expand the palate of colors from which we draw to paint upon the canvas of life the forces that we want to oppose, let us remember that gangsta rap is not simply an objective revelation or narration of the coming racial apocalypse. I don't believe in the moral neutrality of gangsta rap, as I don't believe in the moral neutrality of the senate, as I don't believe in the moral neutrality of the recording industry. All of us must be held responsible for the circulation of vicious, misogynistic, sexist and homophobic lyrics, ideas and ideologies. . . .

I would not dare come here and defend any attempt to, in any way, desecrate black women. But if we are honest about it, Senator Moseley-Braun, Stokely Carmichael, as part of the movement during the 1960s, said that the best position for a black woman [in the movement] was prone. Civil rights organizations were notoriously sexist. Highly trained black women were sent to work in civil rights organizations, and they were made carriers of coffee and pencil sharpeners. [Women, despite] . . . their extraordinary talent, were. . . . sexually objectified, and we know across this culture that women have been treated that way.

So what I argue . . . is that we must deal with an honest assessment of the conditions that lead to gangsta [rap]. If we listen to Snoop Doggy Dogg when he says, "Wake up, jumped out my bed/I'm in a two-man cell with my homie Lil' Half Dead/Murder was the case that they gave me/Dear God, I wonder can you save me"—what you have in Snoop Doggy Dogg is a [male with a] second-generation Mississippi drawl in the post-industrial collapse of L. A. trying to come to grips with . . . the transition from a stable life to one that has been undermined by forces of . . . economic immiseration and class division. Those are the real culprits here.

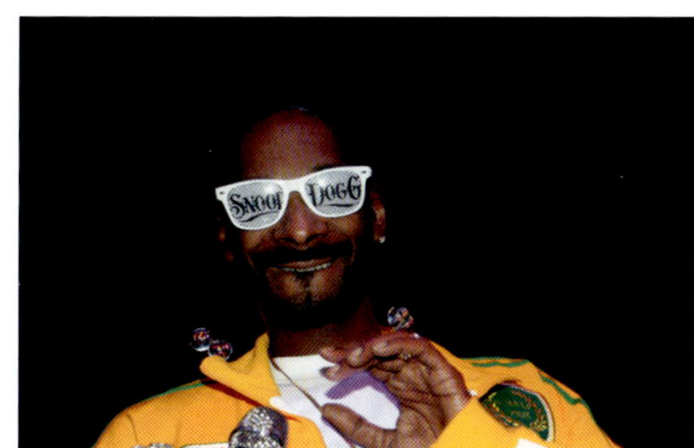

SNOOP DOGG (SNOOP LION), 2011

Although these words were spoken nearly twenty years ago, they communicate a raw passion about the defense of vulnerable black youth that burns in me to this day. The flaws of hip hop must be acknowledged and opposed; rap music's often-poisonous views of women and gays must be resisted. Rap music has too often twisted James Brown's patriarchal cry into a wretched paean to male supremacy and misogyny: "This is a man's world/But it wouldn't be nothin' if we couldn't diss a woman or a girl."

But the best of hip-hop culture looks beyond bigotry to embrace the heroic use of words and beats to cast light on the dark places of the black experience and the American soul. At their noblest hip-hop artists carry the weight of the black and poor in their speech and rhythms and exorcise demons as they encounter them in their own minds and in the world around them. It is in performance that rap's rhetorical royalty often massage the grief and encourage the ecstasy of their audiences and cast word spells over a transfixed constituency.

This is the world that David Scheinbaum captures with effortless brilliance and transcendent beauty. His images stick in the eye for their lean and muscular portrayals of bodies in motion, and for their voluptuous characterizations of mouths in movement. He catches speech the moment it spills from lips fixed around sentences that rush in staccato fury or fall back in asymmetrical repose. Scheinbaum's aesthetic voice and visual language speak through images that zing, blur, haze, identify, splatter, brush, clarify, and even coagulate like celluloid blood on fleshly surfaces. If renowned photographer Roy DeCarava famously shot the sound he saw when Coltrane blew his horn, then David Scheinbaum shoots the music he tastes when his eyes are hungry for poetic truth. If hip-hop artists are ghetto deities born to fly the artistic coop and soar to the musical heavens and back, then Scheinbaum is one of their most faithful chroniclers, recording their ascent and return one gesture, one image, at a time. To paraphrase the holy book: In the beginning was the word, and the word became flesh and spoke among us through pavement prophets. What they said is on record; how they looked when they said what they said is on record, too. Turn these pages and see.

 MASEO, DE LA SOUL, 2009

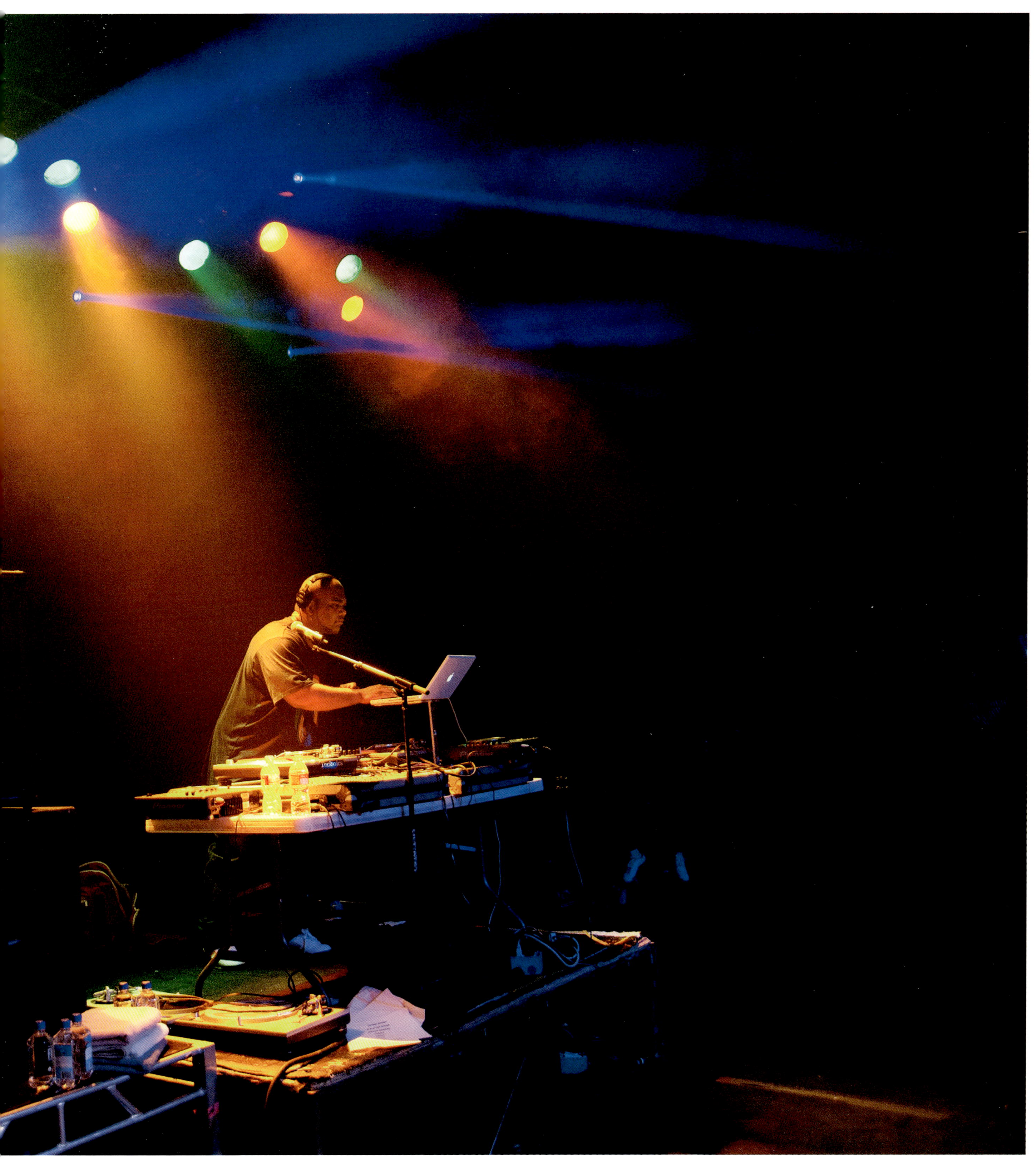

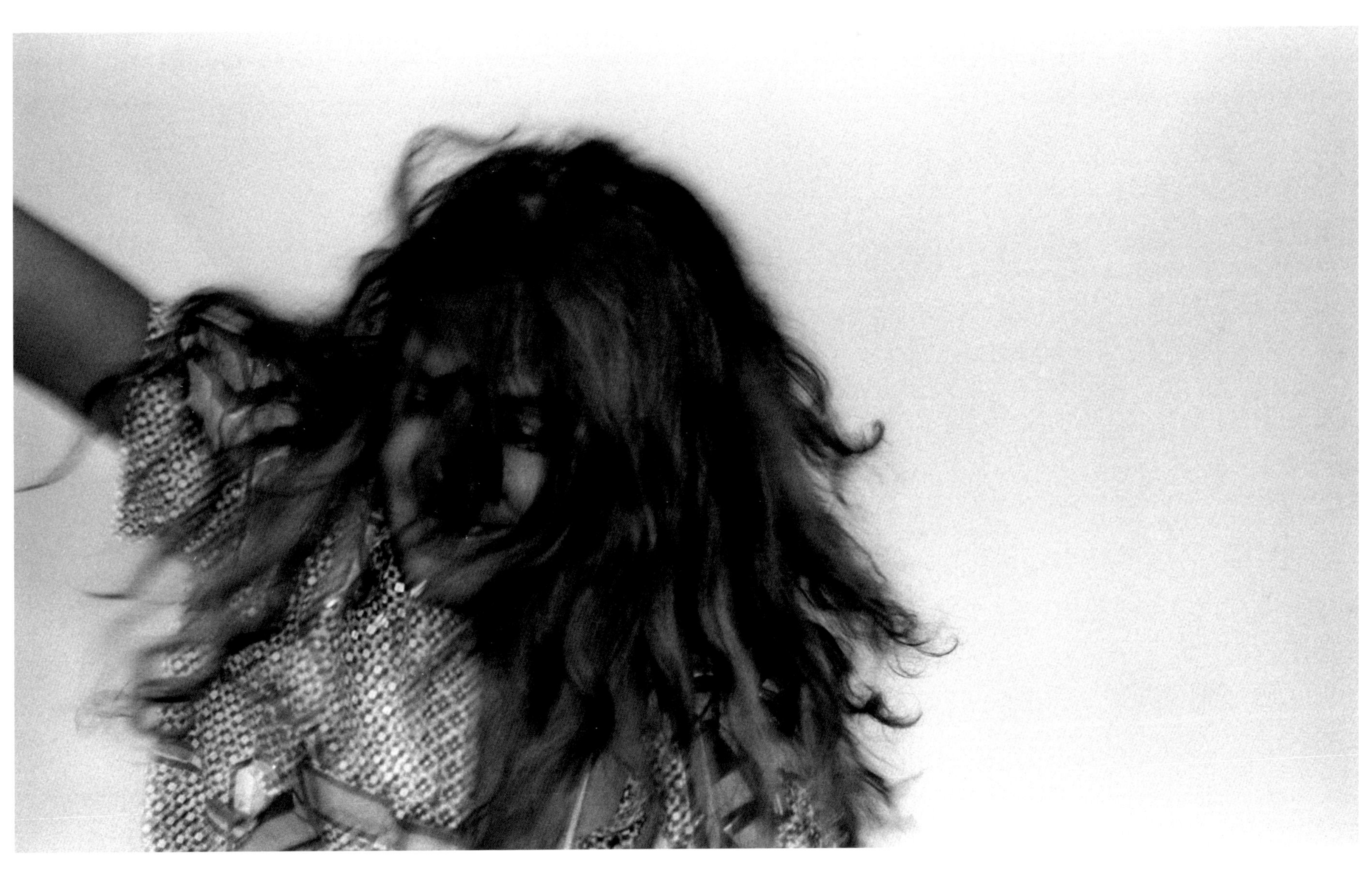

M.I.A., 2005

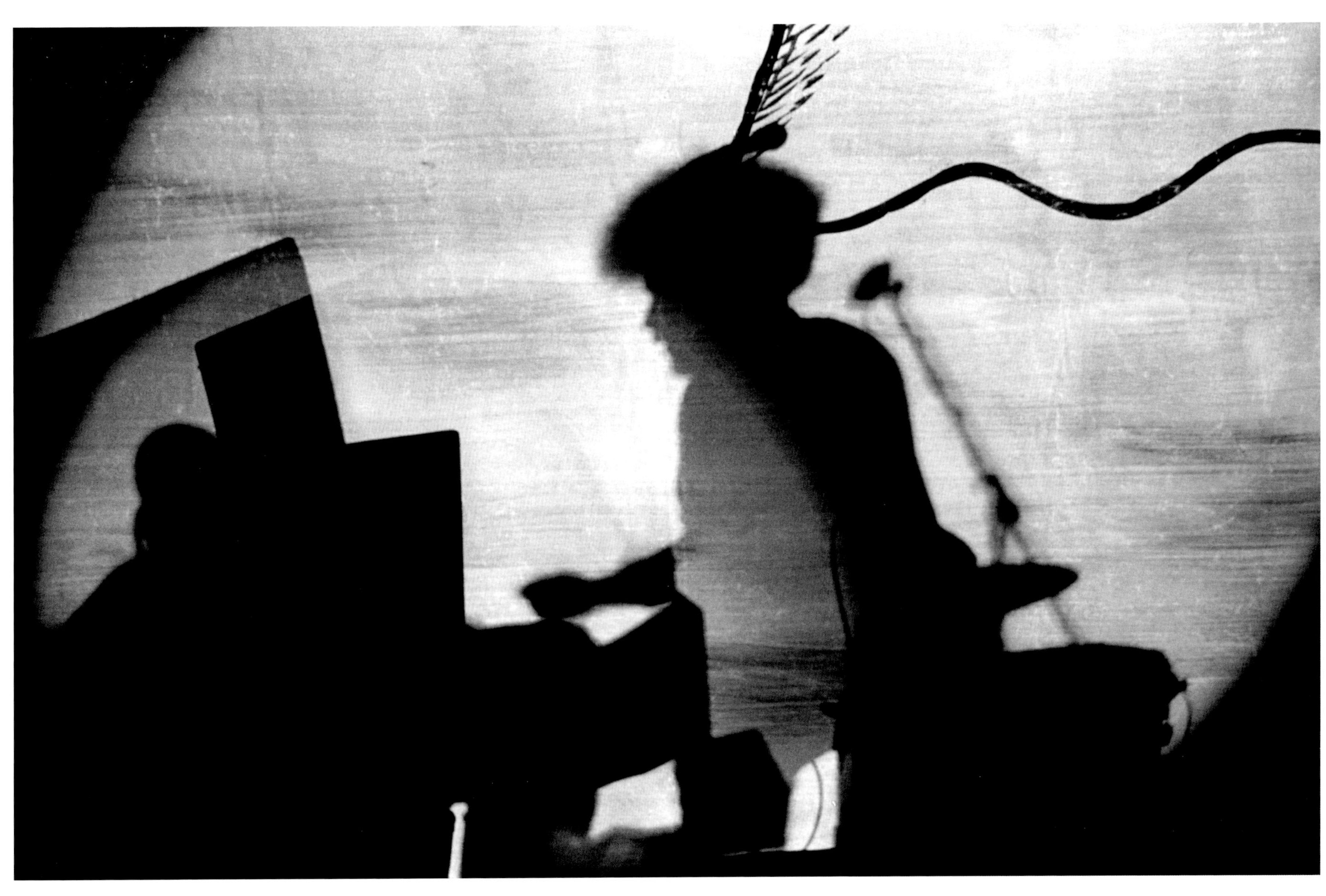

?UESTLOVE, THE ROOTS, 2003

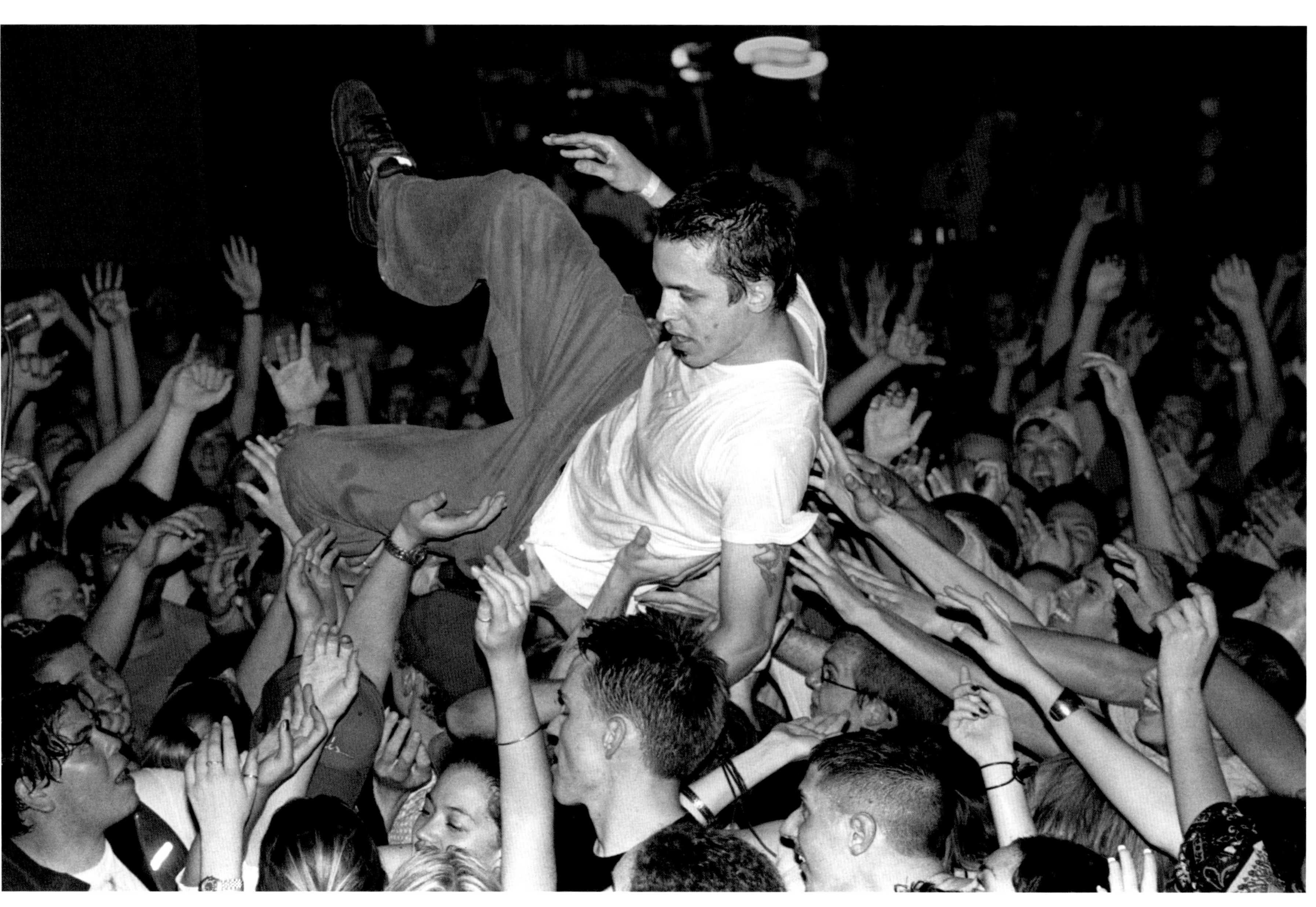

 SLUG, ATMOSPHERE, 2002

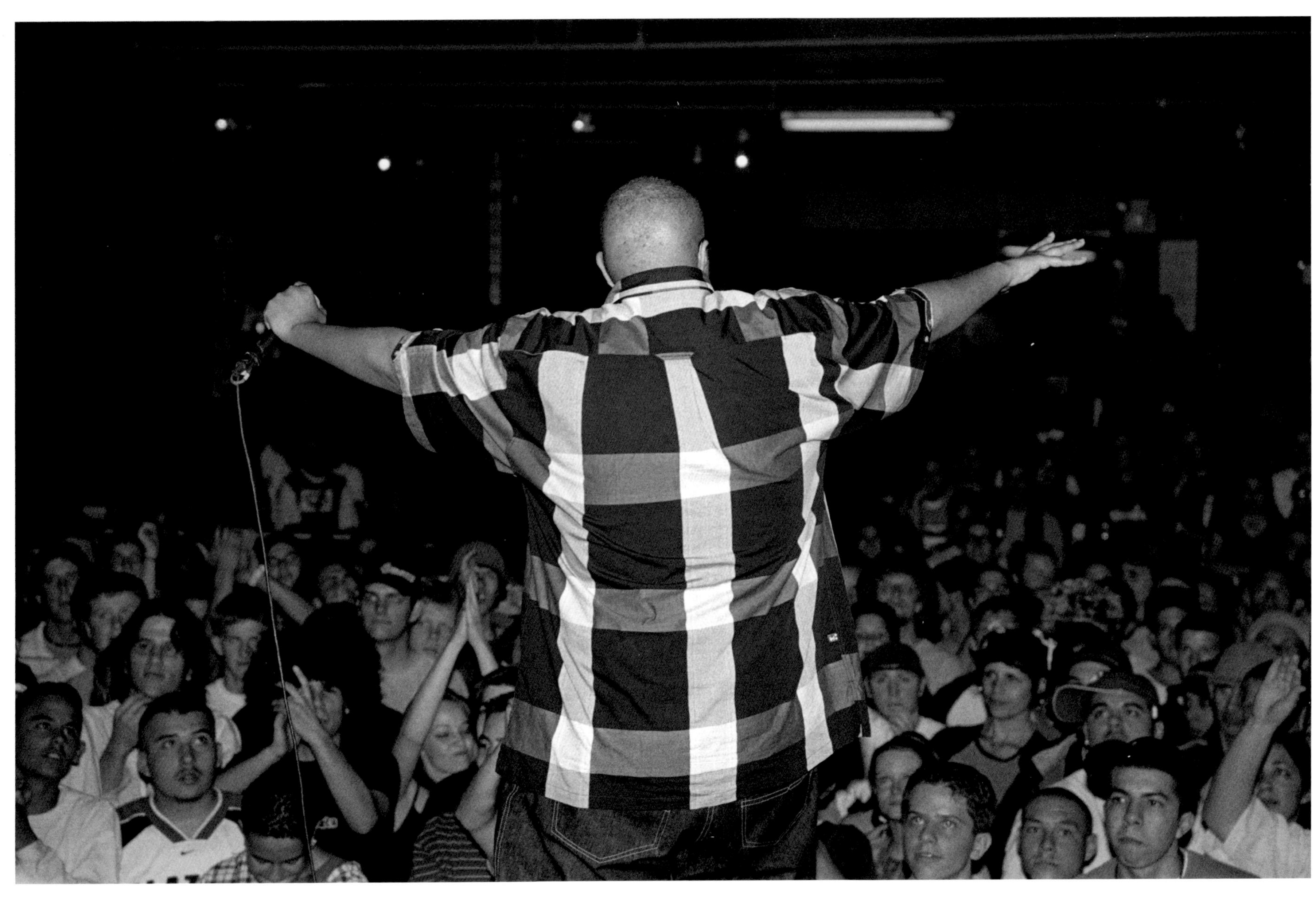

GIFT OF GAB, BLACKALICIOUS, 2005

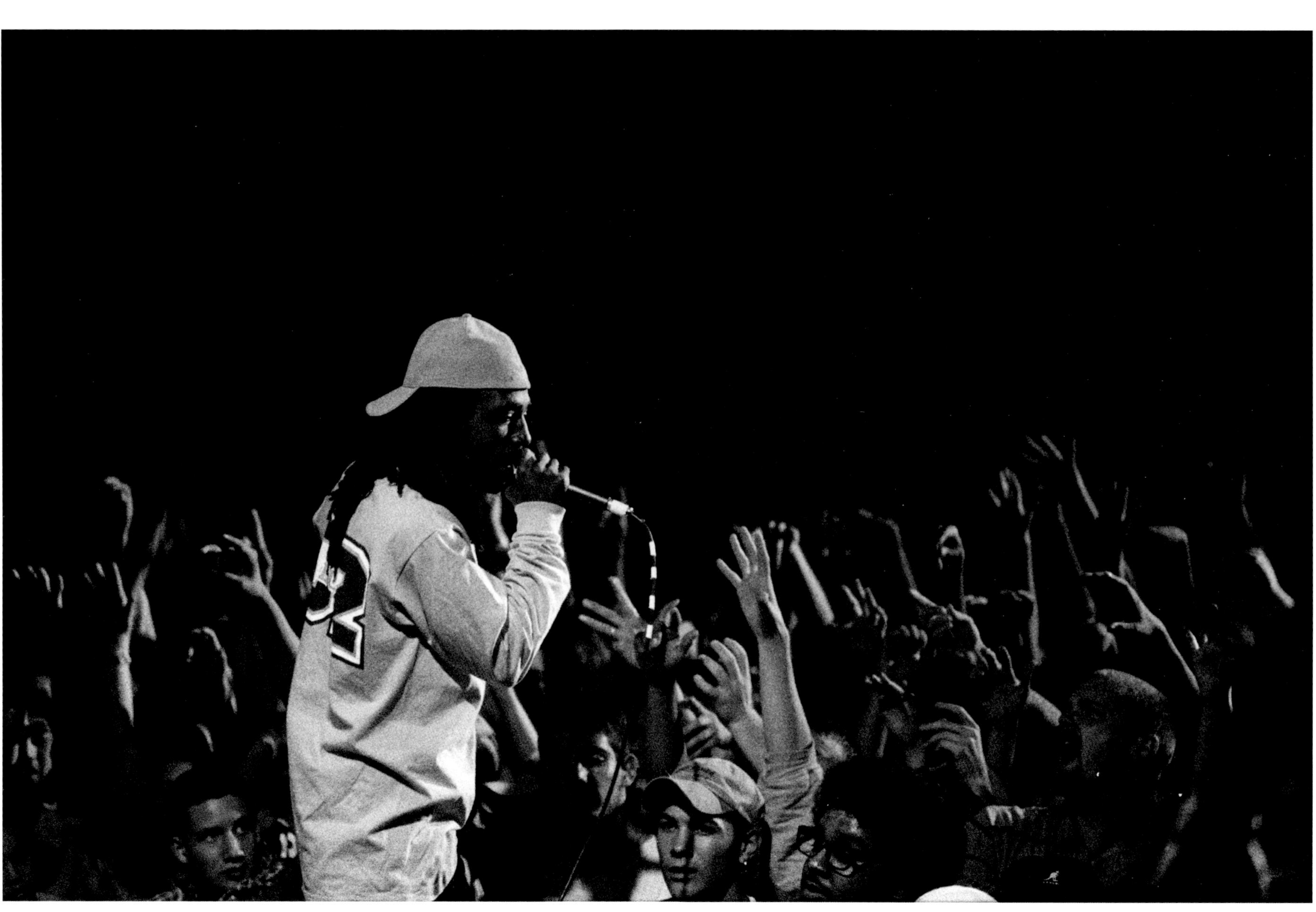

 AKIL, JURASSIC 5, 2000

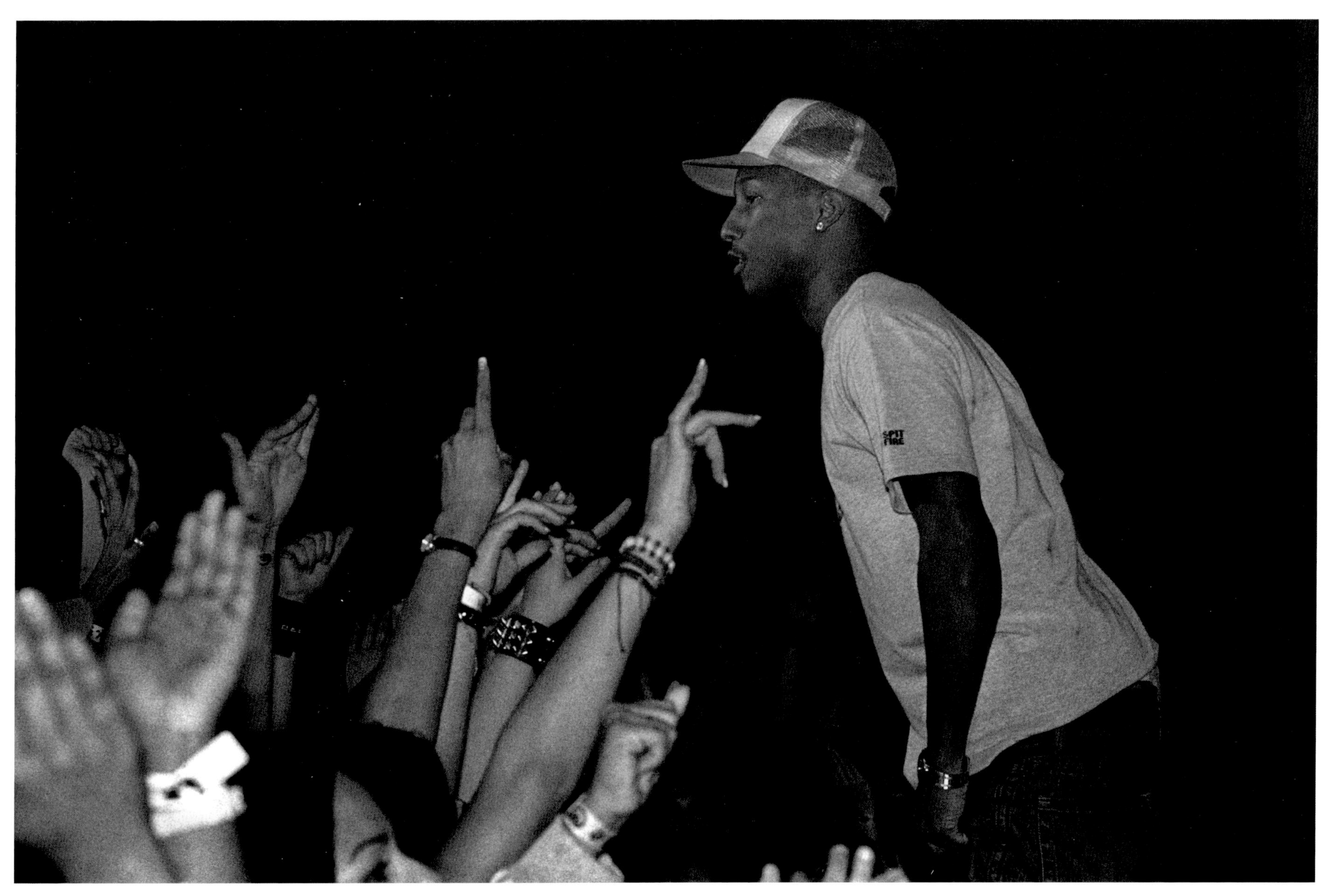

PHARRELL WILLIAMS, N.E.R.D., 2005

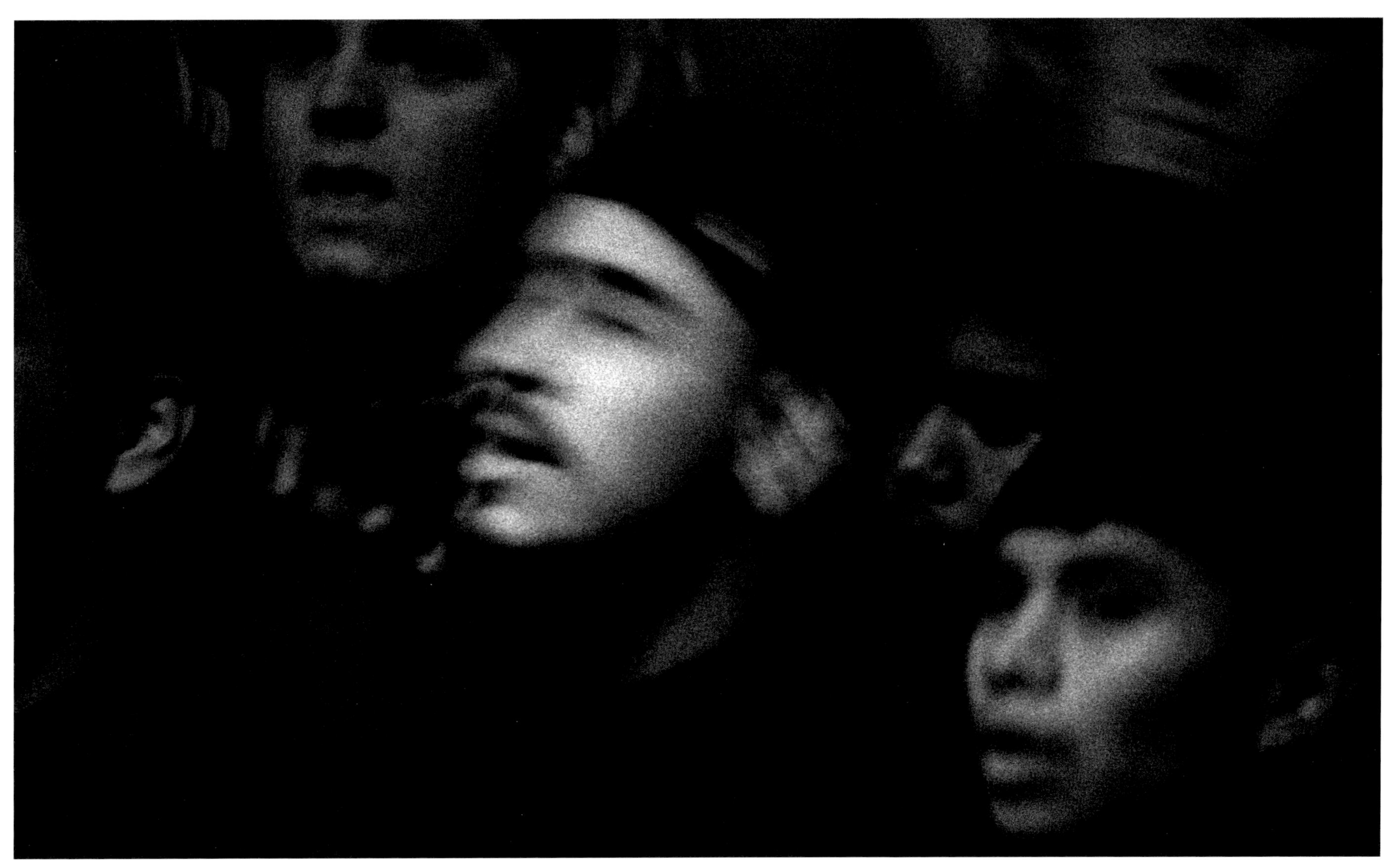

CROWD, SUNSHINE THEATER, 2001

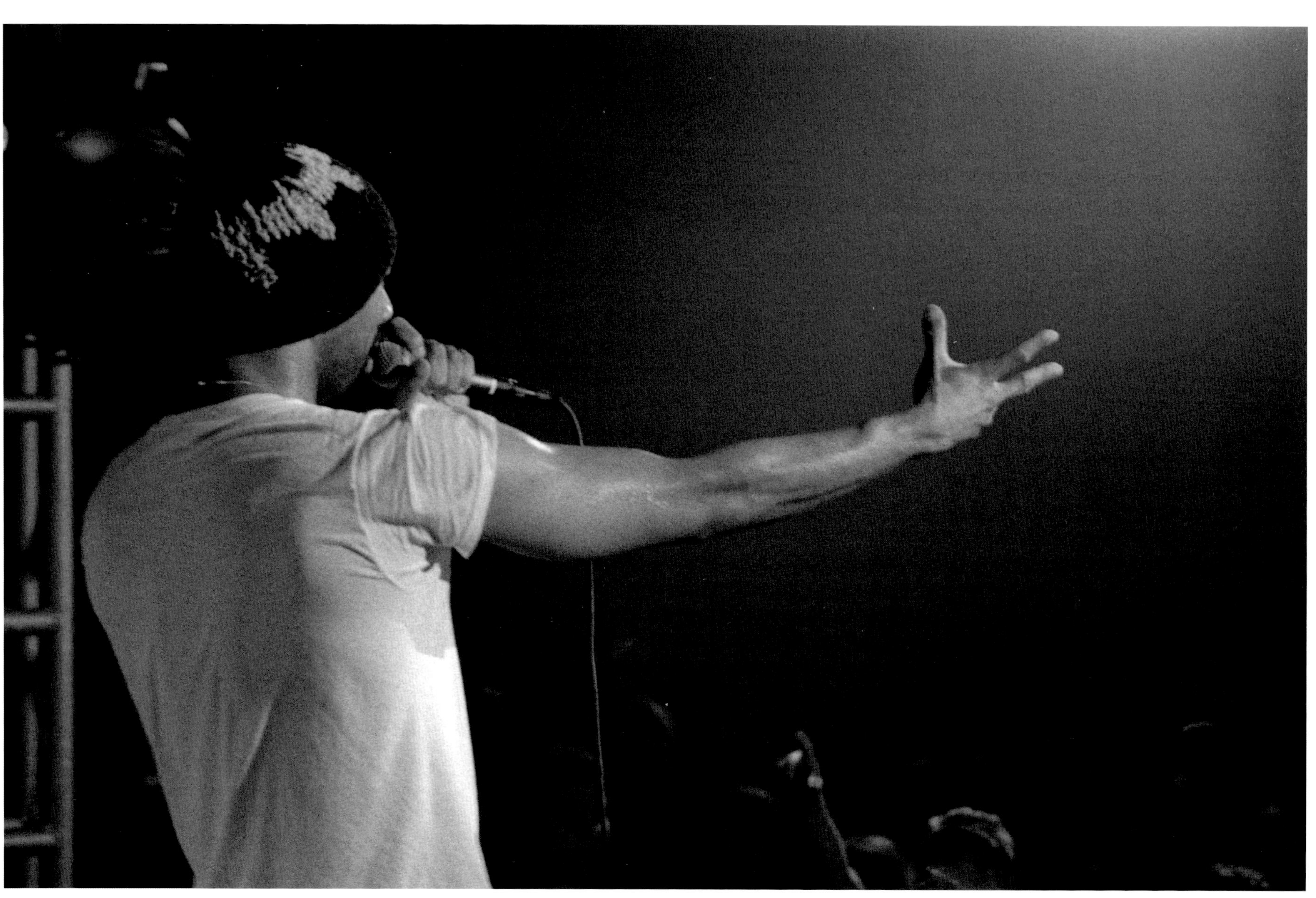

 COMMON, 2003

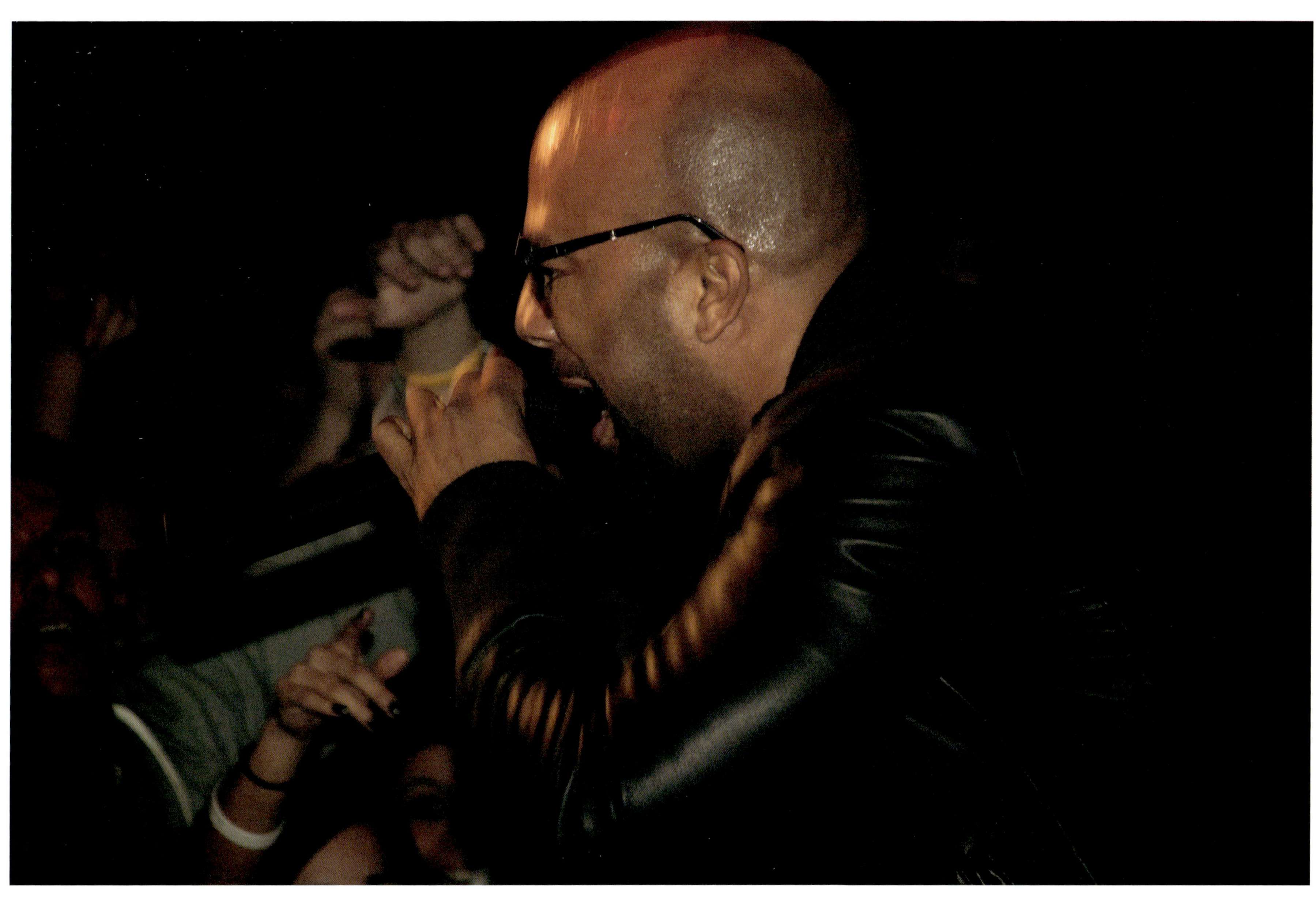

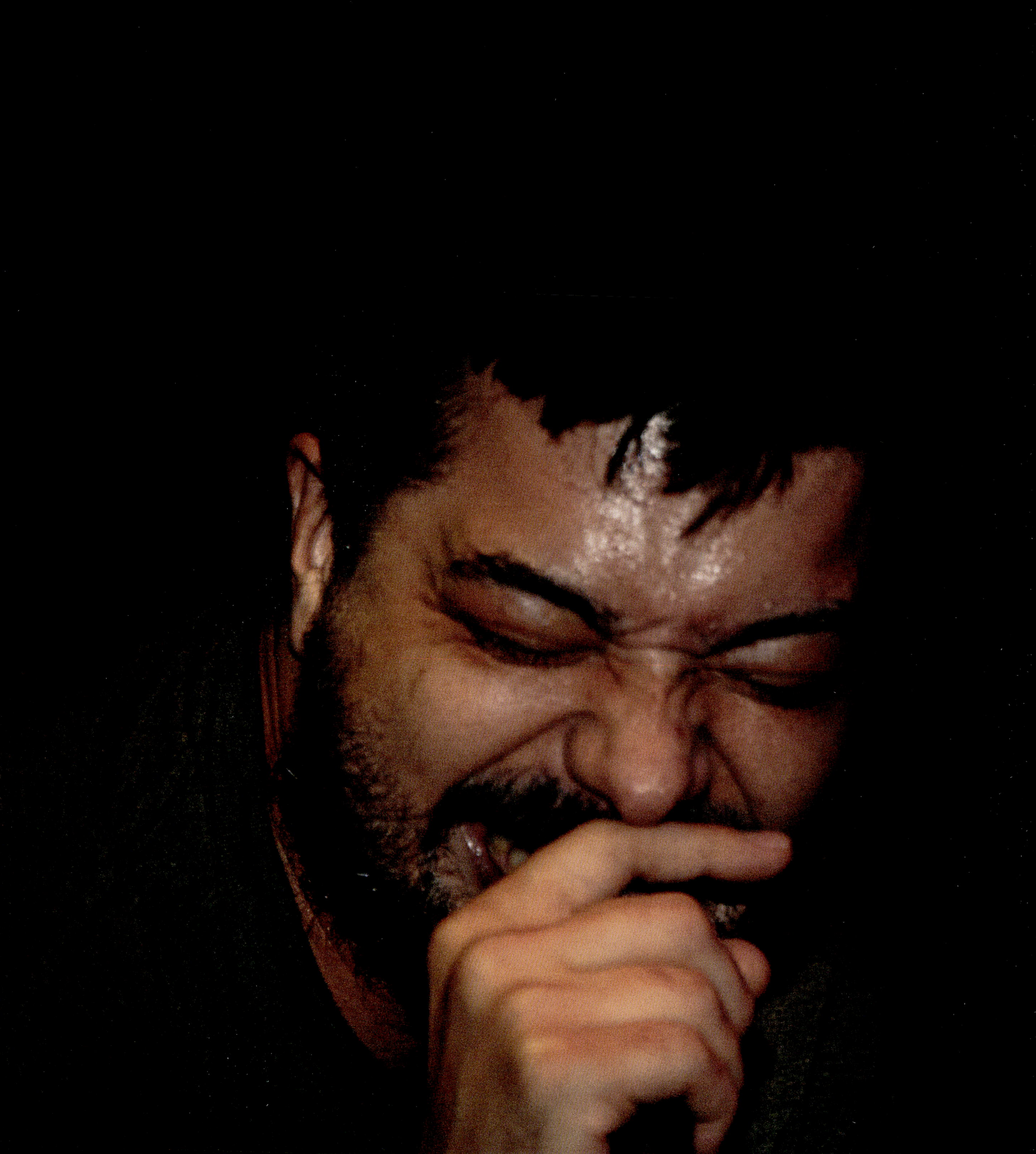

AESOP ROCK, 2012

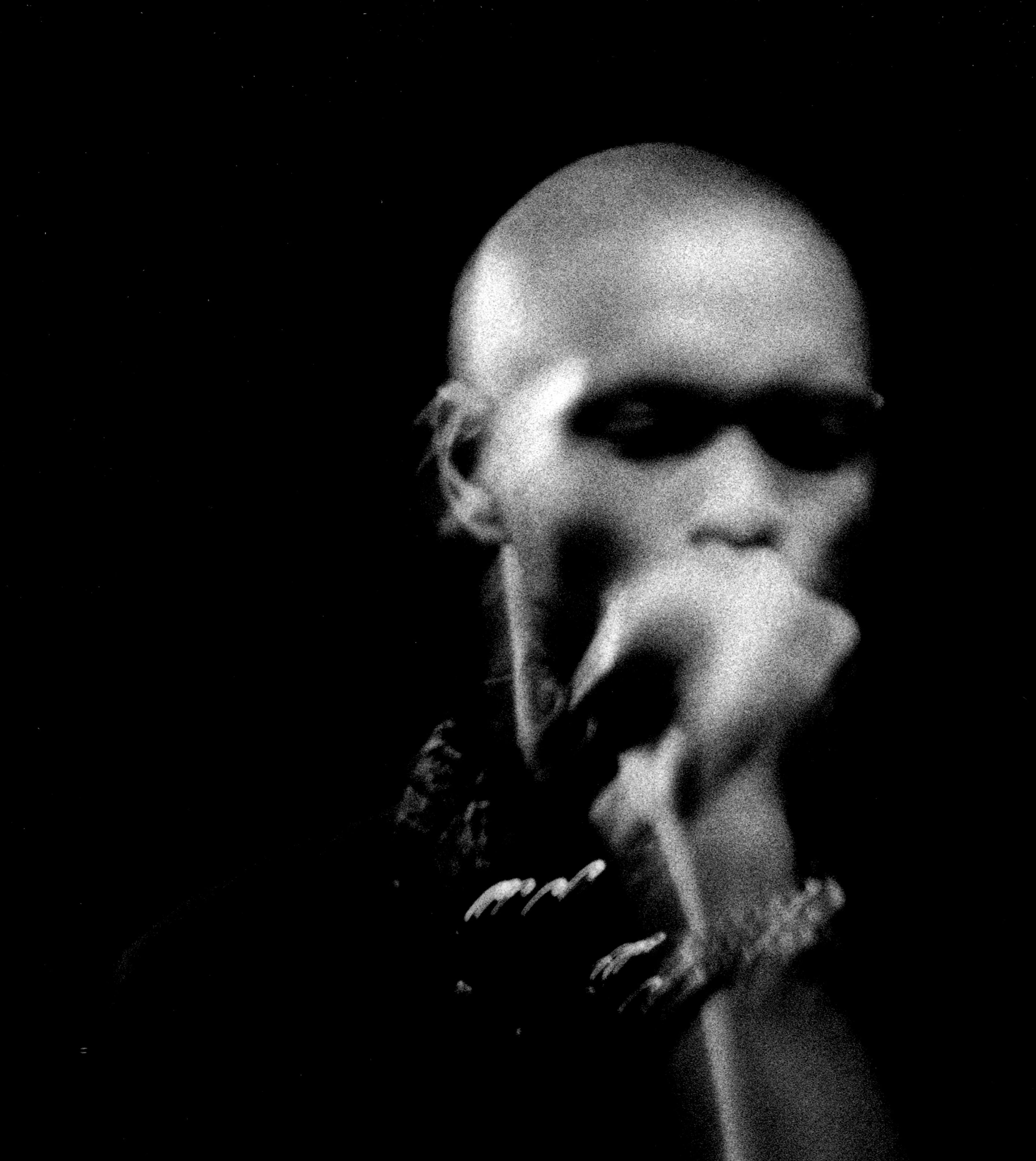

TAJAI, SOULS OF MISCHIEF, 2001

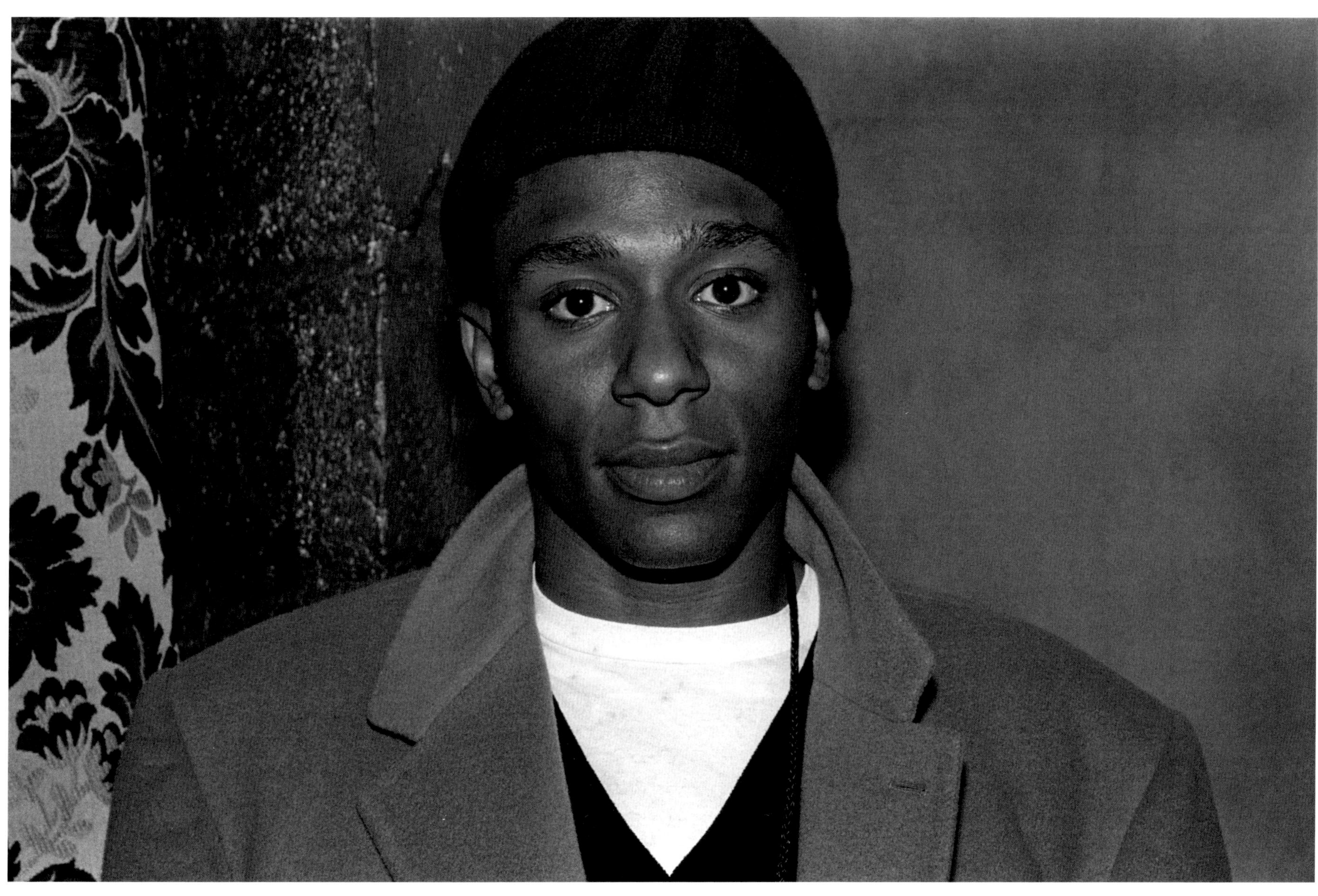

MOS DEF (YASIIN BEY), 2002

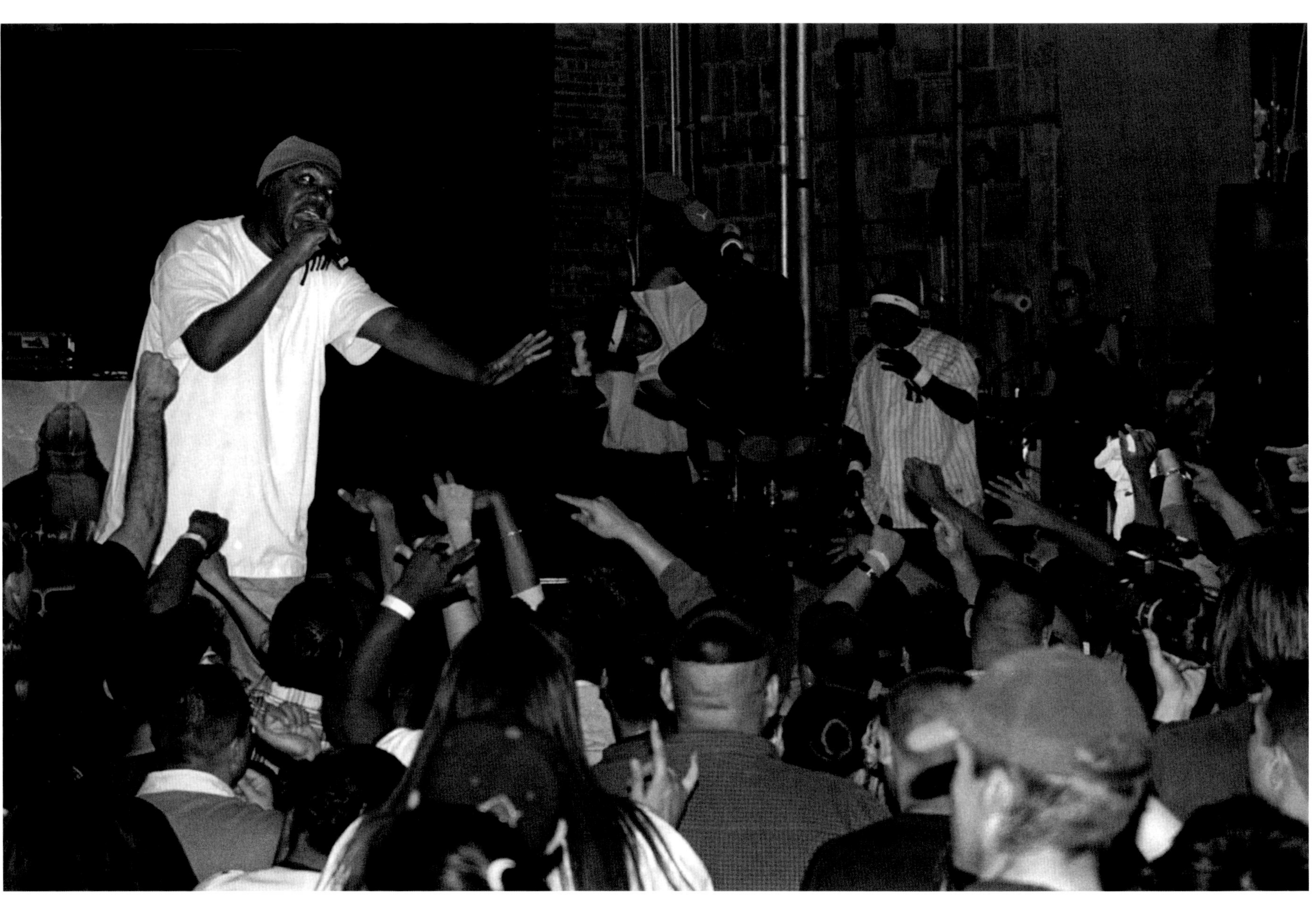

 KRS-ONE, 2002

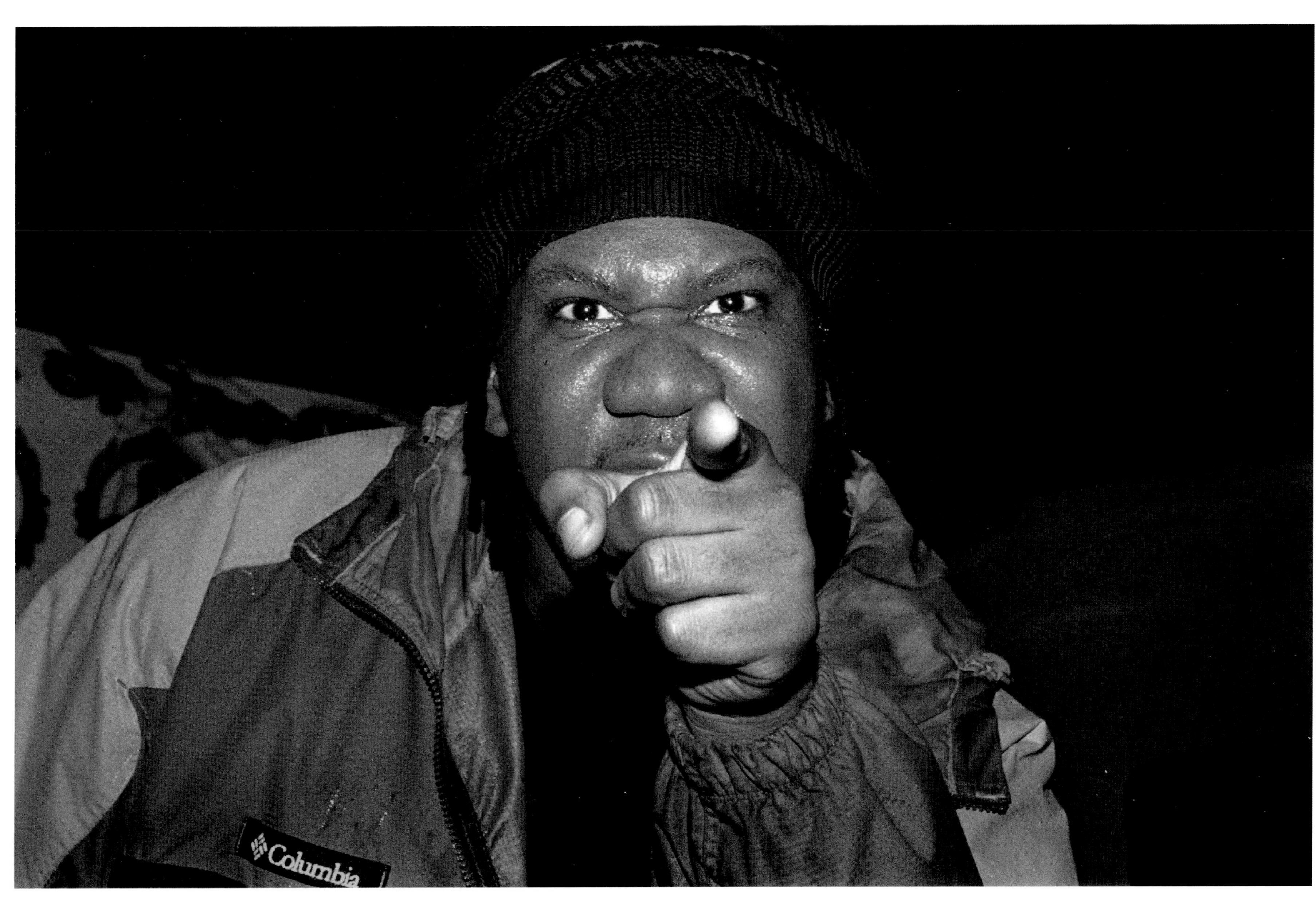

KRS-ONE, 2002

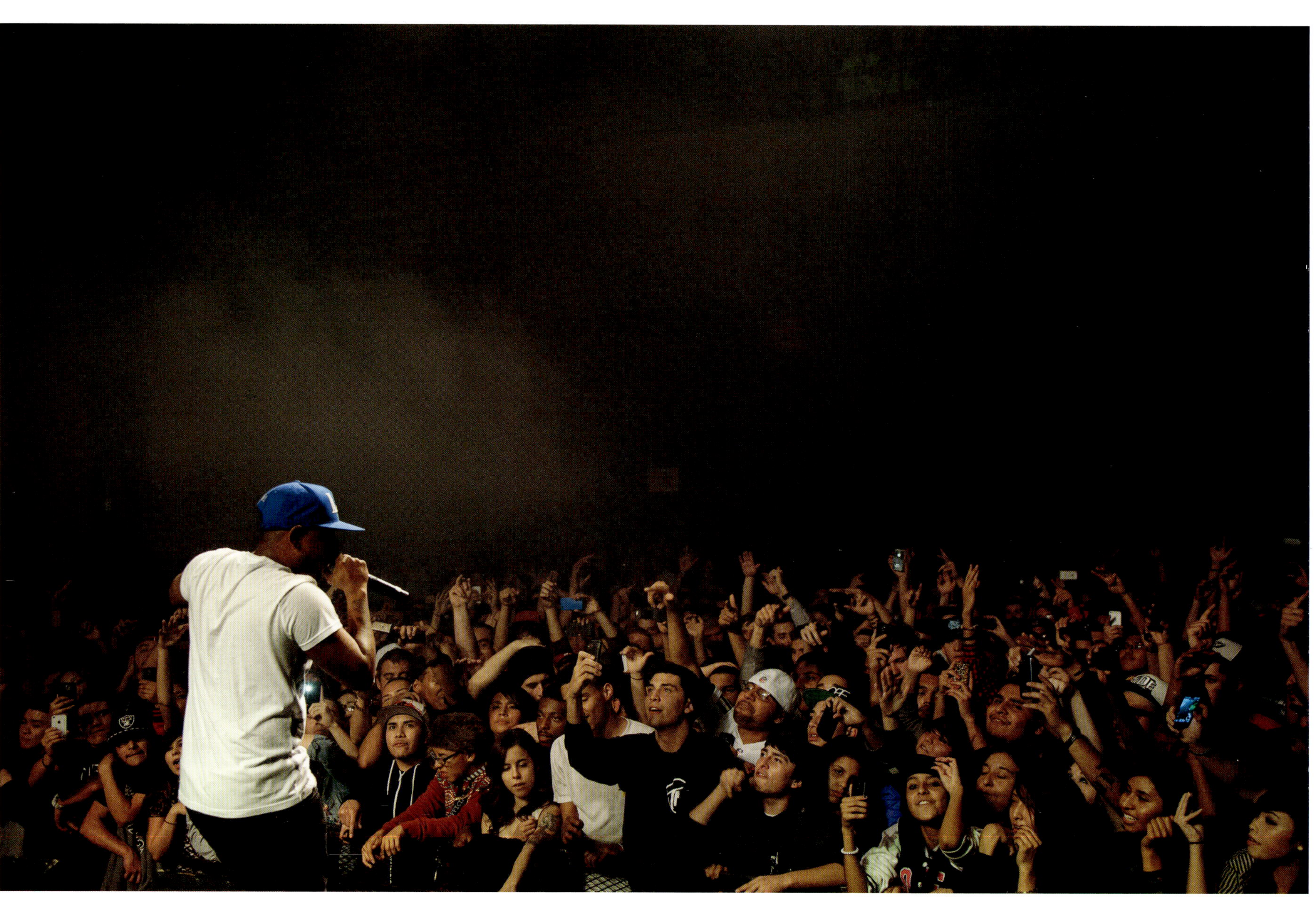

 Above and opposite: KENDRICK LAMAR, 2012

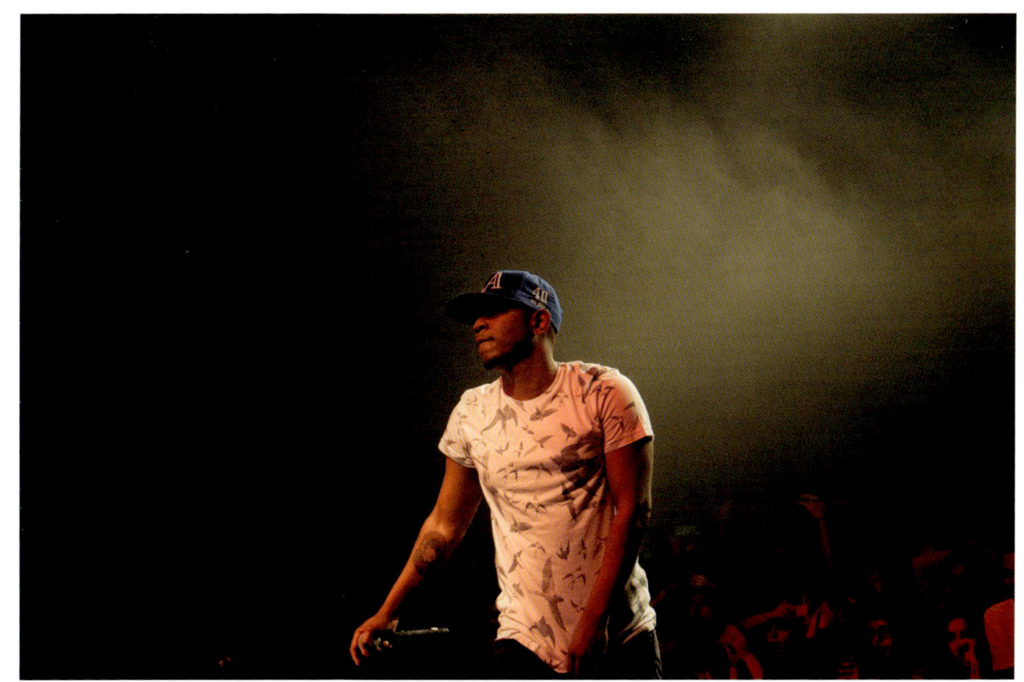

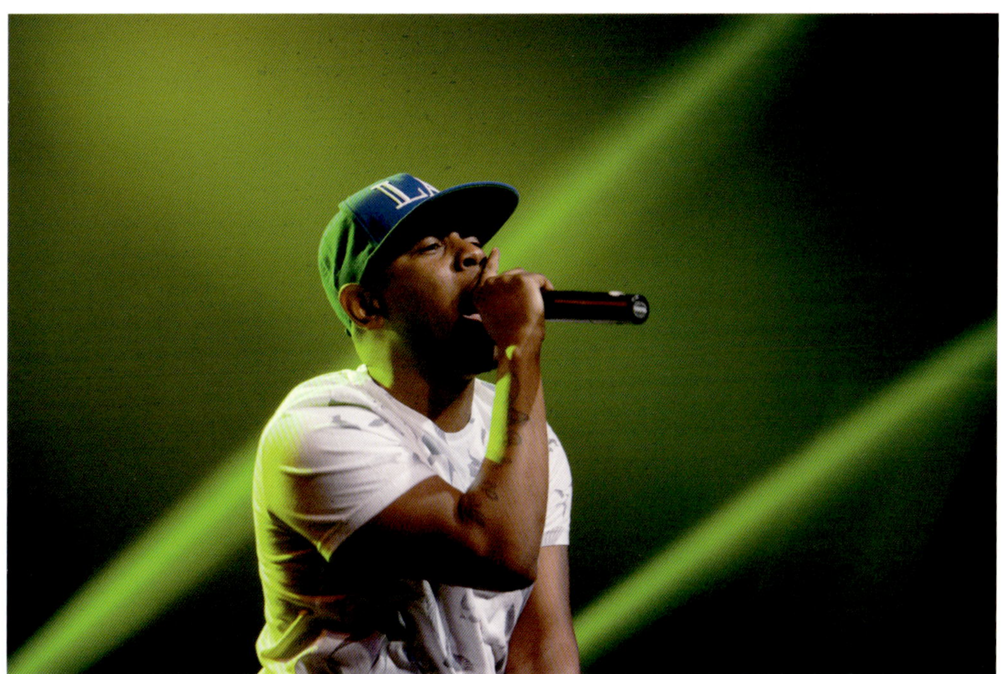

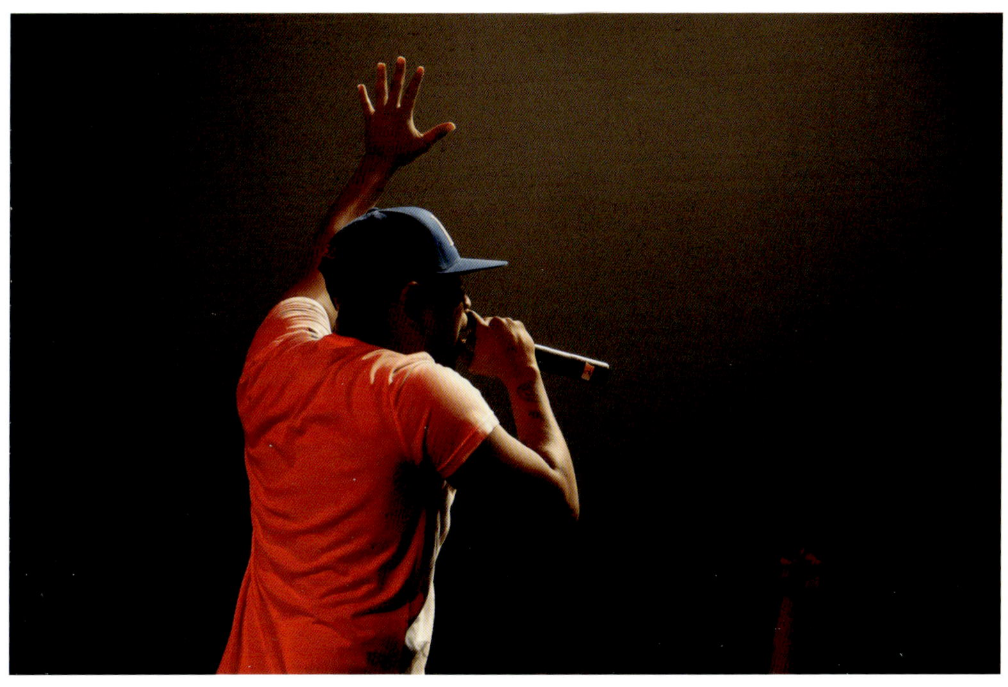

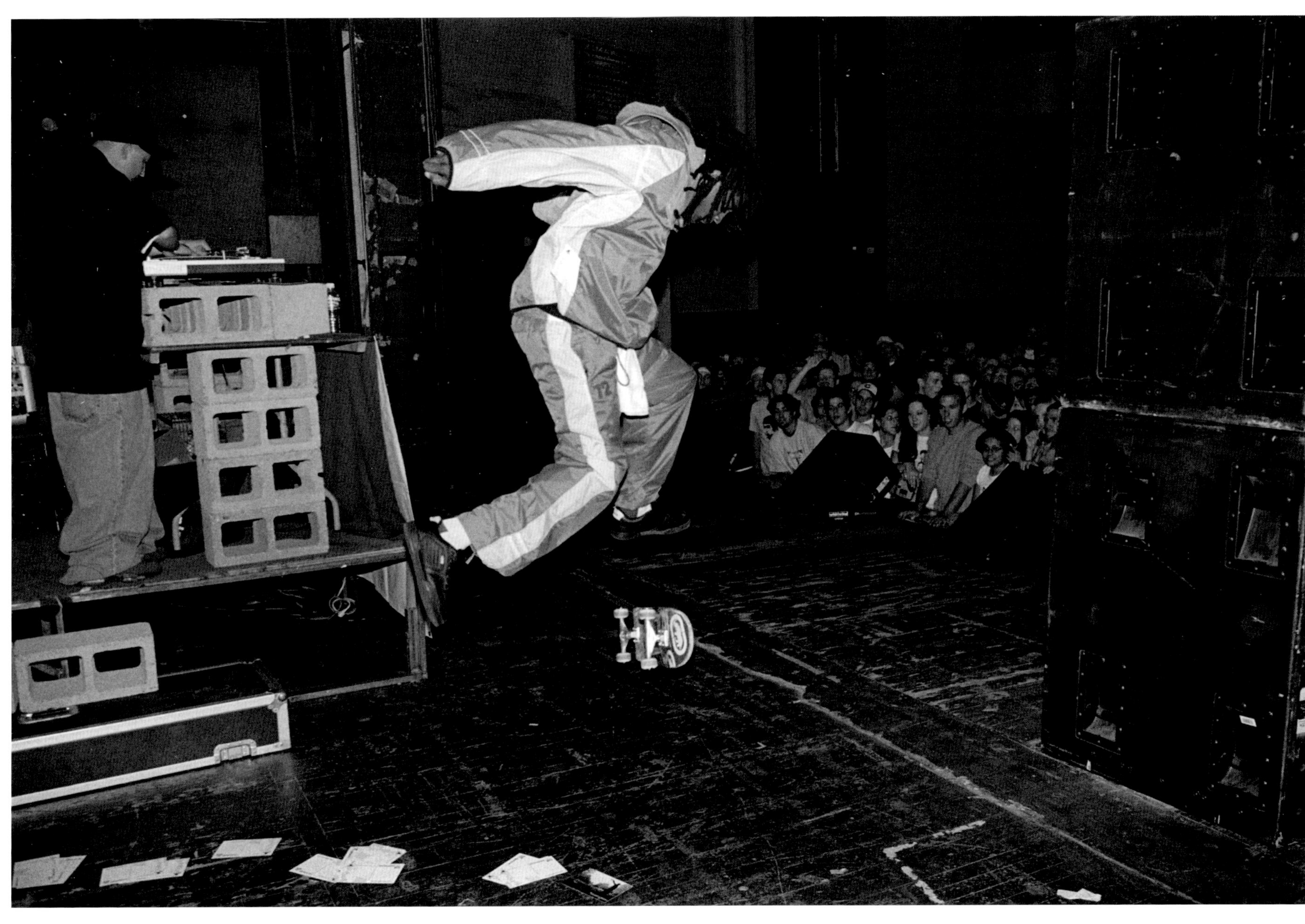

BUKUE ONE, 2002

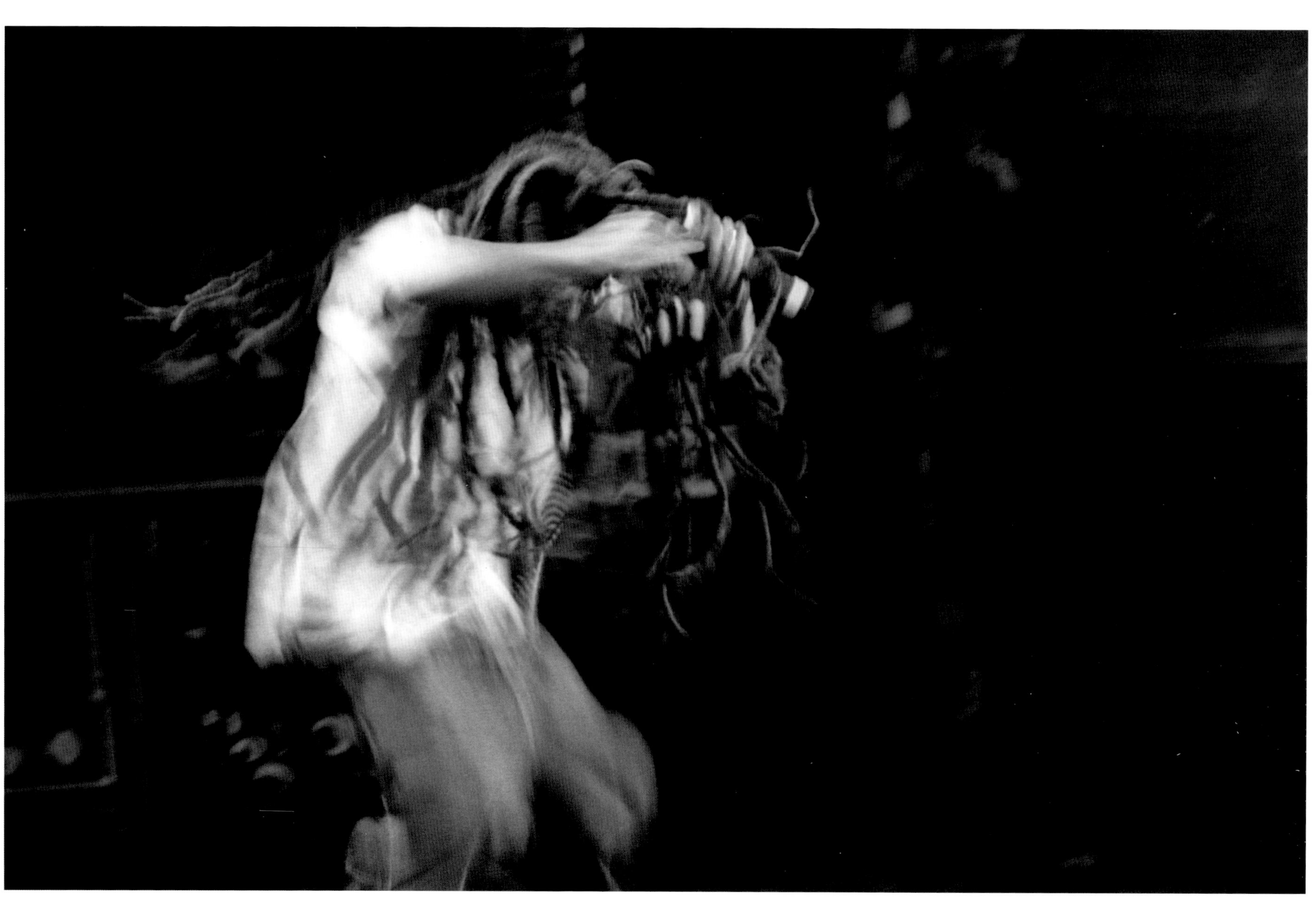

 Z-MAN, 2004

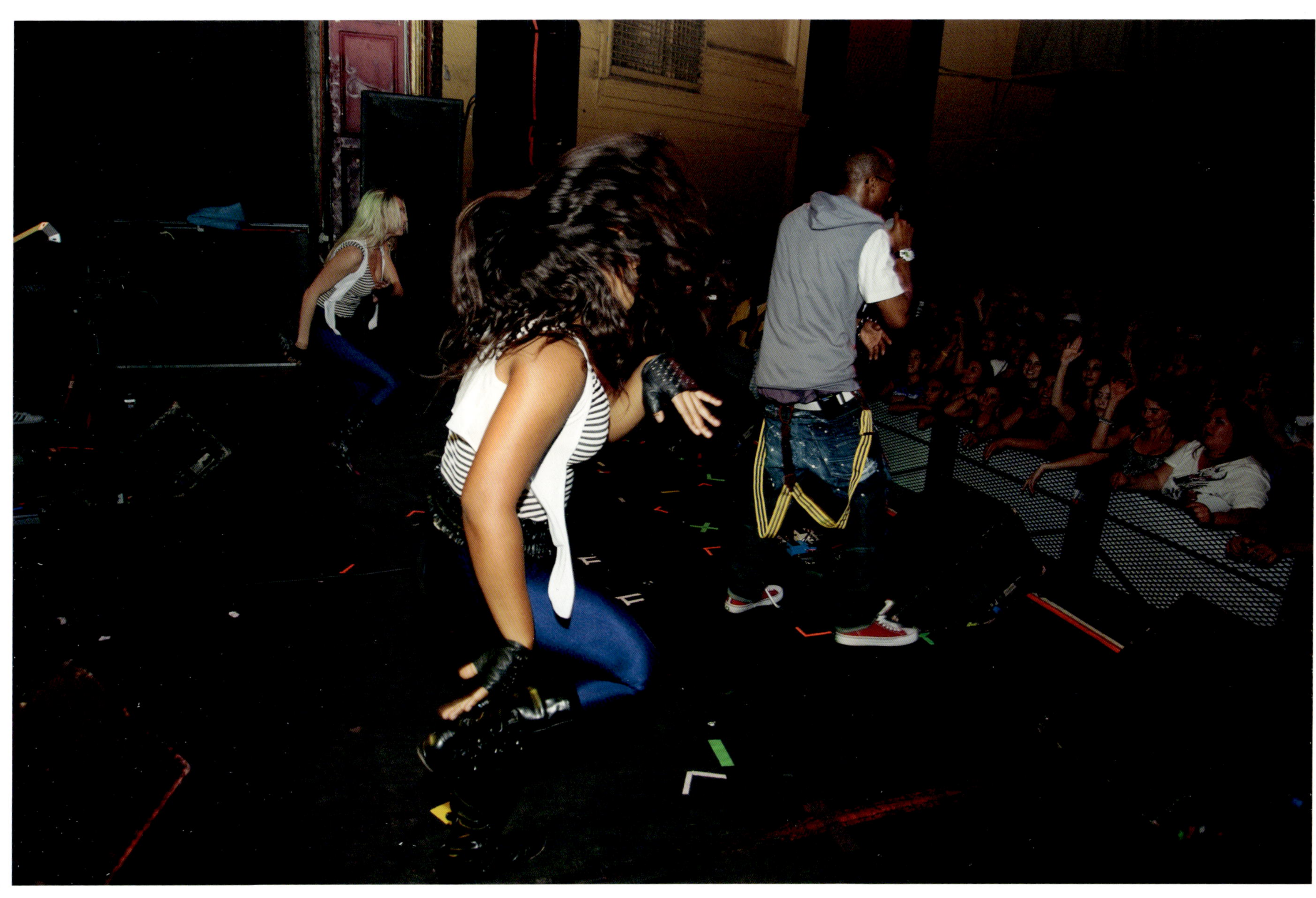

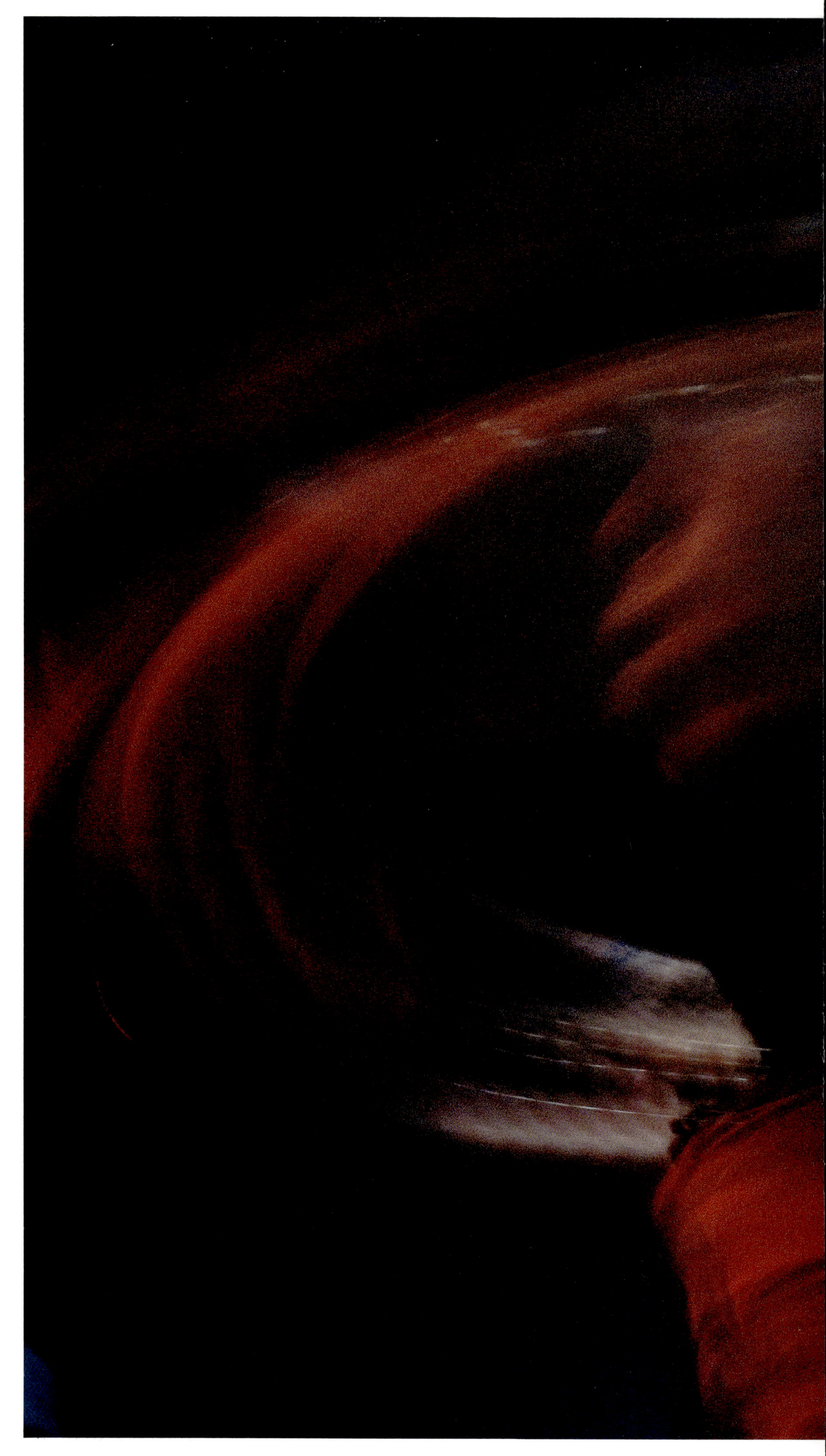

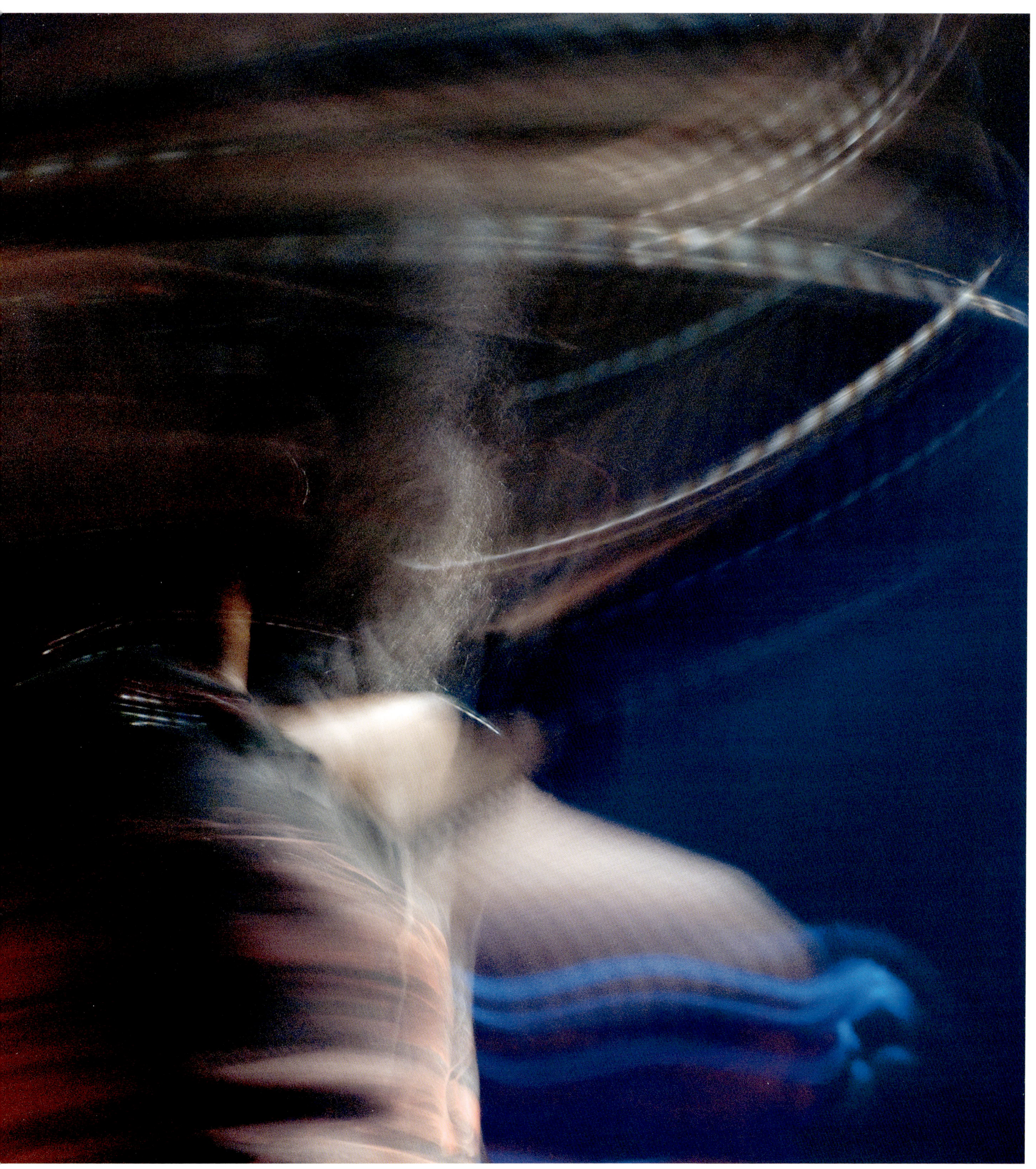

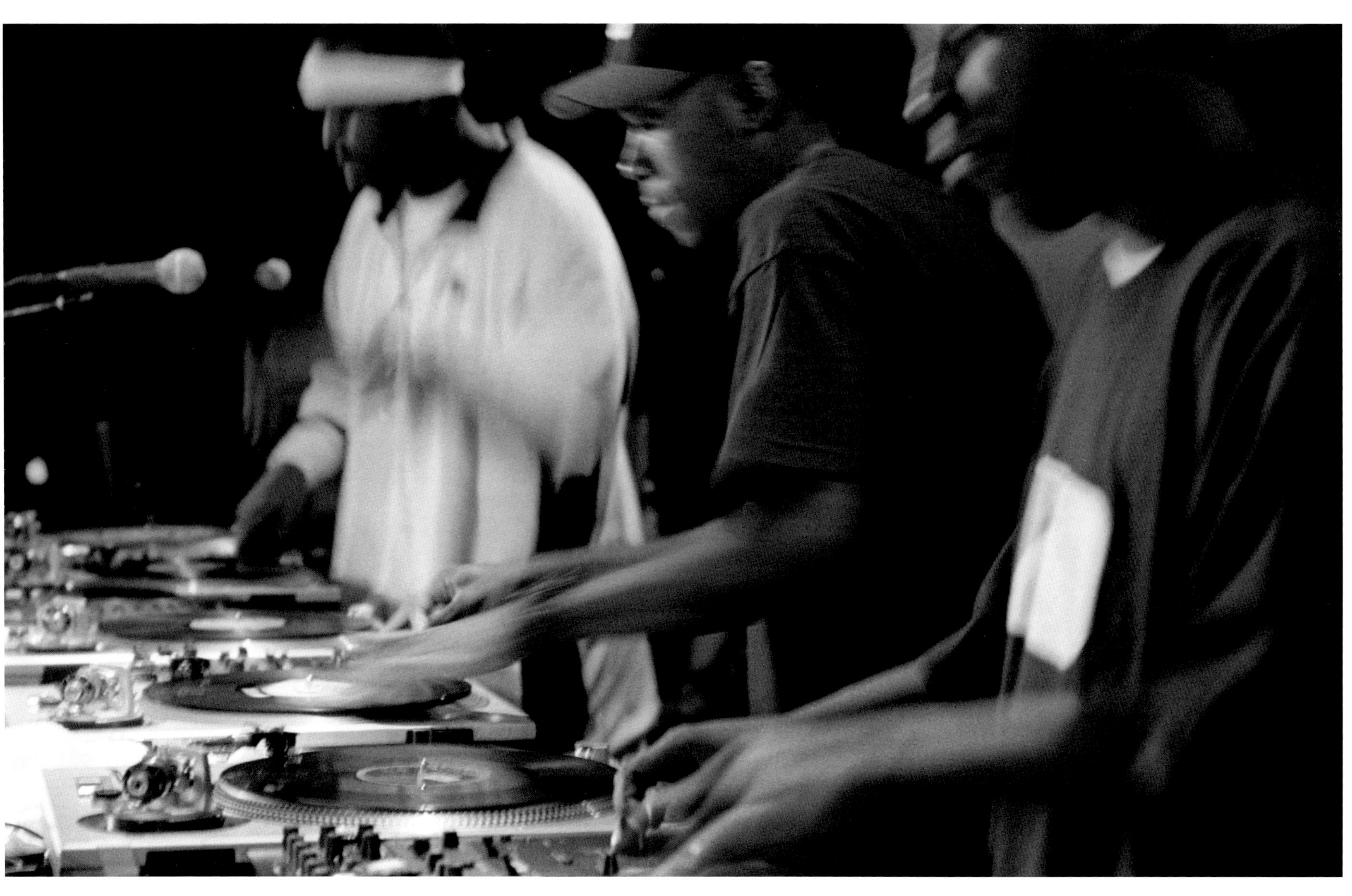

 X-ECUTIONERS, 2004

BEYOND THE PHATITUDE: WHY HIP HOP EXISTS

BY GAYE THERESA JOHNSON

In the 1990s a new sound was emerging from a collective of hip-hop turntablists, fueled by the musical dexterity and competence that DJs must command for their craft. The X-Men (aka X-Ecutioners), comprised of Rob Swift, Diamond Jay, Rock Raida, and Mista Sinister, were debuting a new style of musical production and performance called "beat juggling." Its signature method: to treat the records on turntables like instruments. By isolating drum and snare hits, vocal phrases, or sound effects by the recording artist and "flipping" or combining the sounds with a crossfader, the X-Men took what was already contained in a recording to create new rhythmic patterns. Using two or three turntables each, the artists create a collective expression with each responsible for a different sound. One DJ may isolate the drums behind a particular song, another manipulate a record to make a bass line, and yet another be responsible for a horn riff. In this way, the work of one DJ or sound achieves relevance in joining with other sounds in a collective sonic production.

When multiple DJs beat juggle in one performance, they must manage multiple turntables and crossfaders to break down rhythmic and melodic patterns then recreate them. The records they sample are as diverse and complex as the styles they develope to execute the manipulations quickly and accurately. A turntablist has to *know* records, to have a mental archive not only of songs but of phrases, tempos, lyrics, and instrumentation. Working pitch controls to alter the tempos and tones as well, DJs must be masters of both mixing and memory.[1]

The musical productions that emerge use eclectic combinations of jazz, soul, rock, hip hop, blues, and funk in a fusion not only of musical styles but of sonic patterns associated with different time periods and diverse social spaces. A listener might hear the sounds of Herbie Hancock, Mongo Santamaria, Cannonball Adderley, Isaac Hayes, Al Green, Public Enemy, and the Eagles all in one song. Beat juggling must anticipate audiences' collective memories and produce an appealing soundscape of those memories. The practice encodes and communicates centuries of musical memory, minimizes the distance between diverse geographical spaces, collapses the time elapsed between different albums and songs, and interpolates a wide range of life experiences into a new beat.

We have something to learn from the practice of beat juggling: Instead of turntables and a crossfader, we can use our knowledge of hip-hop history and a commitment to social change to form a new sound,one that situates us as scholars and activists to understand how, like the X-Ecutioners, we might all manipulate past triumphs and present dangers posed by racist public policy and ingrained social prejudices into a new social and political beat.

Hip hop is a brilliant creative production that developed in spite of devastating urban poverty and neglect. In both liberating and damaging ways, it has delivered critical understandings about music, power, and race by intellectuals not always credited with brilliance, by historical actors not credited with action, by artists not celebrated for sophisticated or elegant expressions of situated knowledge. *This* is the framework we have to lead with when we study and learn from hip hop. Because beyond the phatitude of beats and rhymes, hip hop gives us an alternative way to imagine the rich identities that exist beyond the immediately visible, about race, culture, music, space, and sound. And though often burdened with the unfair

1. I was first made aware of beat juggling through a conversation with turntablist Brendan "BK-One" Kelly. I thank turntablist Lord "DJ Lord" Aswod for his instruction on pitch controls and the technicalities of beat juggling.

expectation that it will speak for all things "black," "urban," or "youth," hip hop remains, nonetheless, a unique optic for understanding myriad issues in contemporary society. Its significance persists as one of the most evocative and broadly relevant cultural expressions of all time.

But it isn't the least complicated form of cultural expression, and it keeps getting more complex. Writing about hip hop in this historical moment requires a particular presence of mind, a steadiness capable of pulling together the discord of representation, the increasingly damaging aspects of the genre, and its abundant possibilities.

On the one hand, the spaces and people who inspired its original expression (namely African- and Latina/o-descended folks) have more opportunities than ever in many regards—and less in others. They have more mobility than ever in some regards—and less in others. We see an unprecedented visibility in media representation, but the symbolic imagery is painful, overwhelmingly reduced to scripted reality television archetypes and musical parodies of the "ghetto-fabulous." Anti-immigration policies, economic restructuring, and the prison industrial complex have coalesced to severely curtail the freedom and mobility of black and brown people. Politicians, corporate executives, and moral pundits have displayed such palpable and prolific indifference to human rights on issues of immigration and racial suppression that it can often seem like no one else is speaking. But here is the place where hip hop is critical; here is the reason why it exists. When scholars (formal or not) treat it as a serious source of articulated grievances, it has always instructed us in the tenor and locales of dissent. Paying attention to what these artists and their audiences have contributed, especially the expressed hopes and prescriptions for community progress, offers a significant lesson in animated, motivated, and deliberate commitment to sustaining social protest. This is the best of hip hop. And from its worst there is still much to learn.

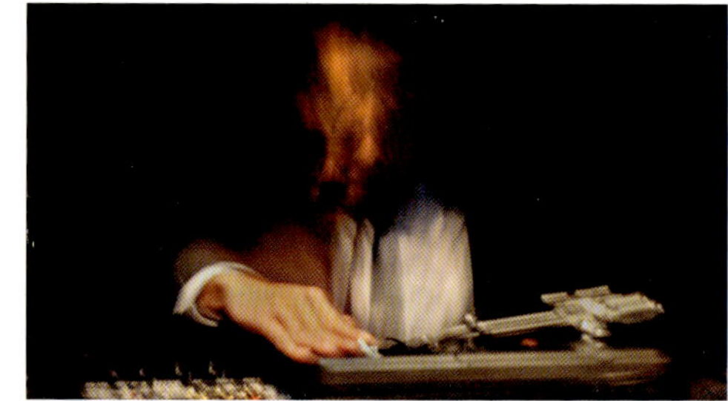

MIKE RELM, 2009

As a working-class subculture, hip-hop artists, their audiences, and their productions divulge more than the terrible costs of economic downsizing and deindustrialization for communities of color. They reveal social identities forged from the collective witness and shared experience of racial and class inequality. They create a new framework of interracial and transnational affiliations rooted in local experiences of racism, struggle, and displacement. In the 1970s and '80s, antiracist politics in these communities were fashioned from the collective memories of displacement because of urban renewal, exile, and labor migration and of struggle in race-based mobilizations for rights, resources, recognition, and peace. Hip hop still tells these stories if we listen closely.

Hip hop evolved much like many other popular cultural forms, as an expression of a particular experience. In the late 1970s, hip hop was in its formative years with Joe Bataan's "Rap-o clap-o" (1979) and the seminal "The Message" released by Grandmaster Flash and the Furious Five in 1982. The Sugarhill Gang's "Rapper's Delight" (1979) expressed the humanism of black life in sophisticated yet humor-filled records that urban listeners were poised to receive. DJs turned the record player into an instrument, manipulating it to create new sounds mirroring new social realities. And these same realities threatened the viability of these communities as much as they determined the subject matter of their expression.

When Reagan took office in 1981, his solution to the worst economic downturn since the Depression was to propose that the "supply side" of the economy be stimulated through tax cuts for the wealthy, providing an opportunity for the upper class to acquire and presumably invest more money. The central theme of Reaganomics was that a reduction in taxes for the wealthy would provide greater investment opportunities to the upper class, eventually leading to the creation of more jobs for the working class.[2] Instead, the United States accrued more debt during the Reagan administration than in any other era. The redistribution and expansion of wealth during this period set the stage for the decline of living standards for the poorest Americans, while incomes of the wealthiest citizens soared.

When rap music first gained mainstream traction in the late seventies, its artists were dismissed and disrespected by politicians, pundits, and the music business itself. But by the late eighties, the same corporate bodies that had previously shunned it were making millions of dollars selling it. By 1990, label executives had created a "gangsta formula," a business hook that repackaged rap's depictions of black urban realities into a titillating buffet of hypermasculinity and glorified violence, relegating women artists to the margins and creating a new outlet of expression for what became its largest consumer demographic: young white men. Increasingly rejected at the industry door were records penned with good-natured depictions of everyday black life, incisive critiques of urban renewal, or songs that illustrated lyrical or beat-boxing genius. Women—as artists, anyway—were rendered nearly extinct under this formula, rarely allowed on screen or on air for any other reason than a sexual one. And somewhere in the sordid history of mainstream rap's promotion and production, the pairing of rap music and black humanity was, for all intents and purposes, lost. Black artists were complicit in this in many ways, but there was nothing more powerful in or more capable of guiding the direction of rap music than record executives, who weren't artists and weren't, with few exceptions, black, for that matter.

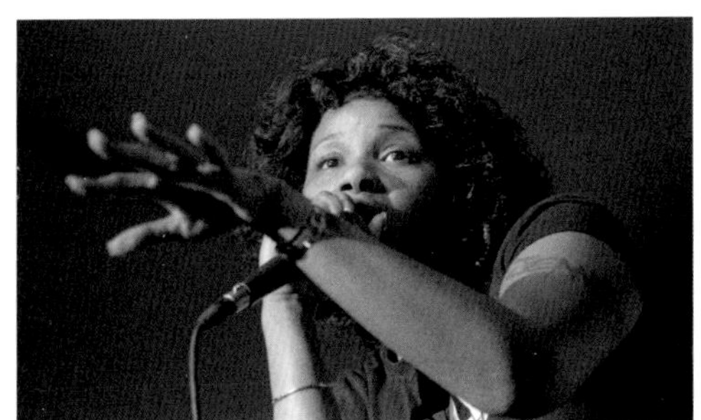

JEAN GRAE, 2005

This is the persistent problem in mainstream hip hop that makes it both painful and liberating to write about. It's a mirror on some of the most denigrating social ills of our time. The sexism, heterosexism, and misogyny already existent in broader society are often magnified in hip hop. And the fullness of our highest potential is, likewise, often mirrored here. Hip hop is a record of how marginalized people have worked under injurious conditions to produce, elaborate upon, and defend emancipatory identities. And this, in all its awkward, wretched beauty, is what makes it something that has lessons for a broad spectrum of learning, about representation and social justice, as well as about some of the worst aspects of our society.

Ask an audience of hip-hop listeners to name two female hip-hop groups in the contemporary scene, and you'll be met with silence. But the roll call of women hip-hop artists is vast: the list of Bgirls merely begins with Jeskilz, Renegade, Headspin Janet, Honey Rockwell, Baby Love, Asia One, Masami, Bonita, B-Girl Mega, Feenix, Mari Coda, Bubbles aka Hanifa Queen, Lady Julez, Tiger Bintu, ABgirl, Beta, Marcella, Jazzy Jes, Hurricane, Karima, Mis Lee, Lady Champ, Bibiche, Pebblee Poo, Pauline, and Miss Twist. Hip-hop artists responsible for the strong genesis that is poppin', lockin' and rockin' include Tangerine, Medusa, Peach, Pandora, Wandee

2. A. Scott Piraino, "Reaganomics at War" in *The Populist: Essays on Politics, Economics, and Military Affairs* (October 8, 2003): 3.

Pop, Snapshot, Pringles, Lockadelic, Toni Basil, Lolipop Sanchez, Lockeroo, Yoshie, Angie, and Pepsi. Graffiti artist Lady Pink remains one of the most important visual artists in hip hop.

Most people miss the fact of hip hop's function as an umbrella term for four critical elements of the genre: graffiti, dance, DJing, and emceeing. Nearly all treatments of hip hop only address the last of these, but to do so exclusively misses the breadth of the form and, significantly, the tremendous involvement of women as cultural workers in hip hop. Women artists have always had to create and remake what it means to be feminine, masculine, sexual, successful, talented, and indeed, merely present in hip hop. Lil' Kim, Foxxy Brown, and artists with shared corporate backers and social aspirations advanced images that both aided and damaged women's images in rap music. Yet there were also less-recognized women artists who created personas that embraced fluid identities of gender and cultural expression. The struggles these women have endured to be represented, to remain visible, to produce under injurious conditions have often been collective but also excruciatingly solitary. And they've often resulted in revolutionary artistic creations that have been rendered invisible in the genre and in the industry as a whole. Yet these creations and practices by women in hip hop hold the possibility for equality in creativity and community, if we listen carefully enough, if we look closely enough.

Hip hop holds expressive politics worth documenting as a record of the everyday circulation of sonic politics among black and brown youth. These practitioners have always found ways to increase the mobility of their sonic expression. Swap meets, informal production and distribution, and spaces of musical congregation and innovation have often been the most articulate challenge to the staggering mobilization of state force against people and communities of color. Within this framework, hip hop becomes a struggle for social membership and human rights by and among local populations, as well as a larger, more just, and more complex discussion about style politics.

It deserves to be noted that while sharing the experiences of containment and confinement, black and brown people have also been pitted against each other constantly, manipulated to compete with each other for jobs, housing, prestige, and political power. Yet they deserve to hear and tell a better story about themselves as people and as a collective seeking freedom, a better story than the one that now dominates the discourse on youth and minority relationships. Like the practice of beat juggling, hip-hop history benefits from the rich repository of histories and cultural productions enacted by black and brown people.

History has shown that hip hop can be as demoralizing as it is powerful. The social problems and internal tensions that plague it can feel overwhelming at times. We have to rewrite the story we've been told about who we are and about our value to each other. There are places, as the work of David Scheinbaum demonstrates, where humanity, dignity, and beauty still exist, still thrive, still inspire. Scheinbaum has captured these moments, and they encourage us to rediscover the most important and moving possibilities that hip hop has to offer. Hip hop began as a desire to represent communities of color—the true, the ugly, the beautiful—with equity and humanity. These photographs help us reconnect to the freedom dreams of hip-hop's creators and to the desire to have those dreams met with equity and social justice.

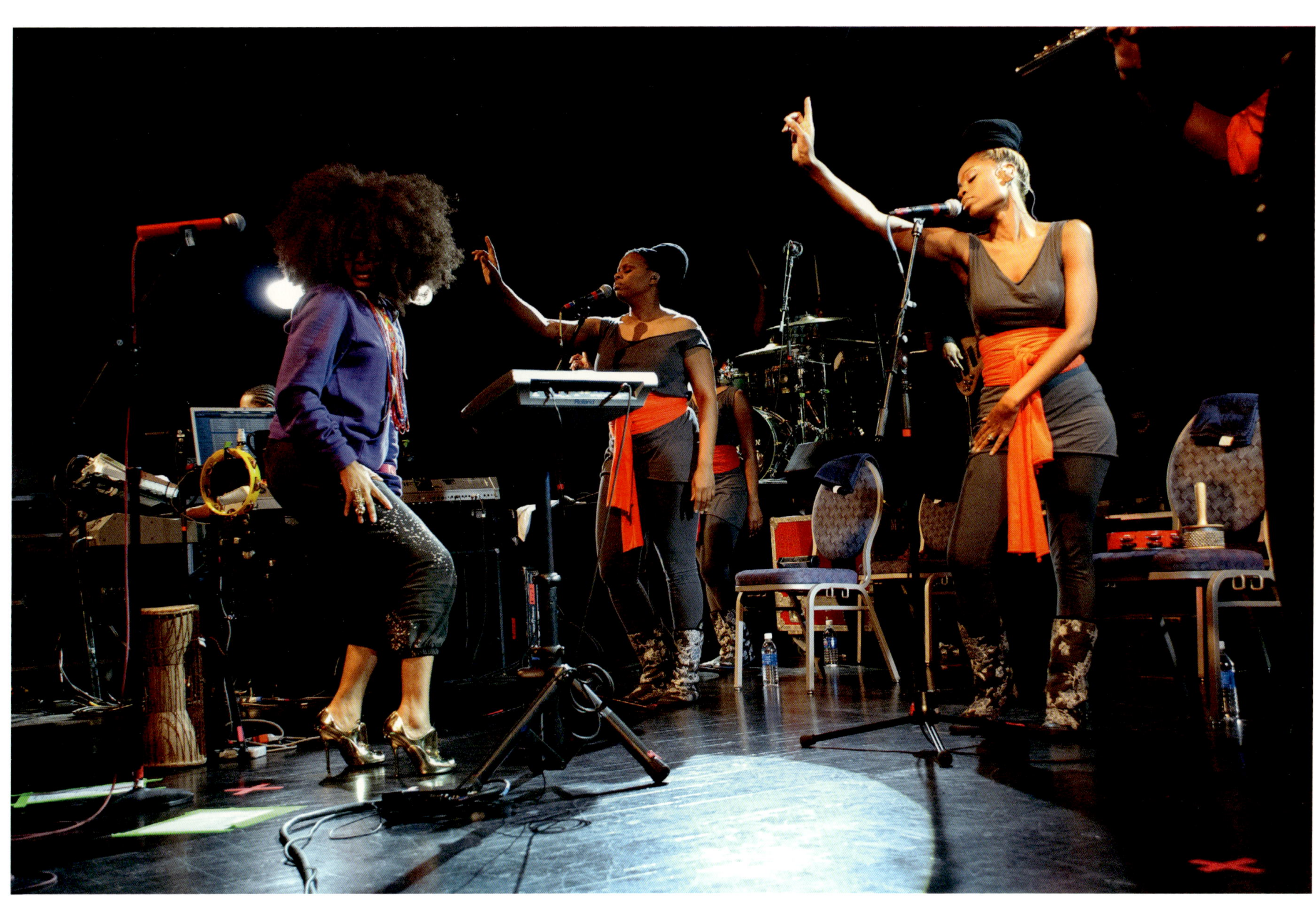

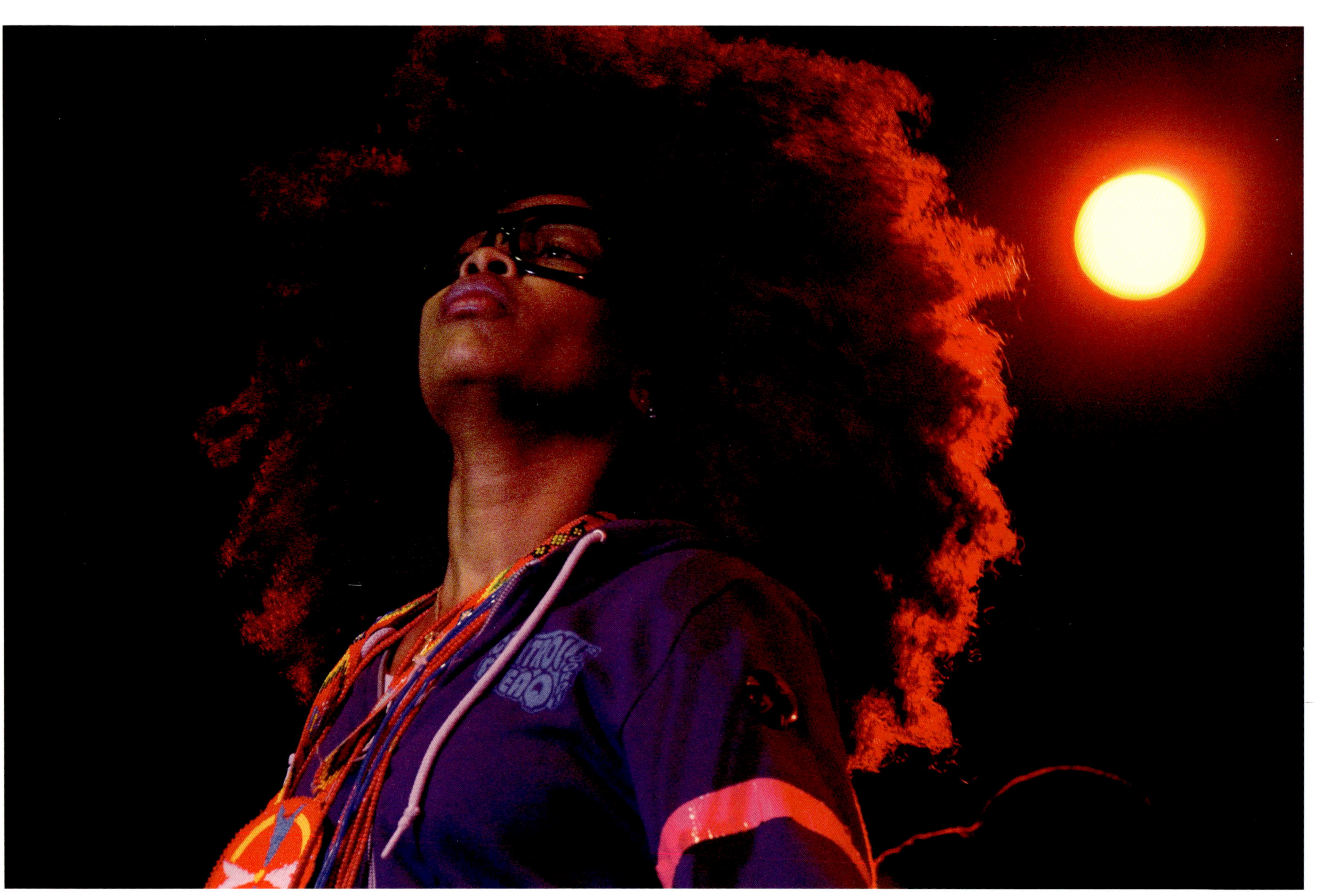

 ERYKAH BADU, 2009

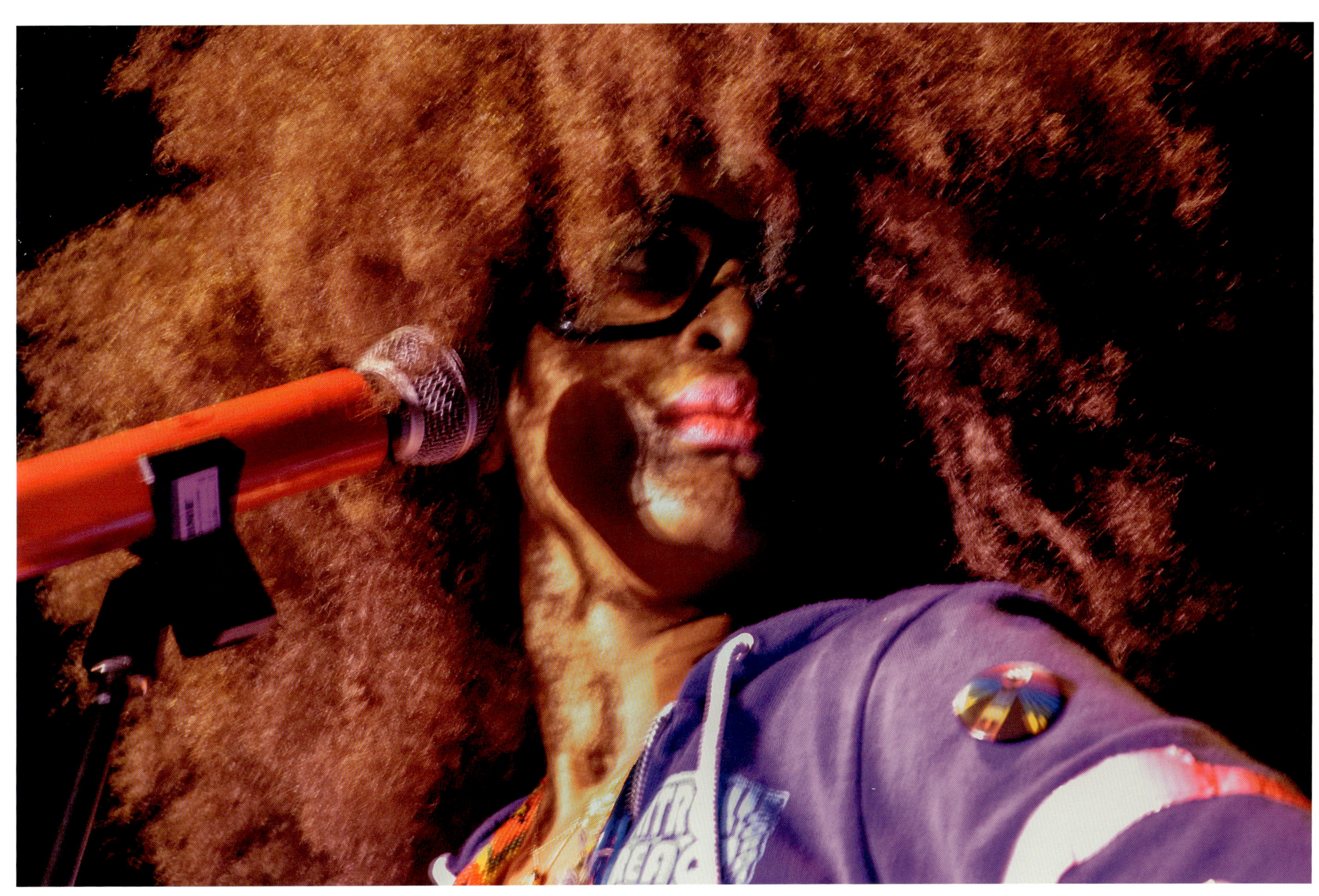

ERYKAH BADU, 2009

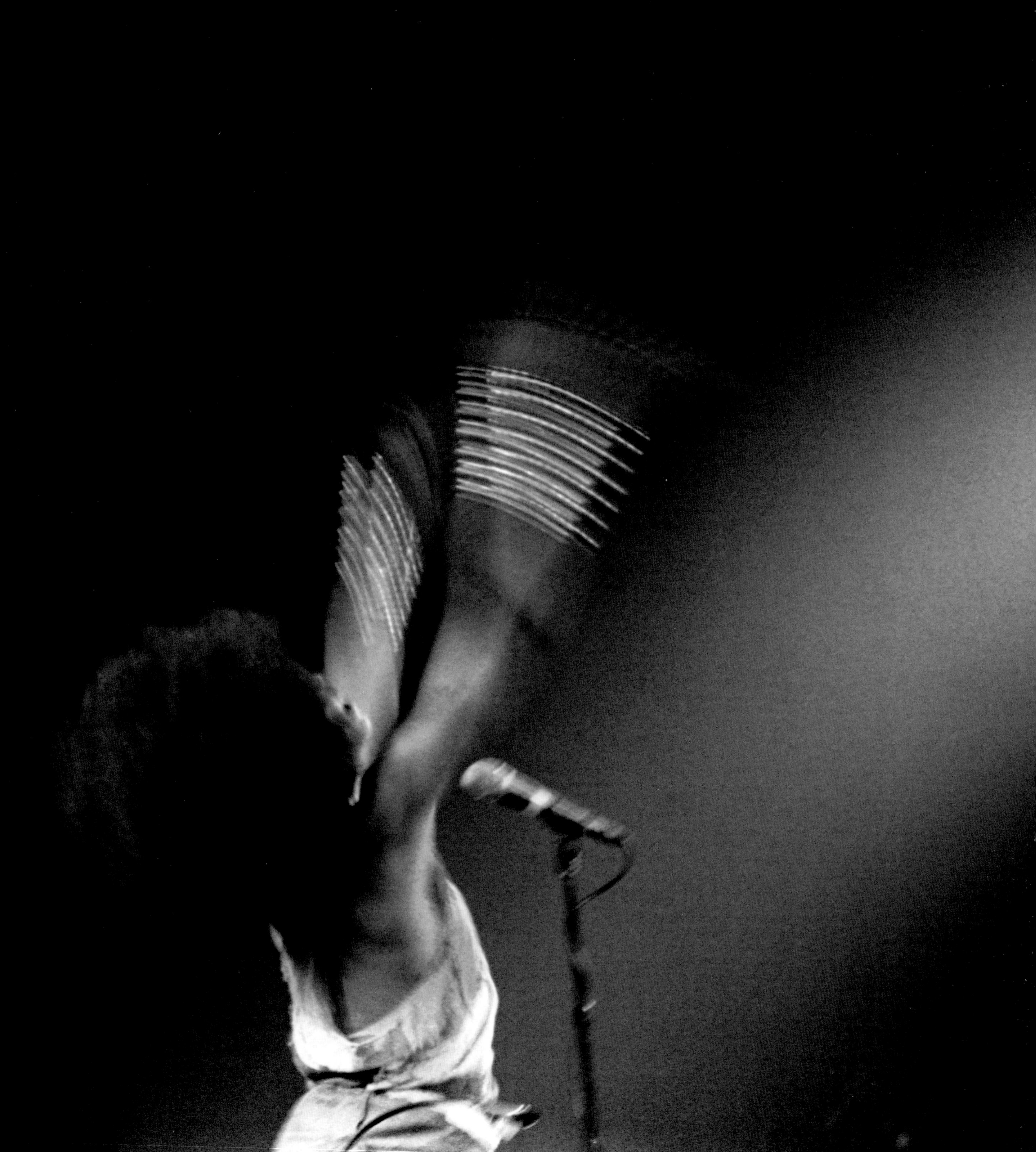

ERYKAH BADU, 2003

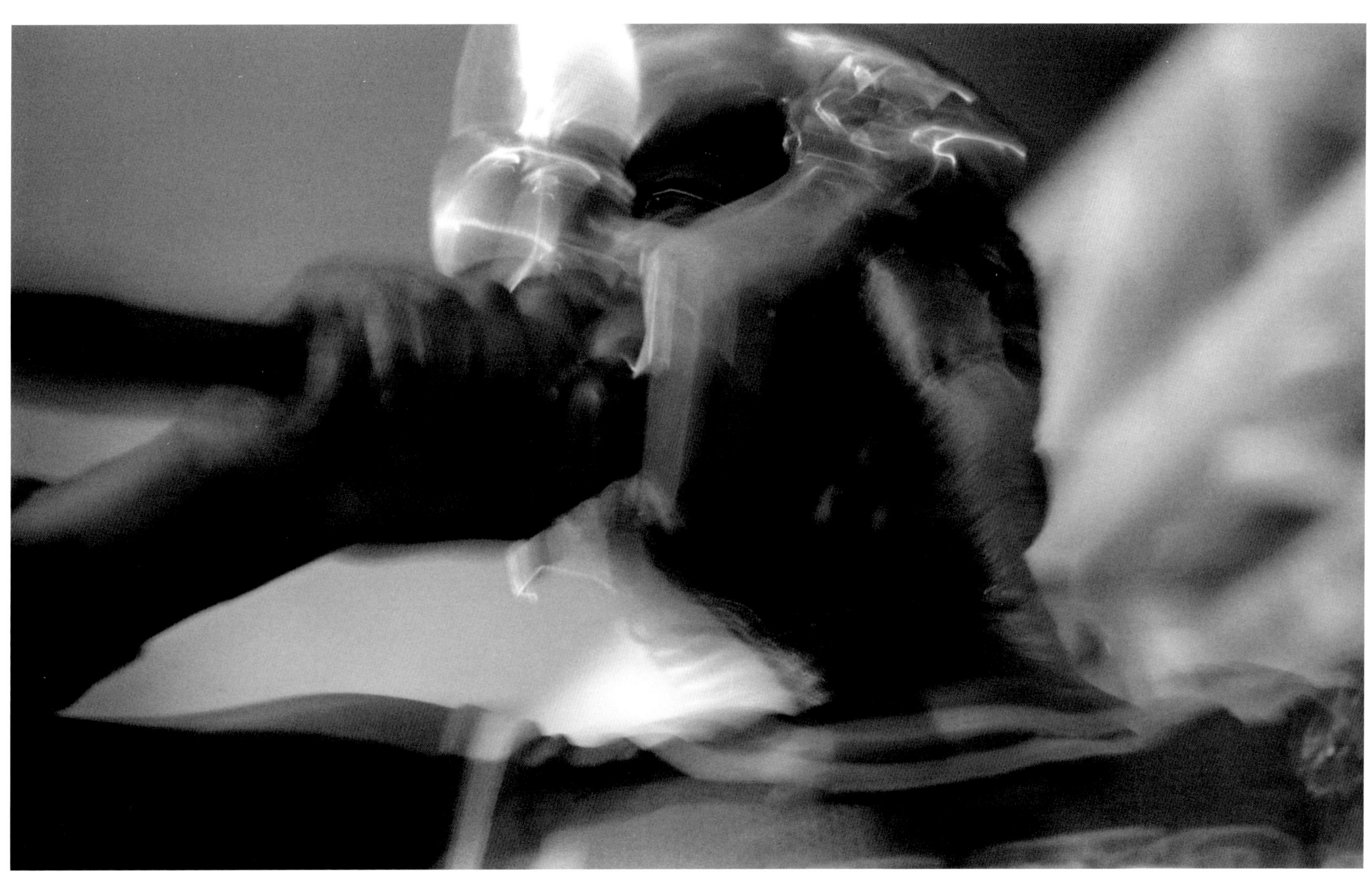

MF DOOM, 2005

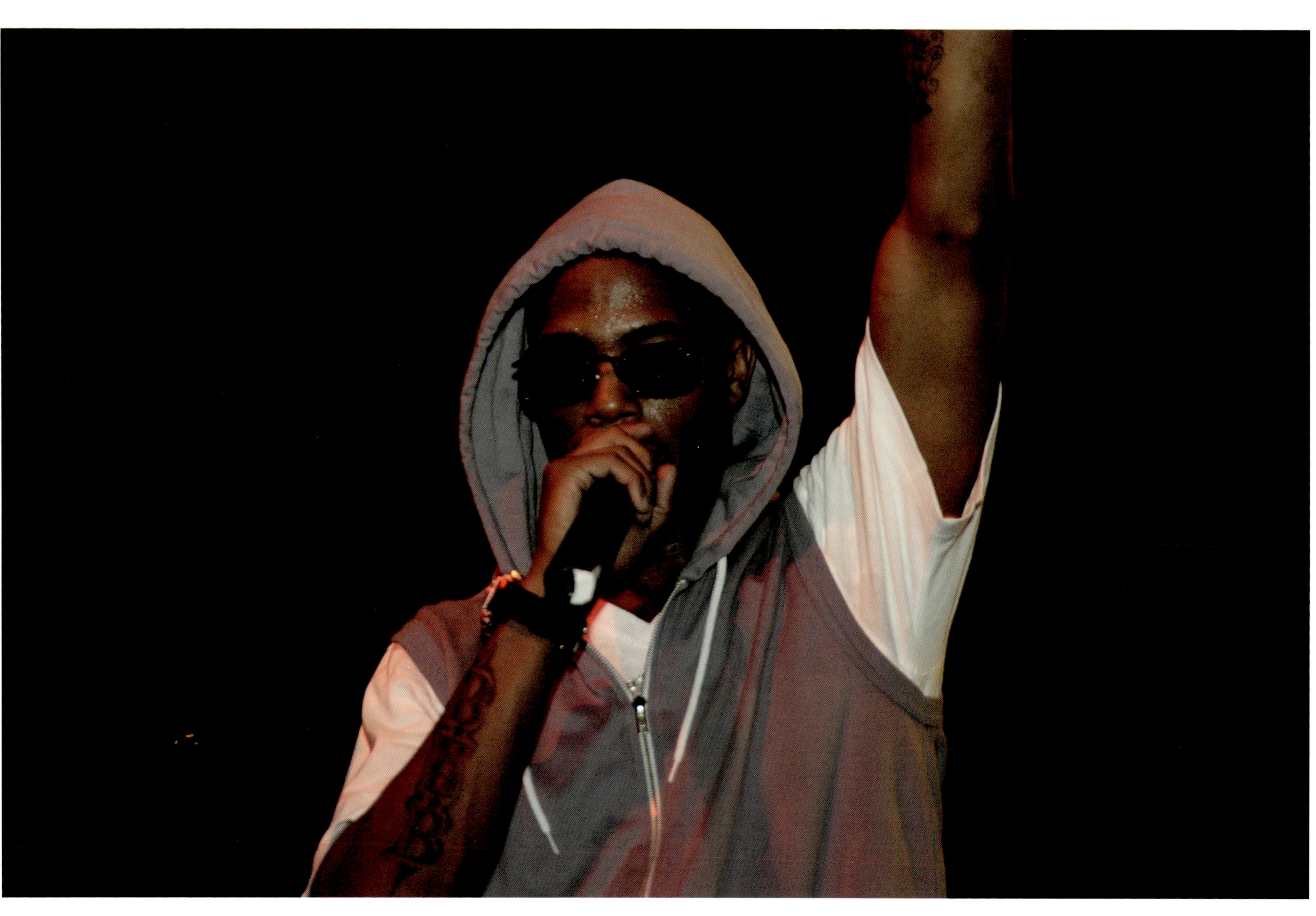

 B.O.B., 2010

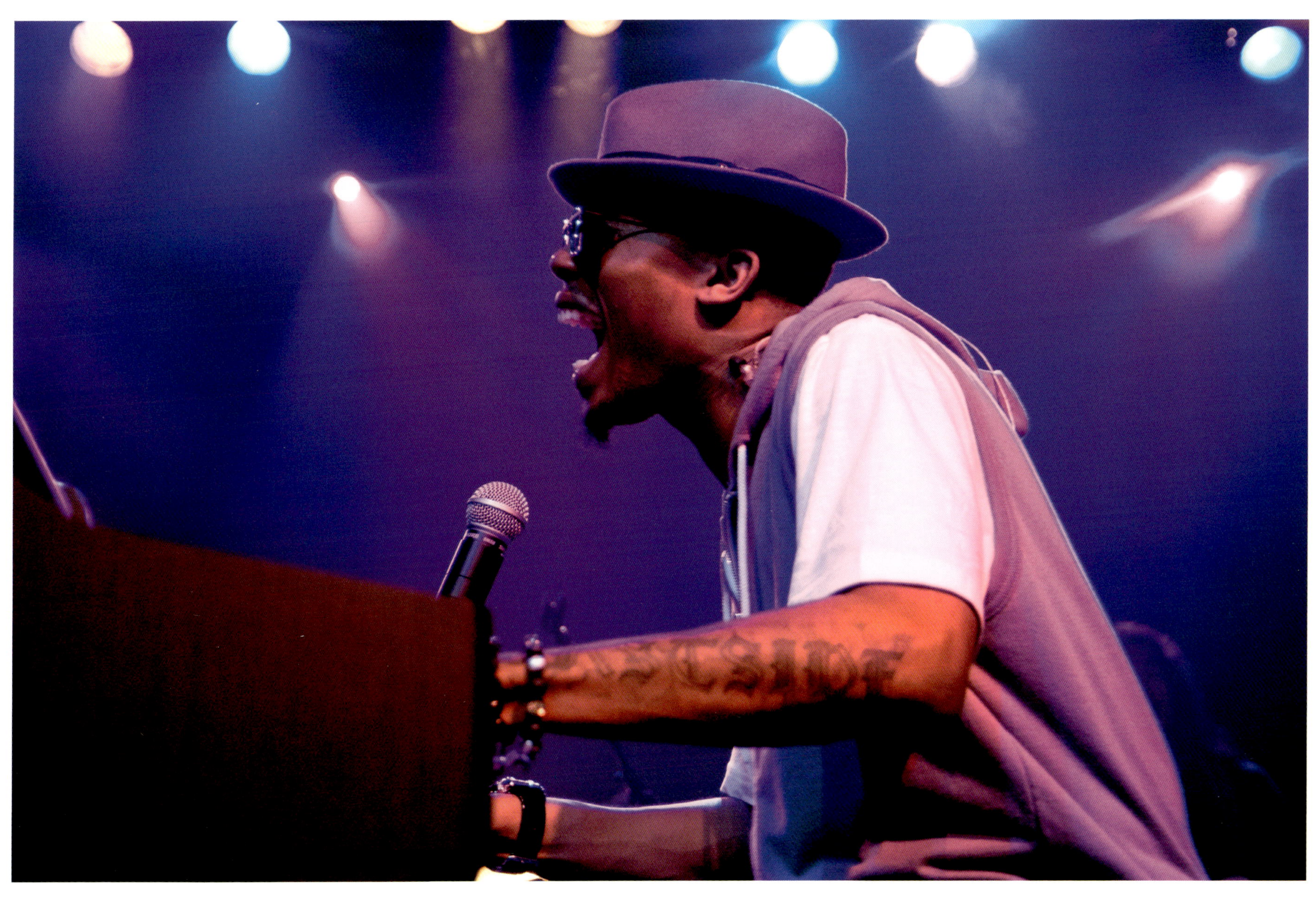

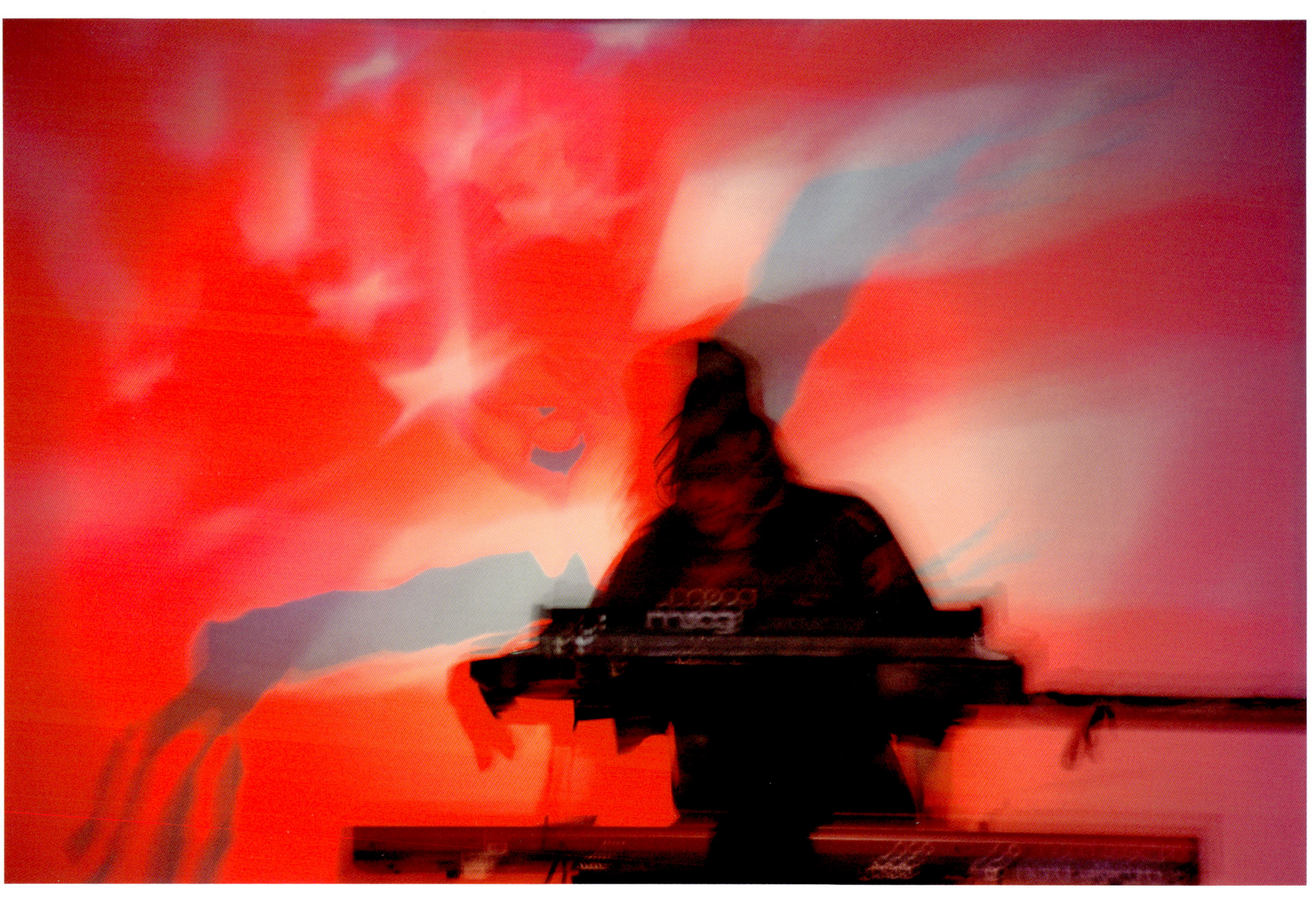

KEYBOARDIST, EL-P, 2007

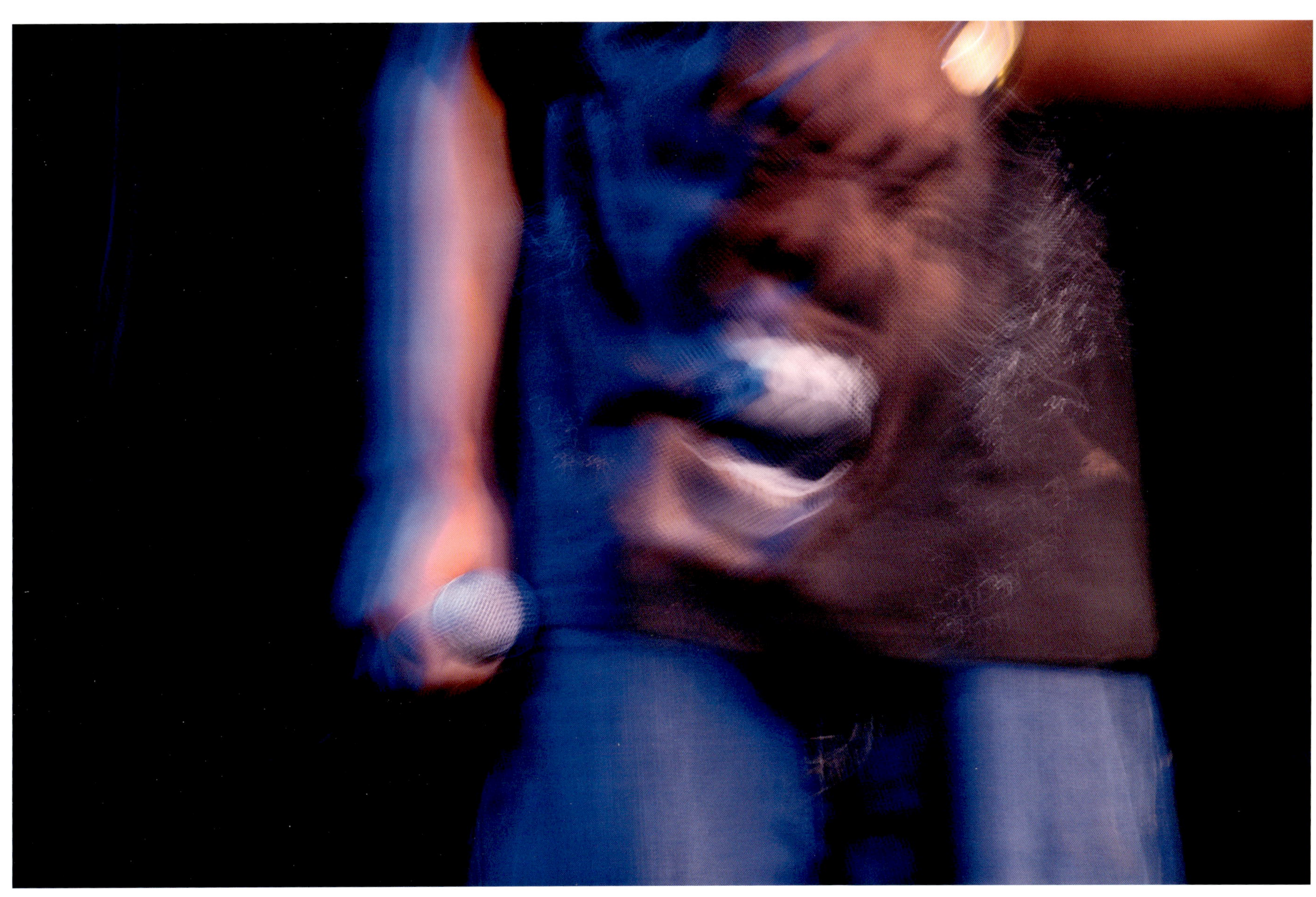

DEL THA FUNKY HOMOSAPIEN, 2009

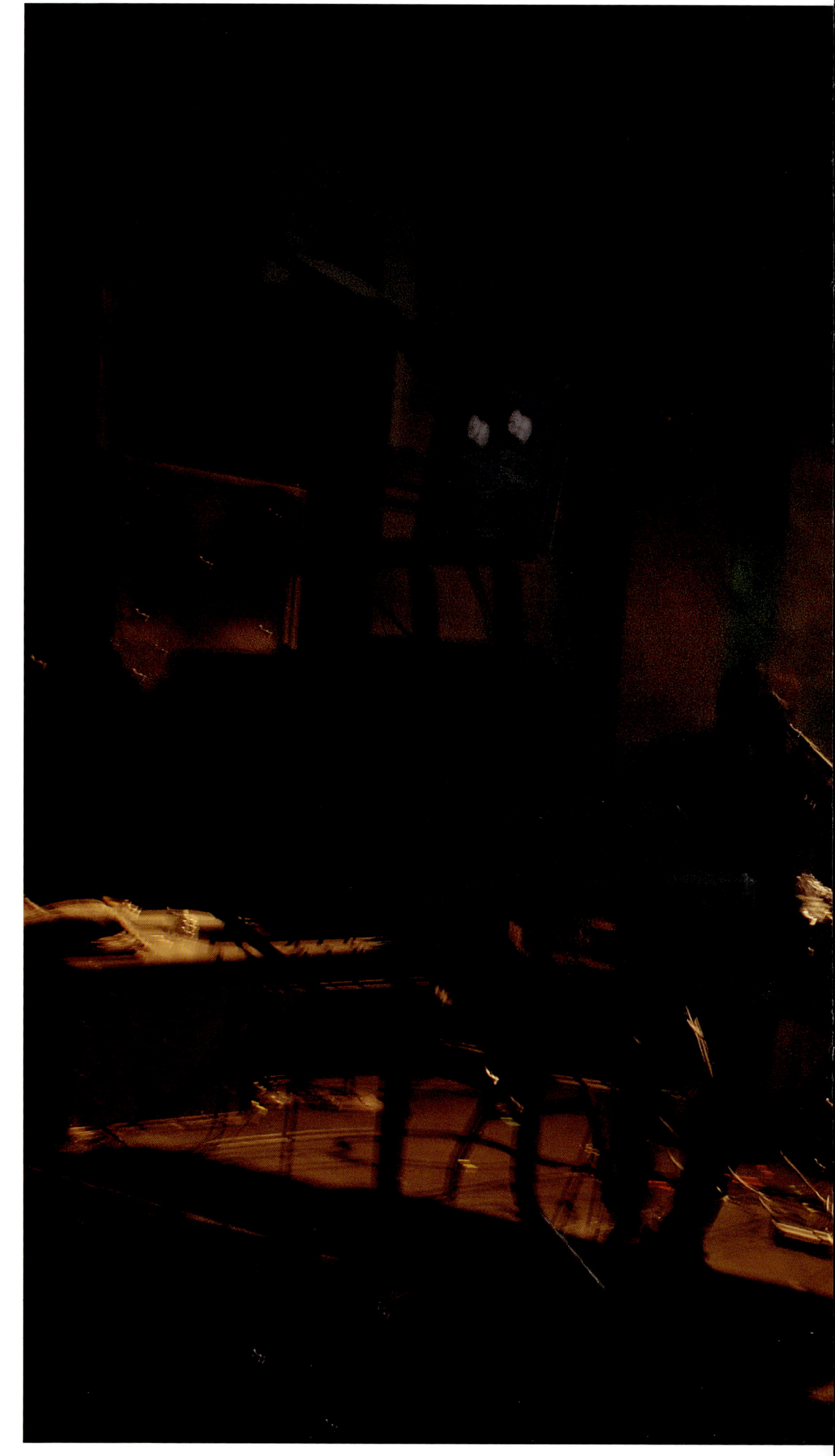

 MIKE RELM, 2009

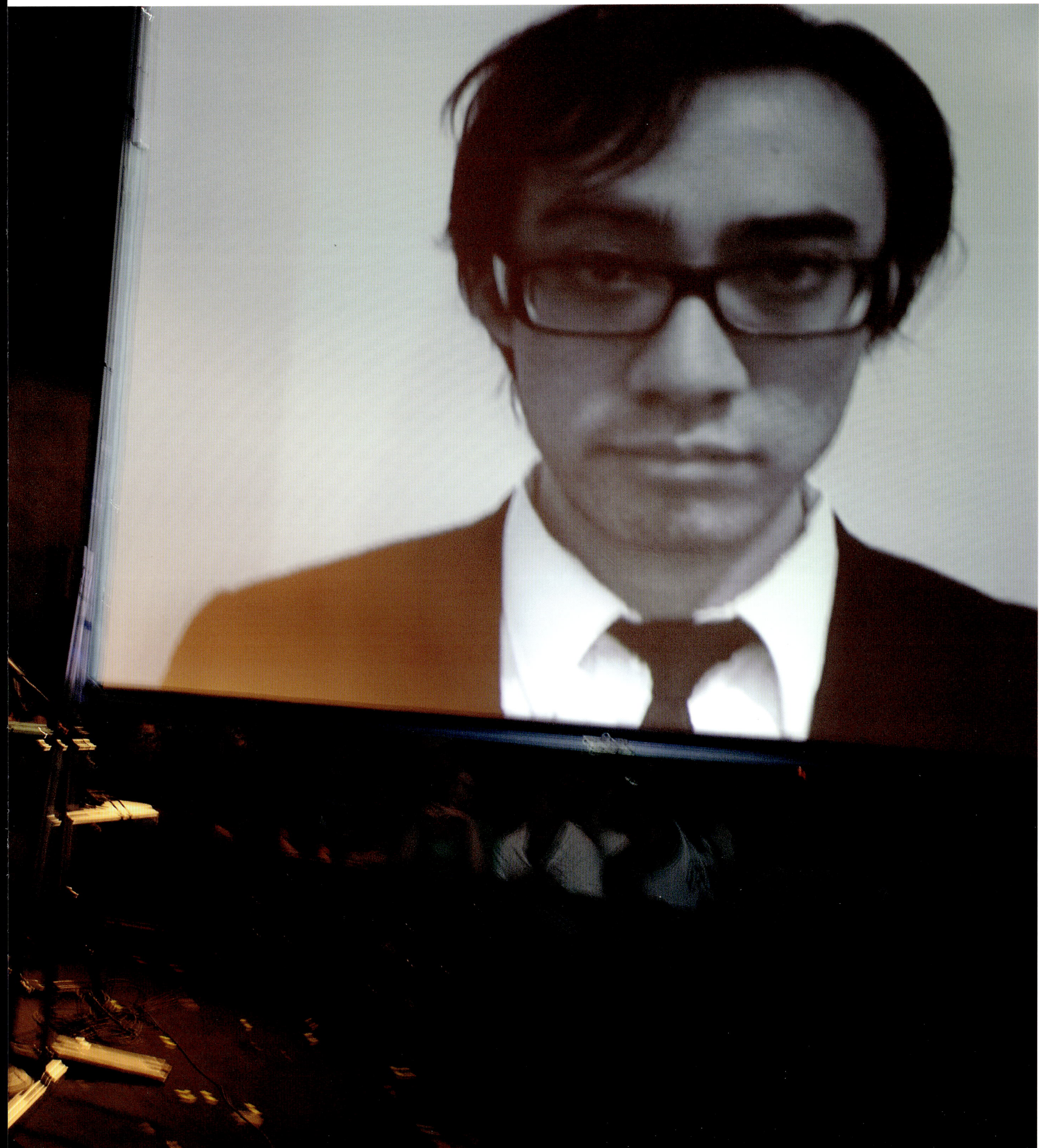

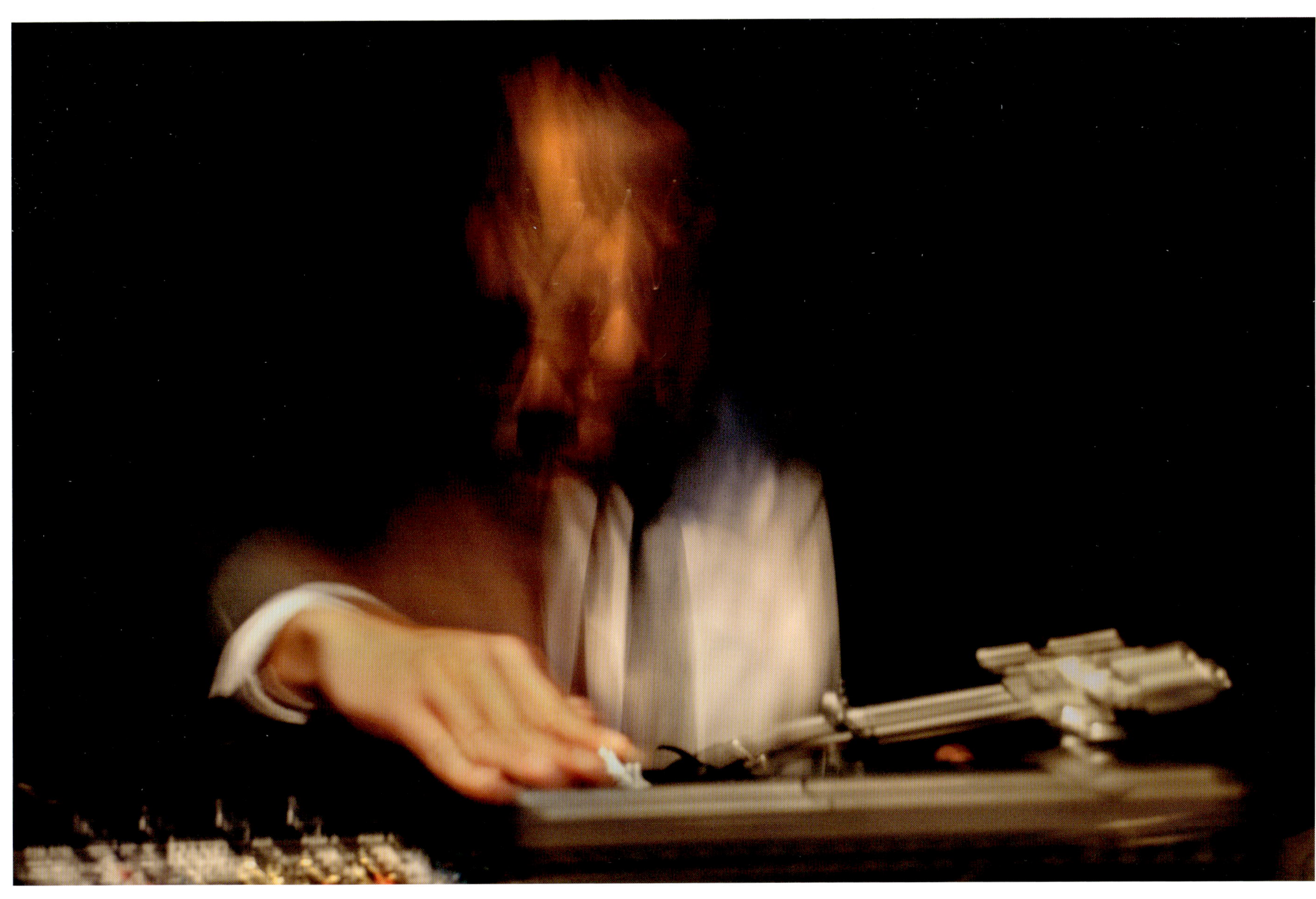

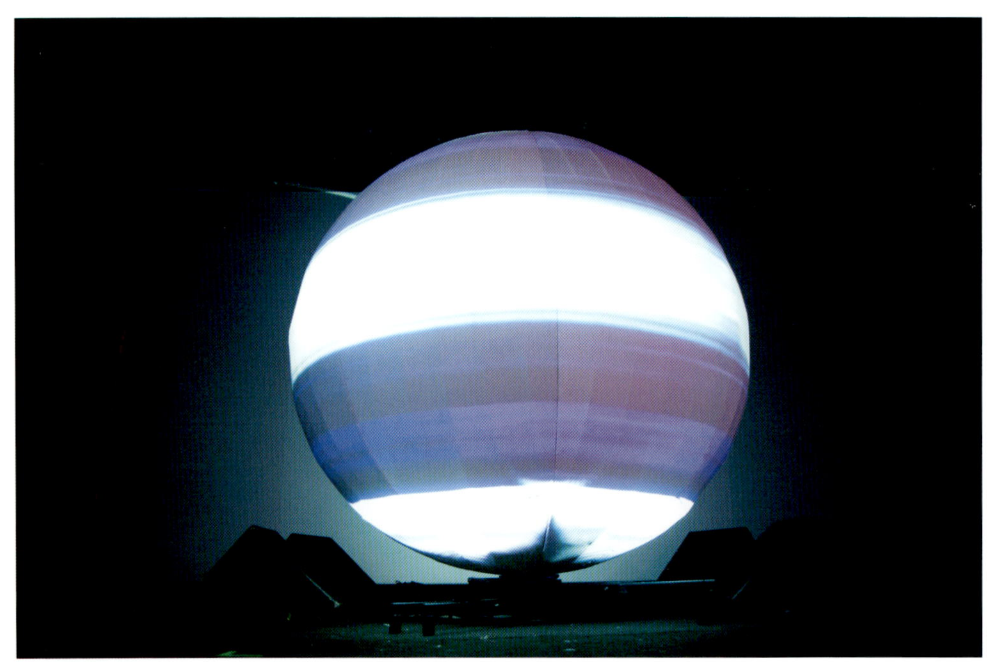

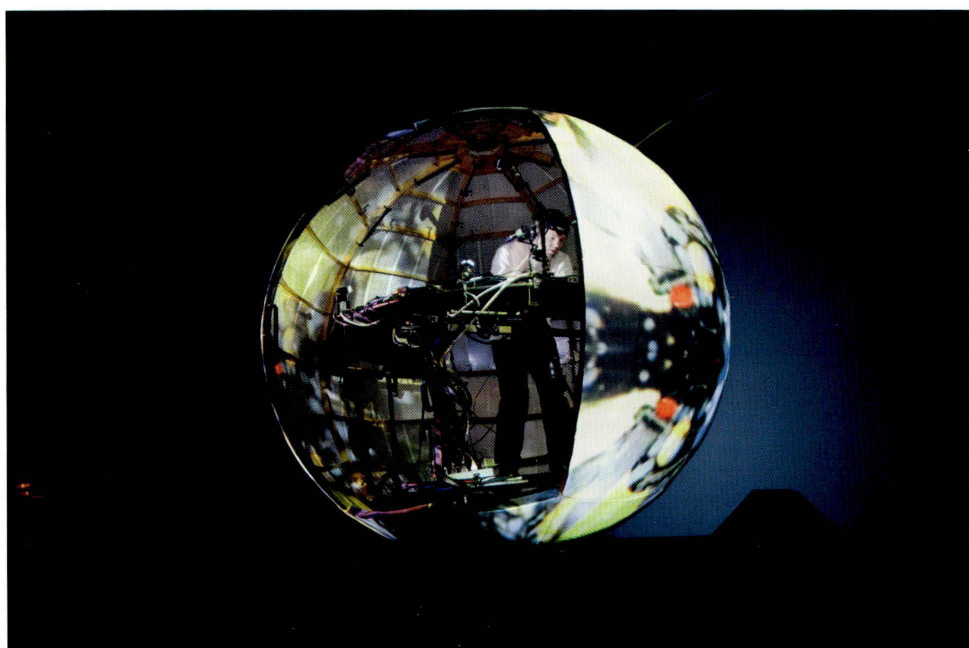

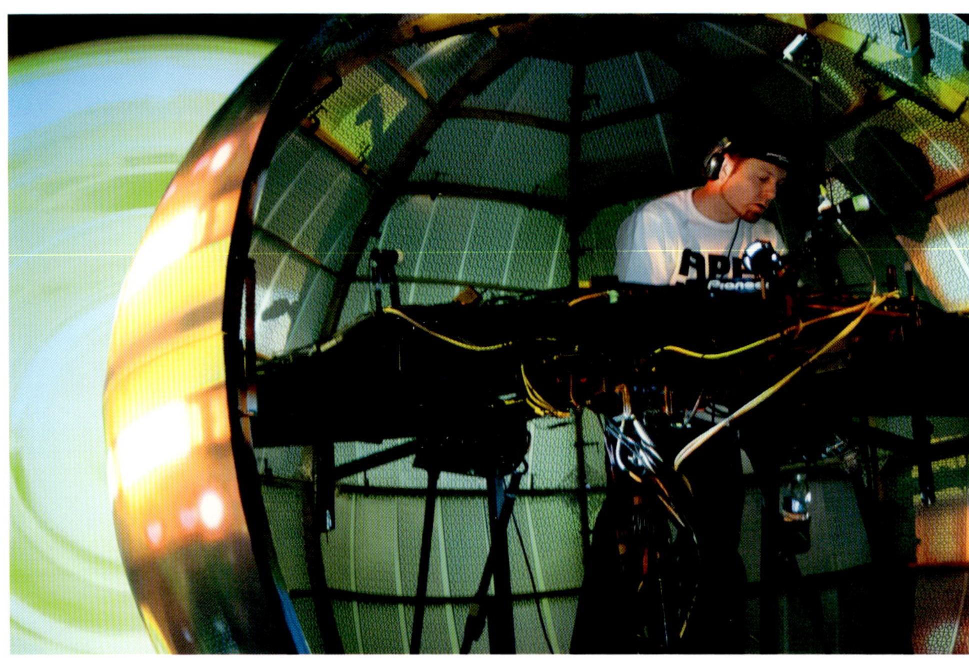

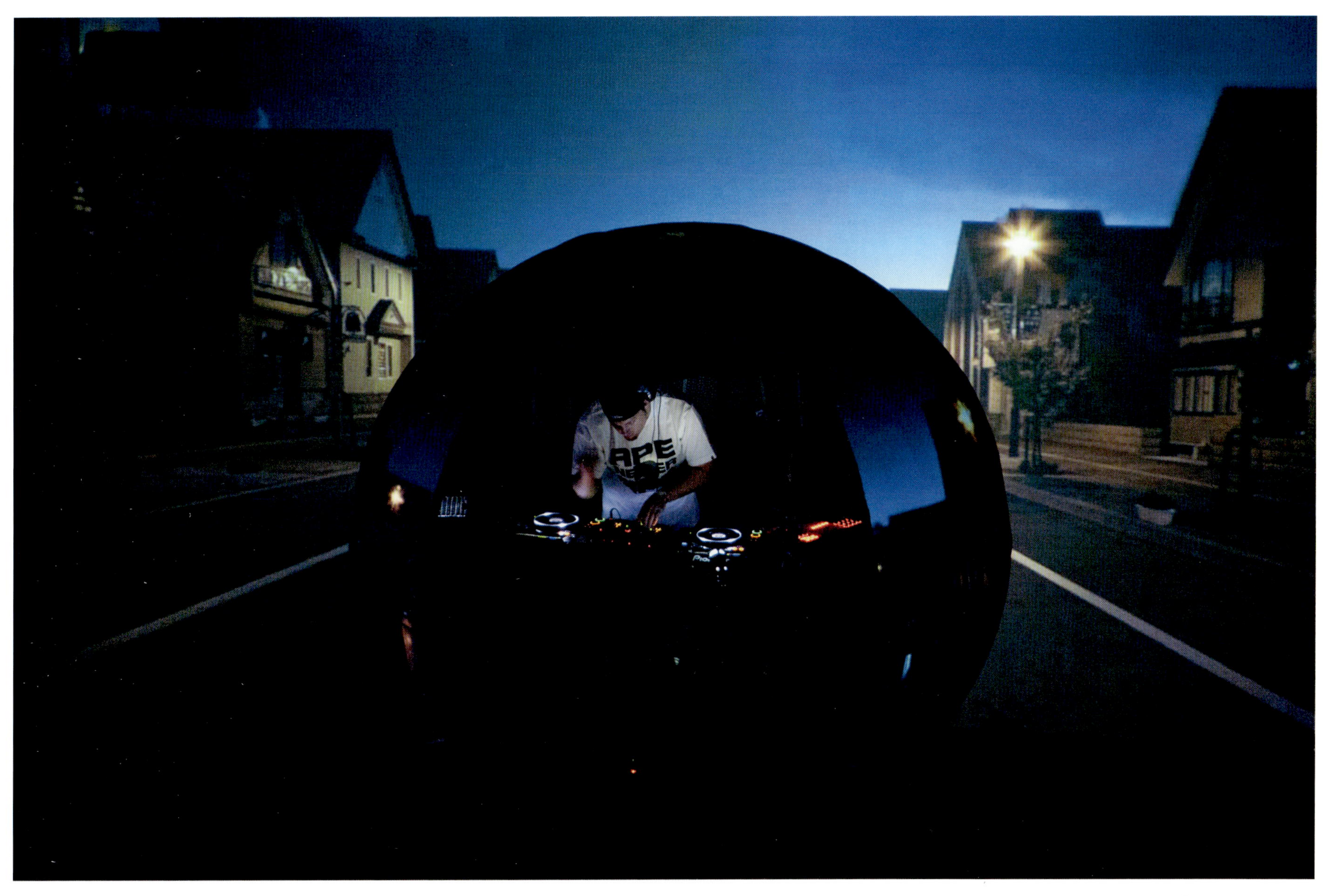

Above and opposite: DJ SHADOW, 2010

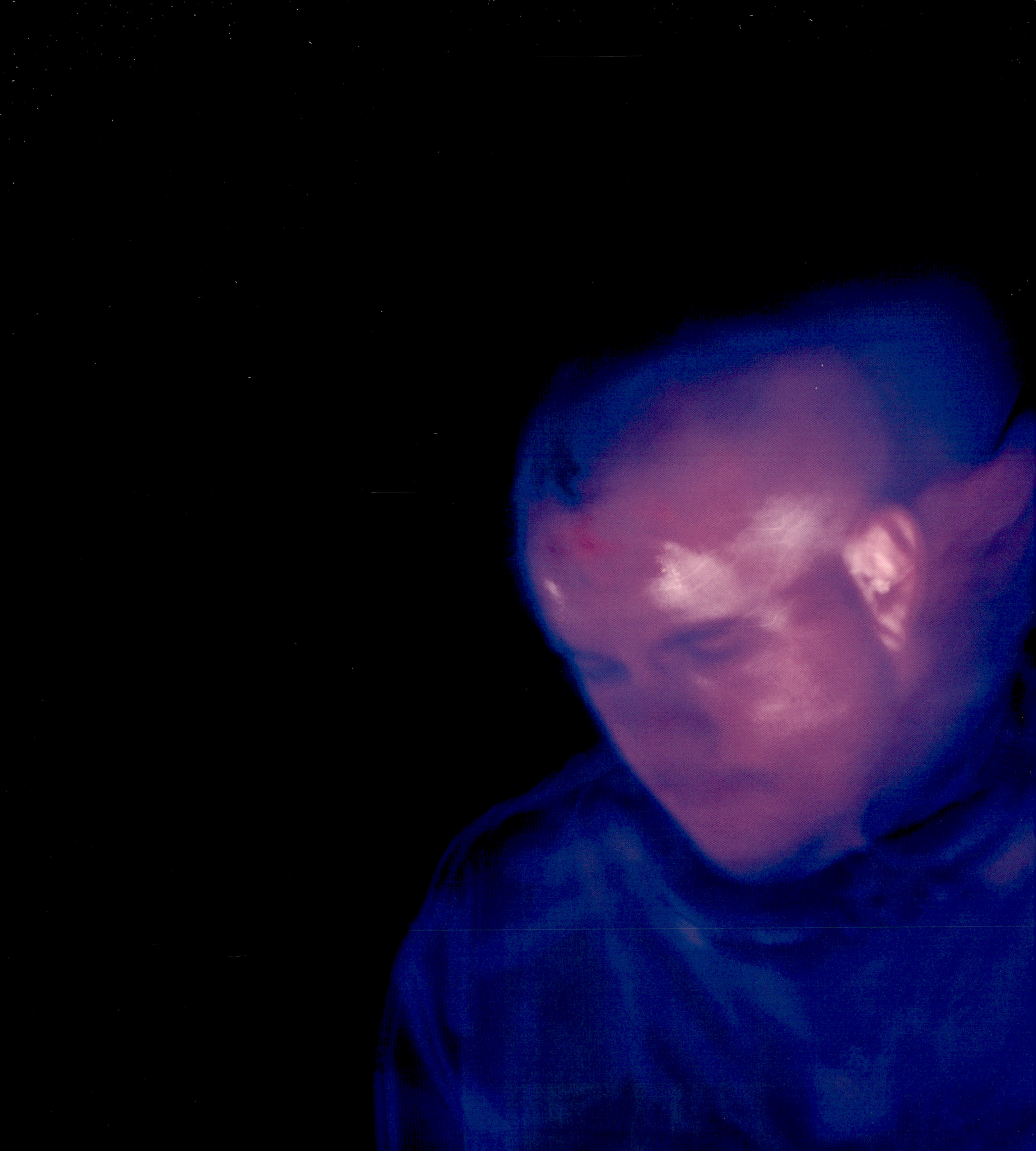

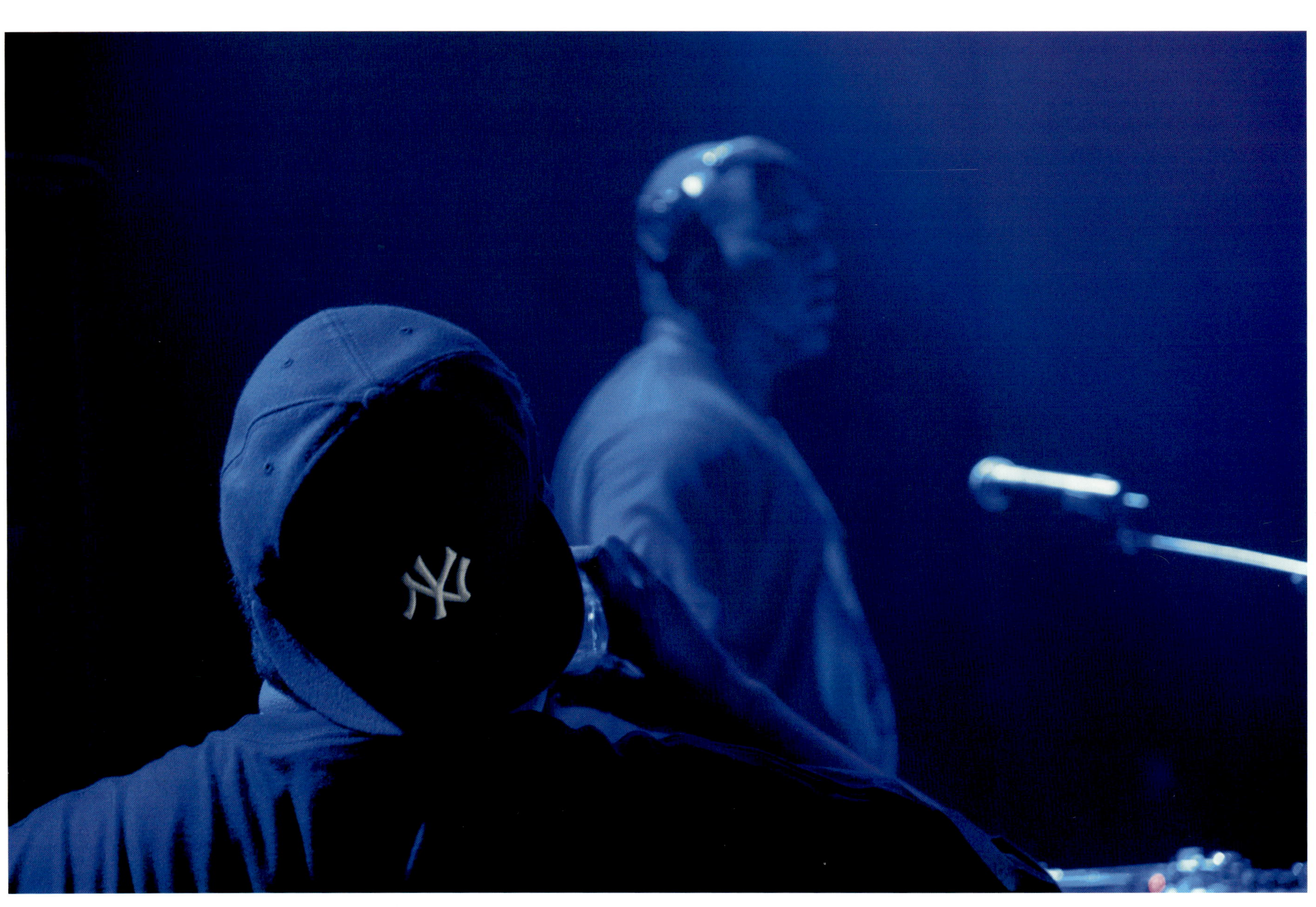

 DAVE (left), MASEO (right), DE LA SOUL, 2009

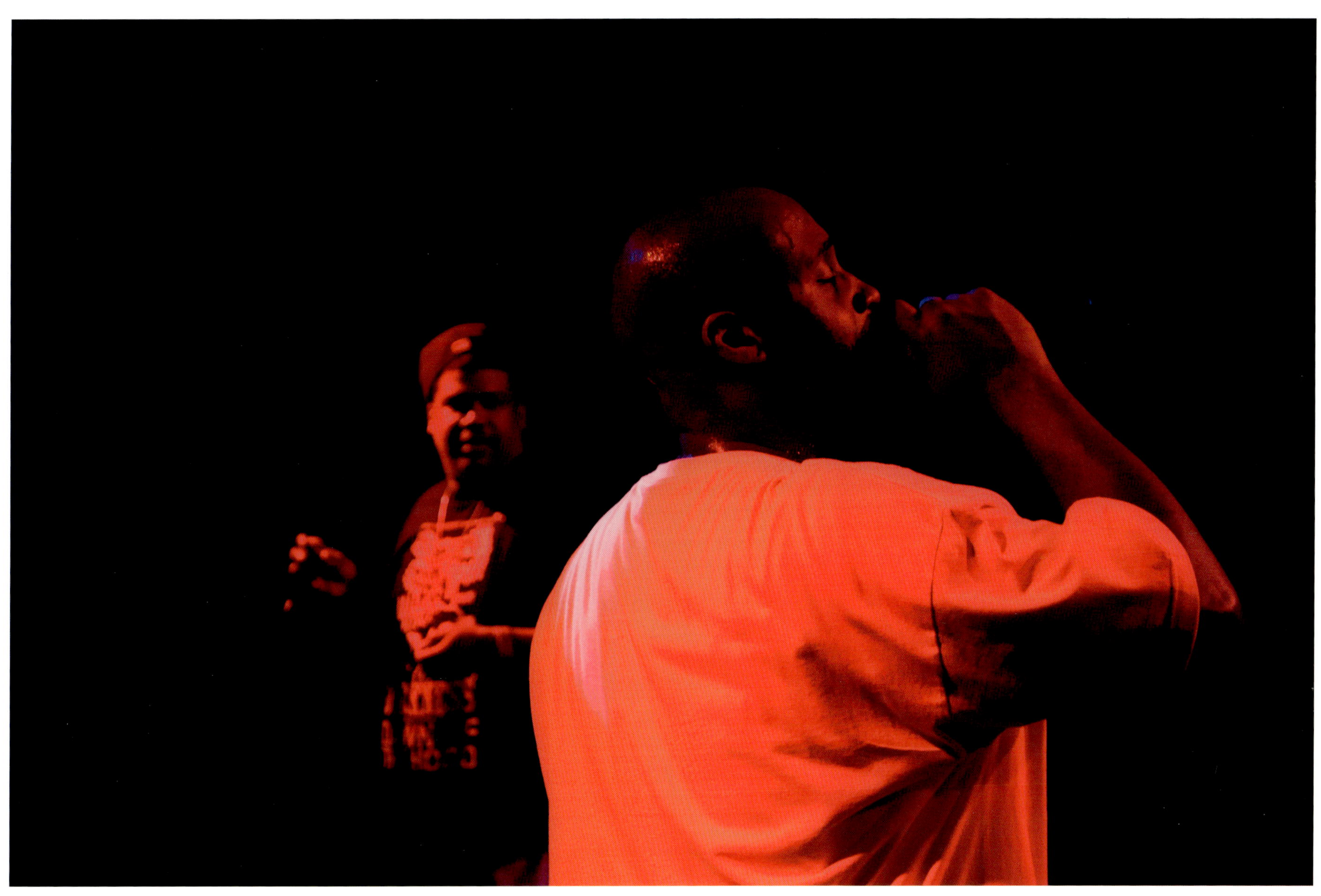

DAVE (left), POSDNUOS (right), DE LA SOUL, 2009

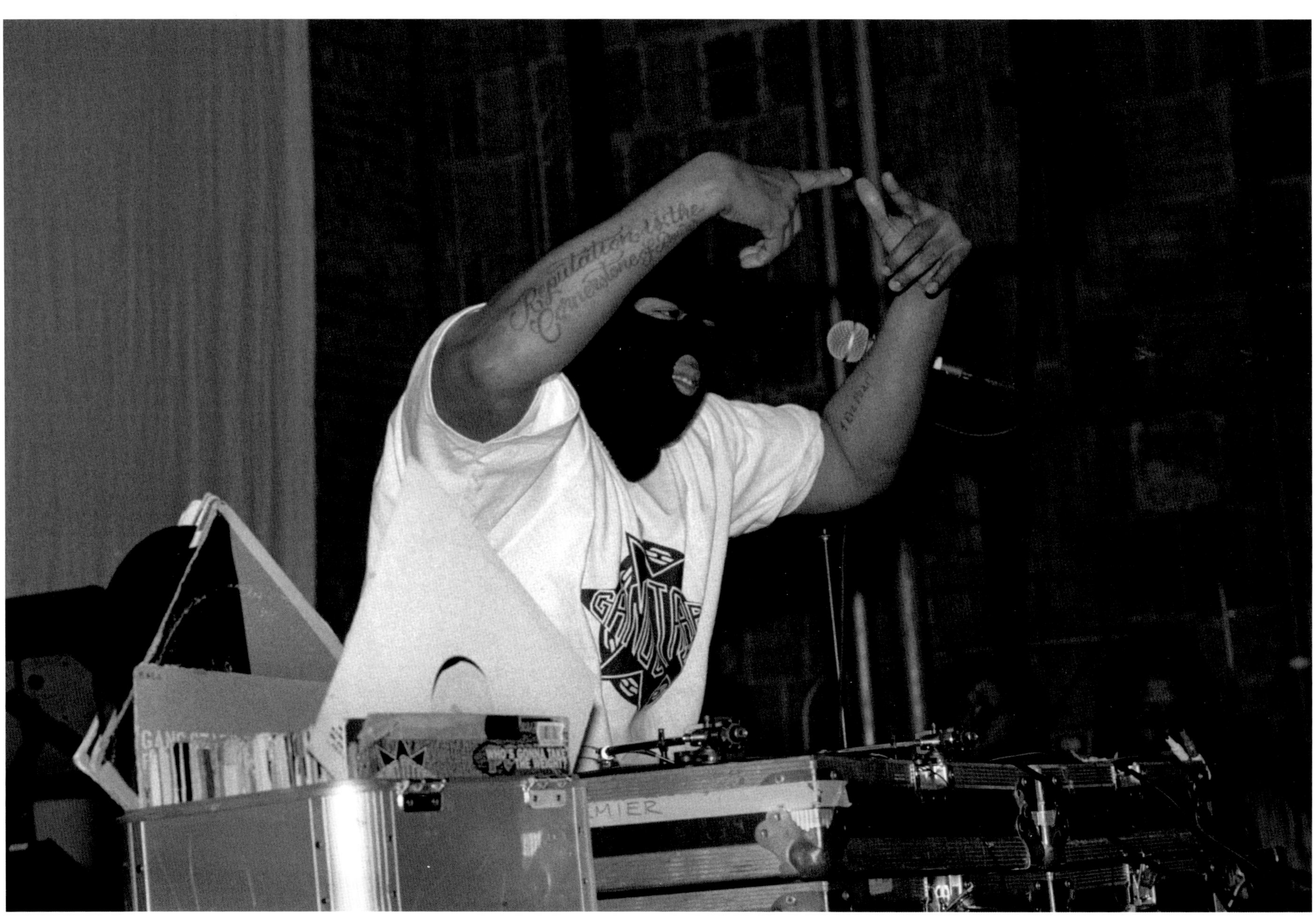

 DJ PREMIER, GANG STARR, 2005

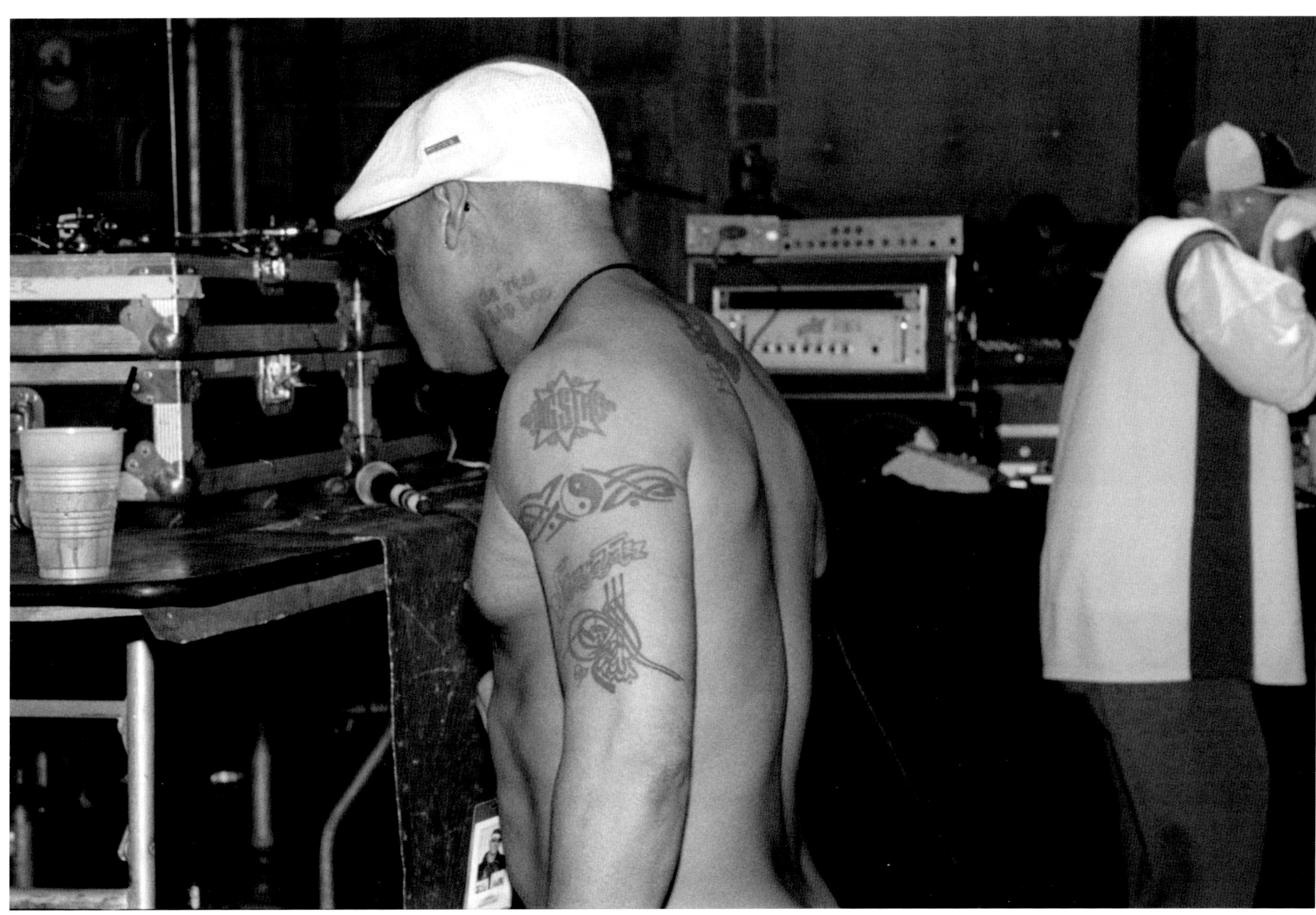

GURU, GANG STARR, 2005

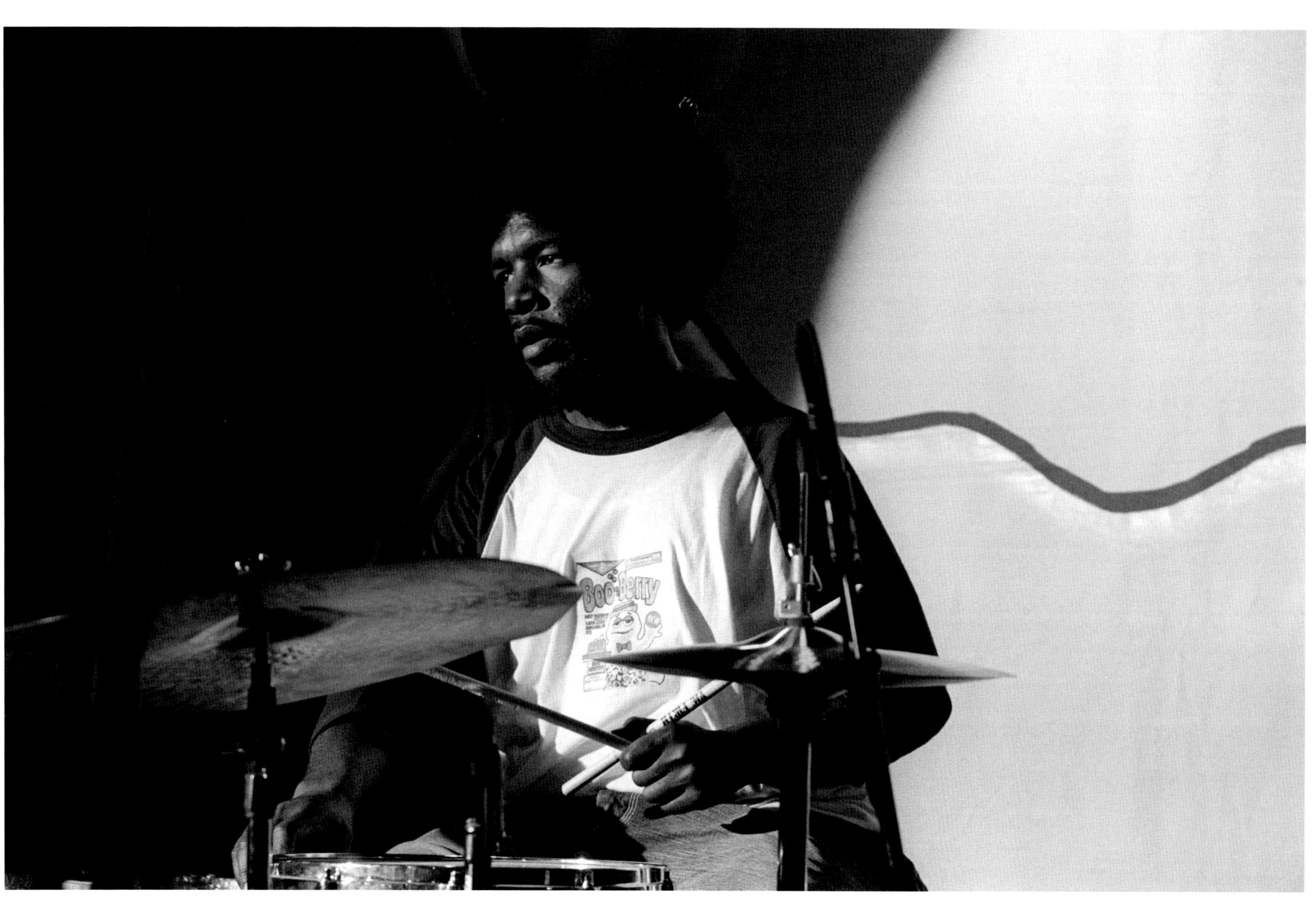

 ?UESTLOVE, THE ROOTS, 2003

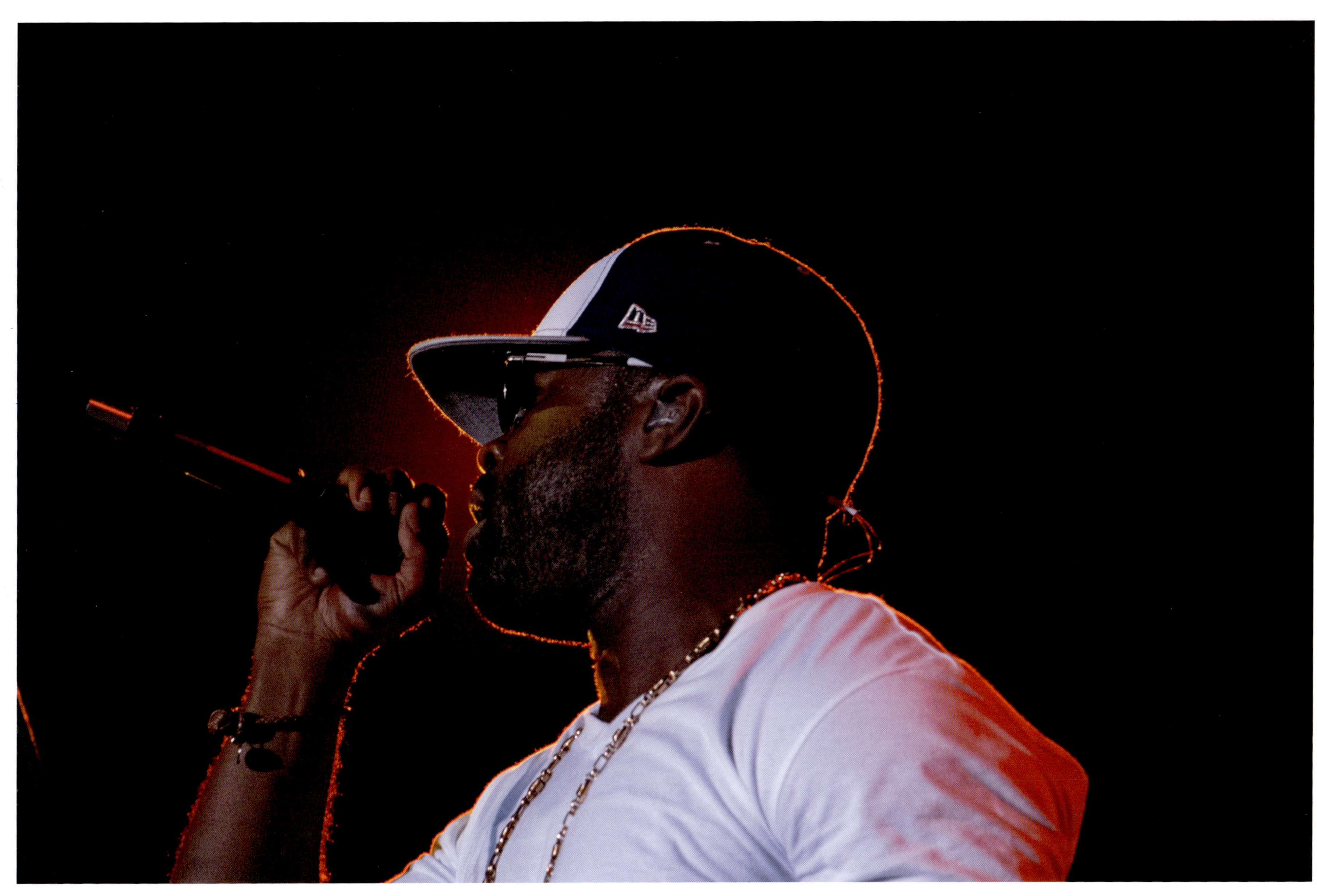

BLACK THOUGHT, THE ROOTS, 2008

 CHUCK D, PUBLIC ENEMY, 2007

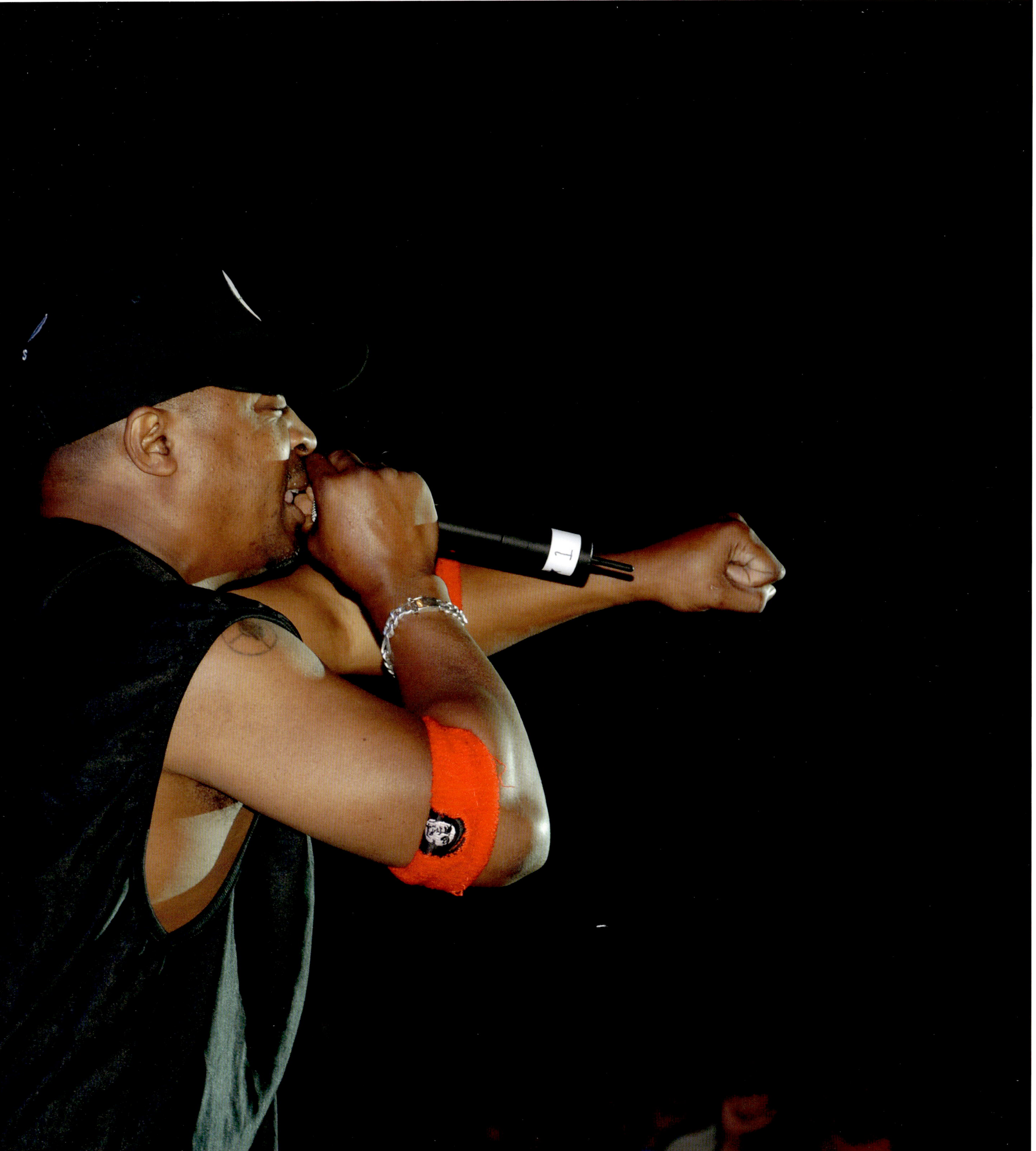

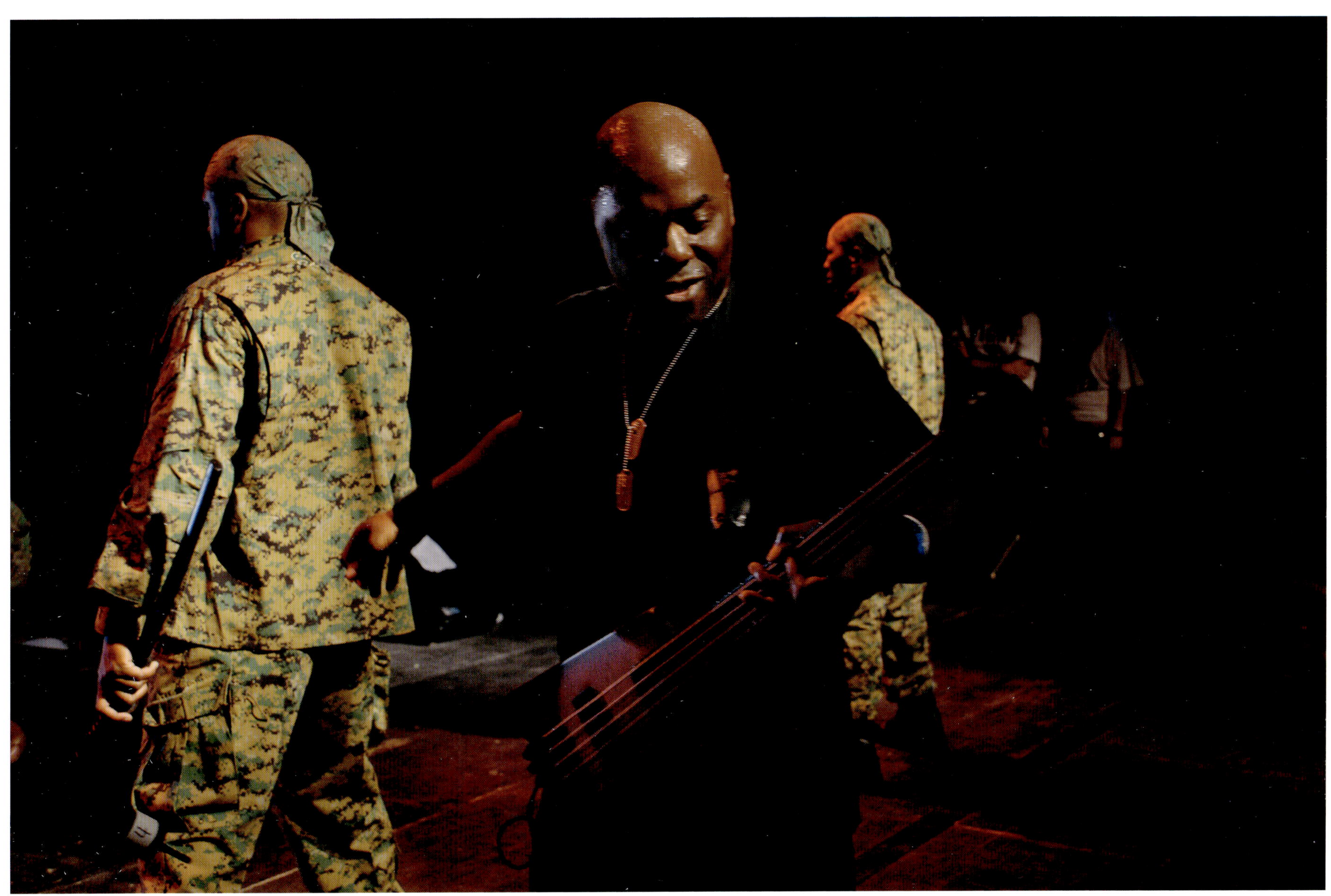

BRIAN HARDGROOVE (center), POP DIESEL S1W (left), JAMES BOMB S1W (right), PUBLIC ENEMY, 2007

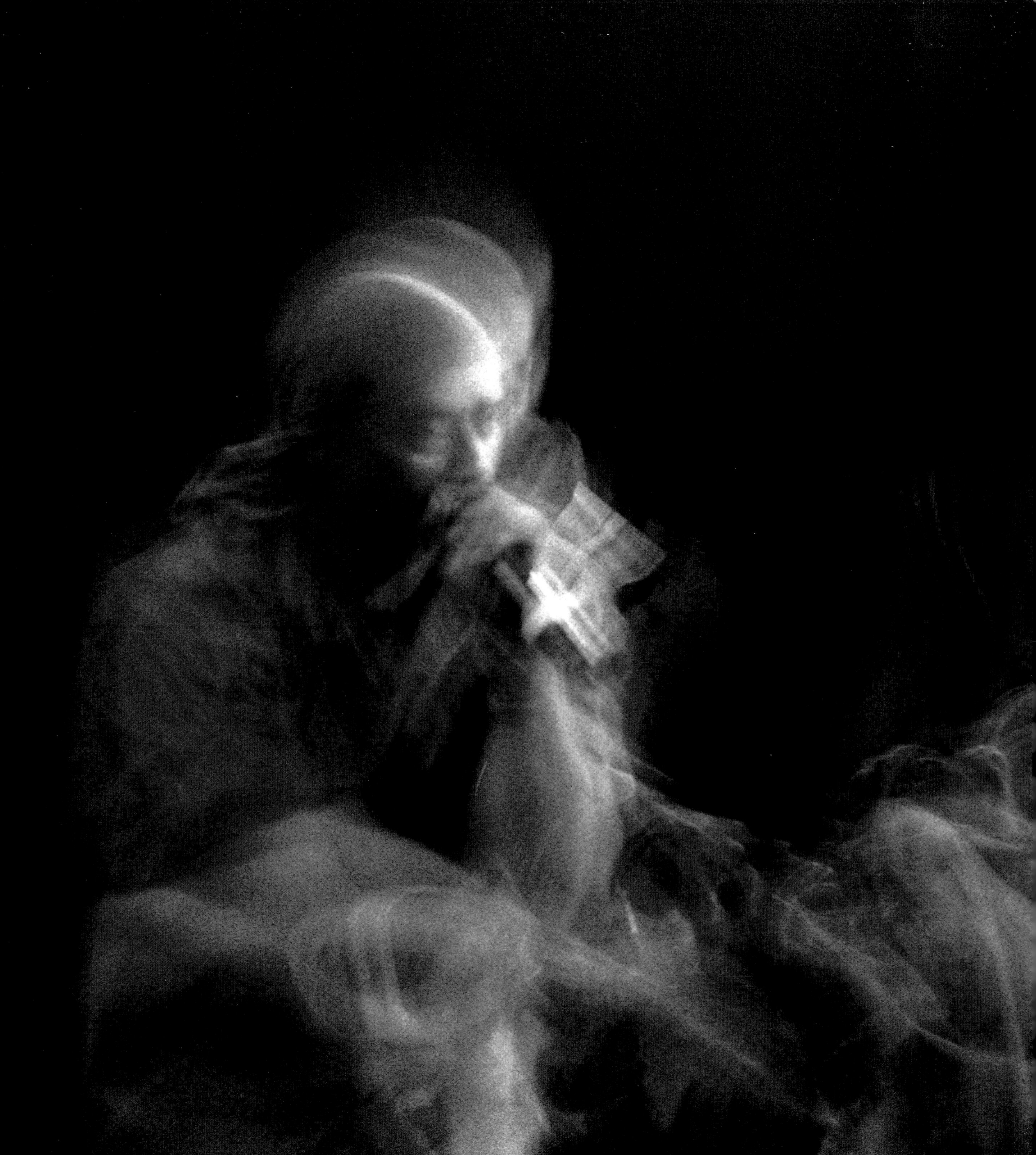

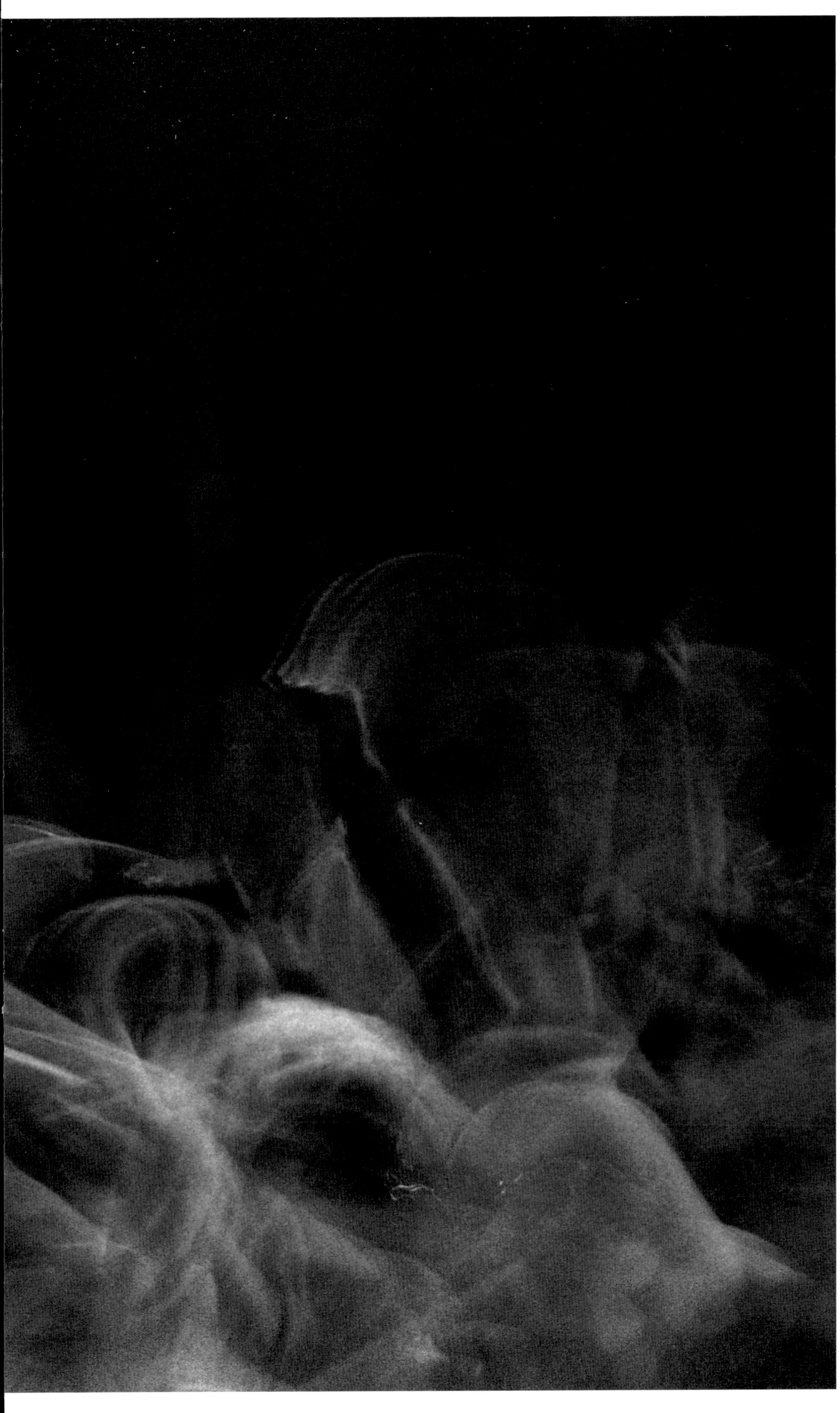

PROFESSOR GRIFF, PUBLIC ENEMY, 2002

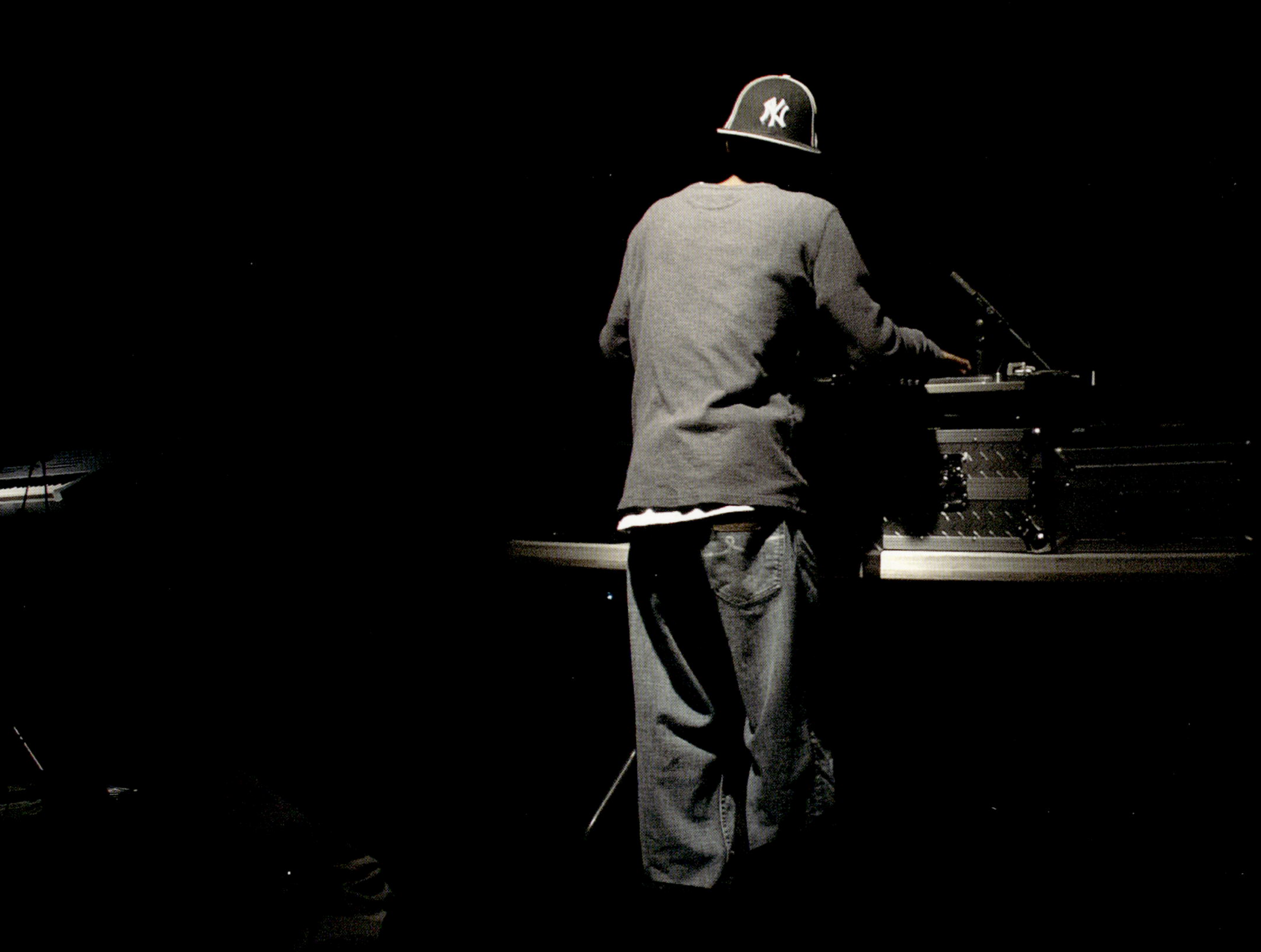

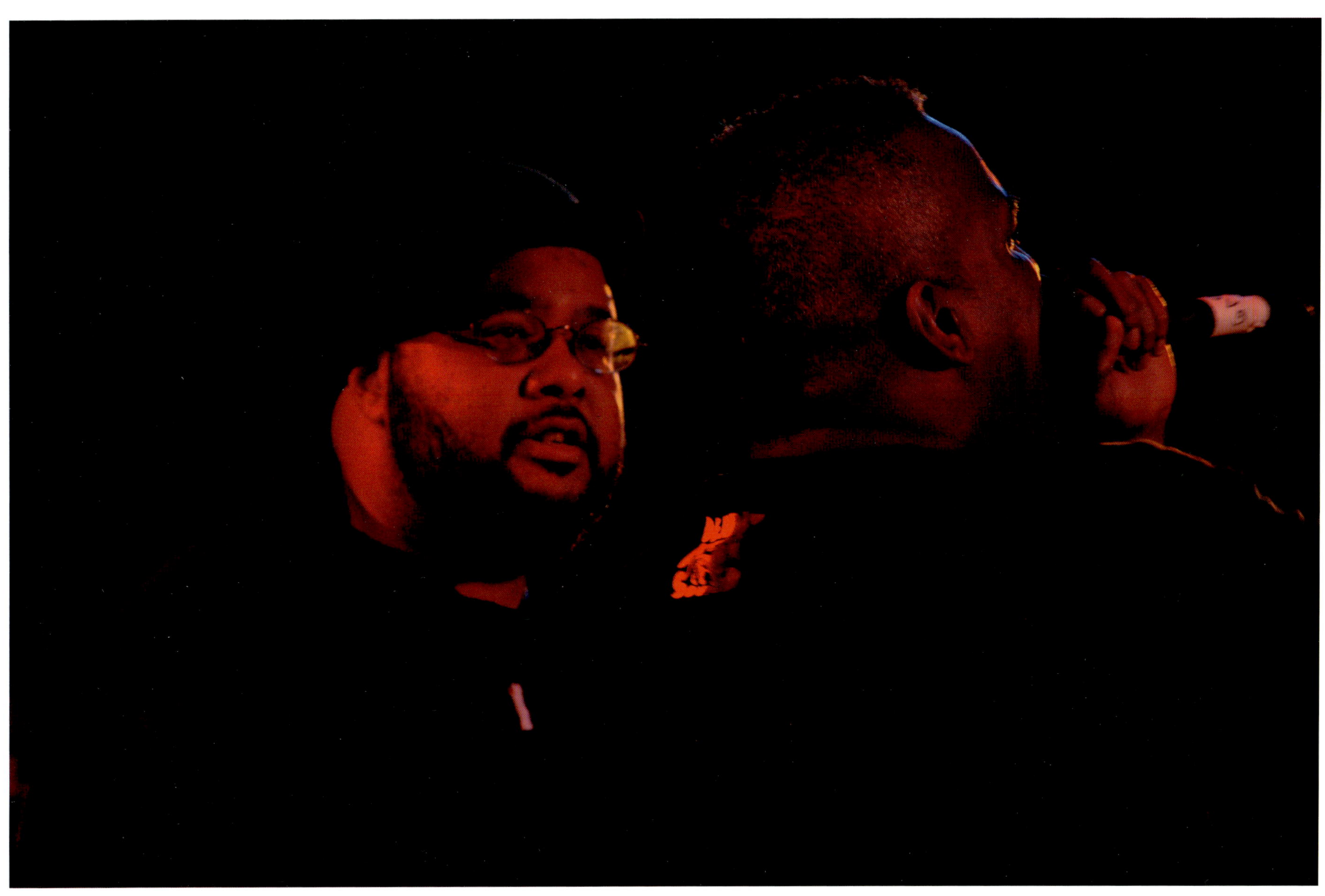

GIFT OF GAB (left), ACEYALONE (right), 2007

 METHOD MAN AND REDMAN, 2009

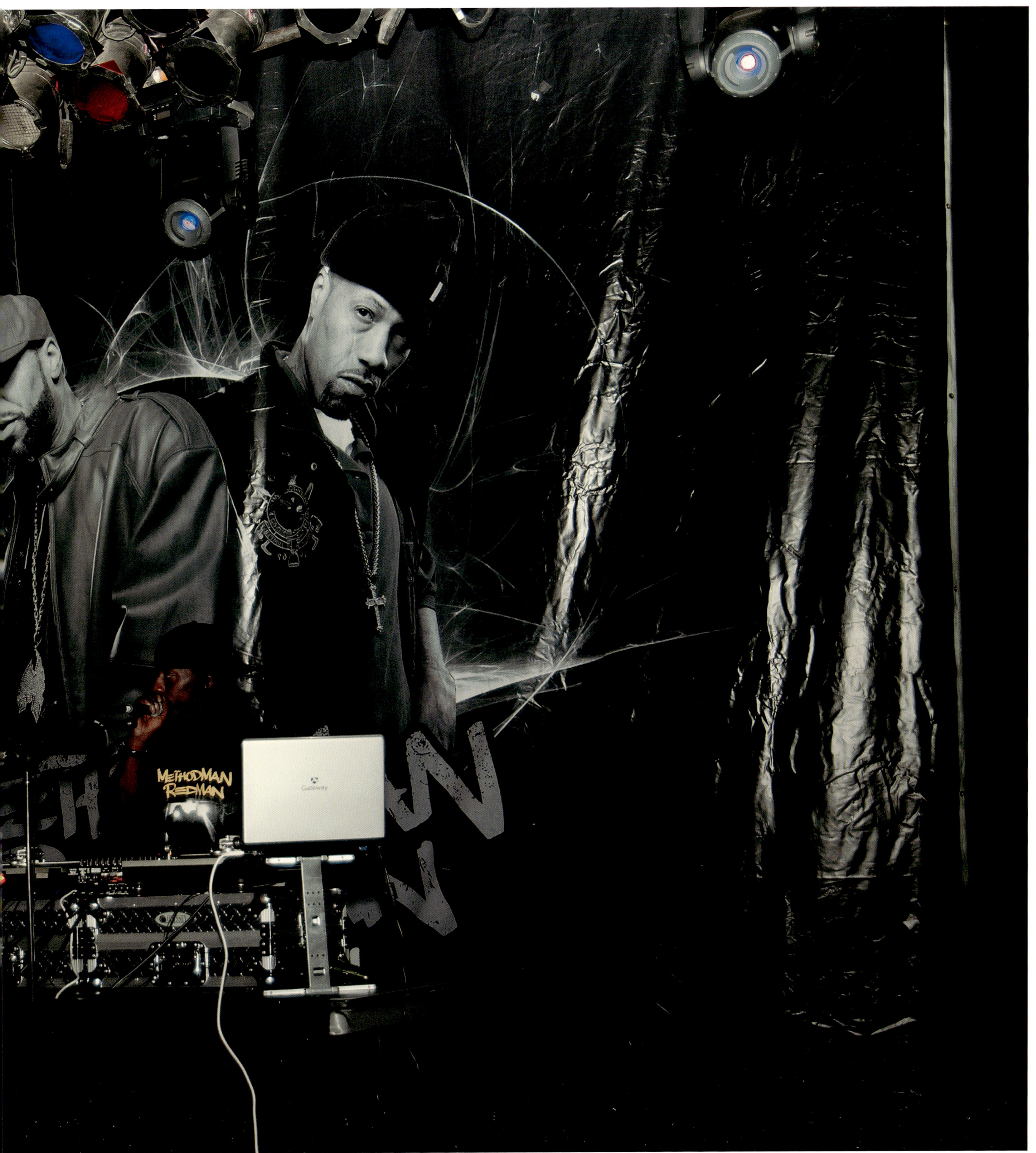
METHODMAN
REDMAN
Gateway

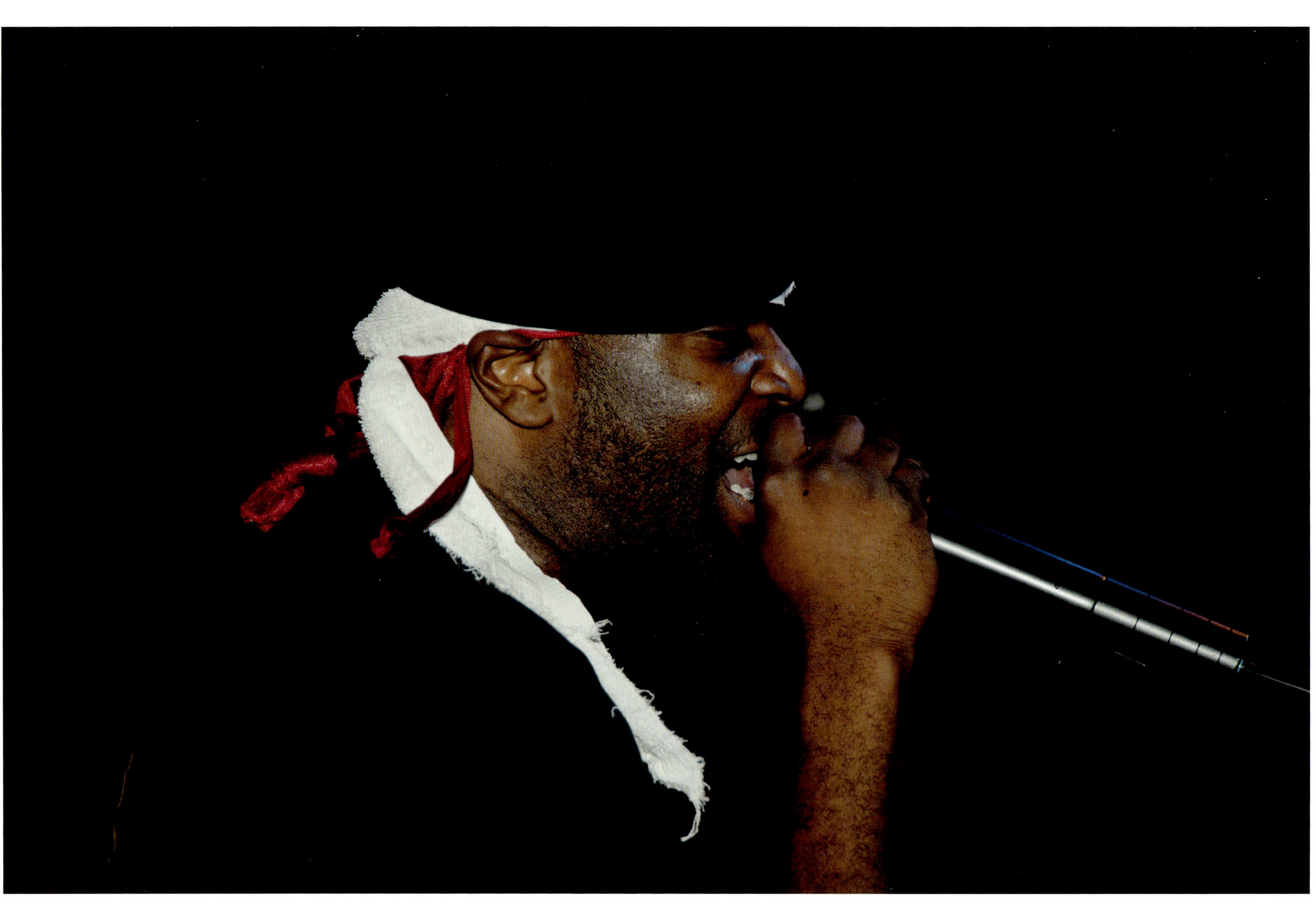

 METHOD MAN, 2009

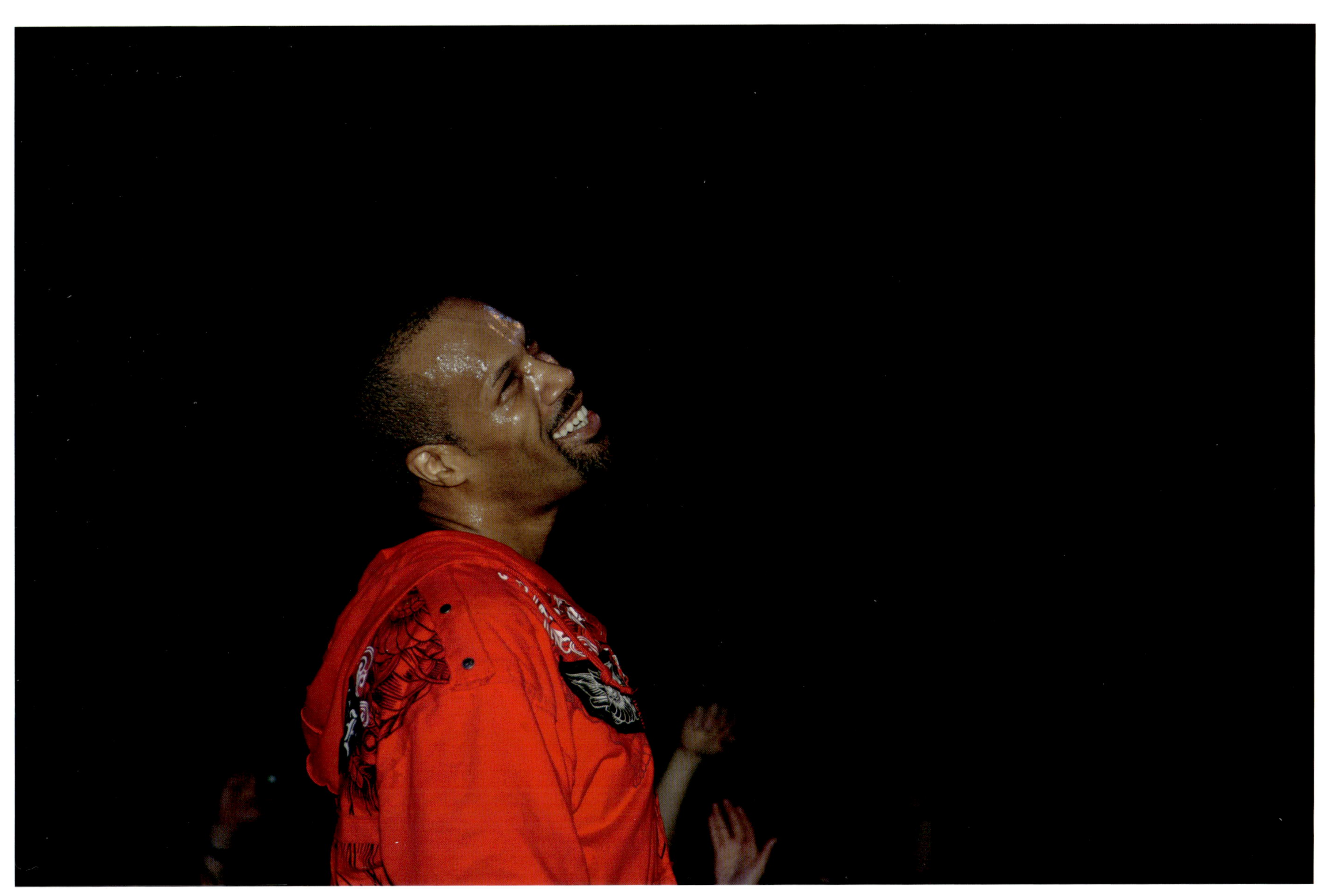

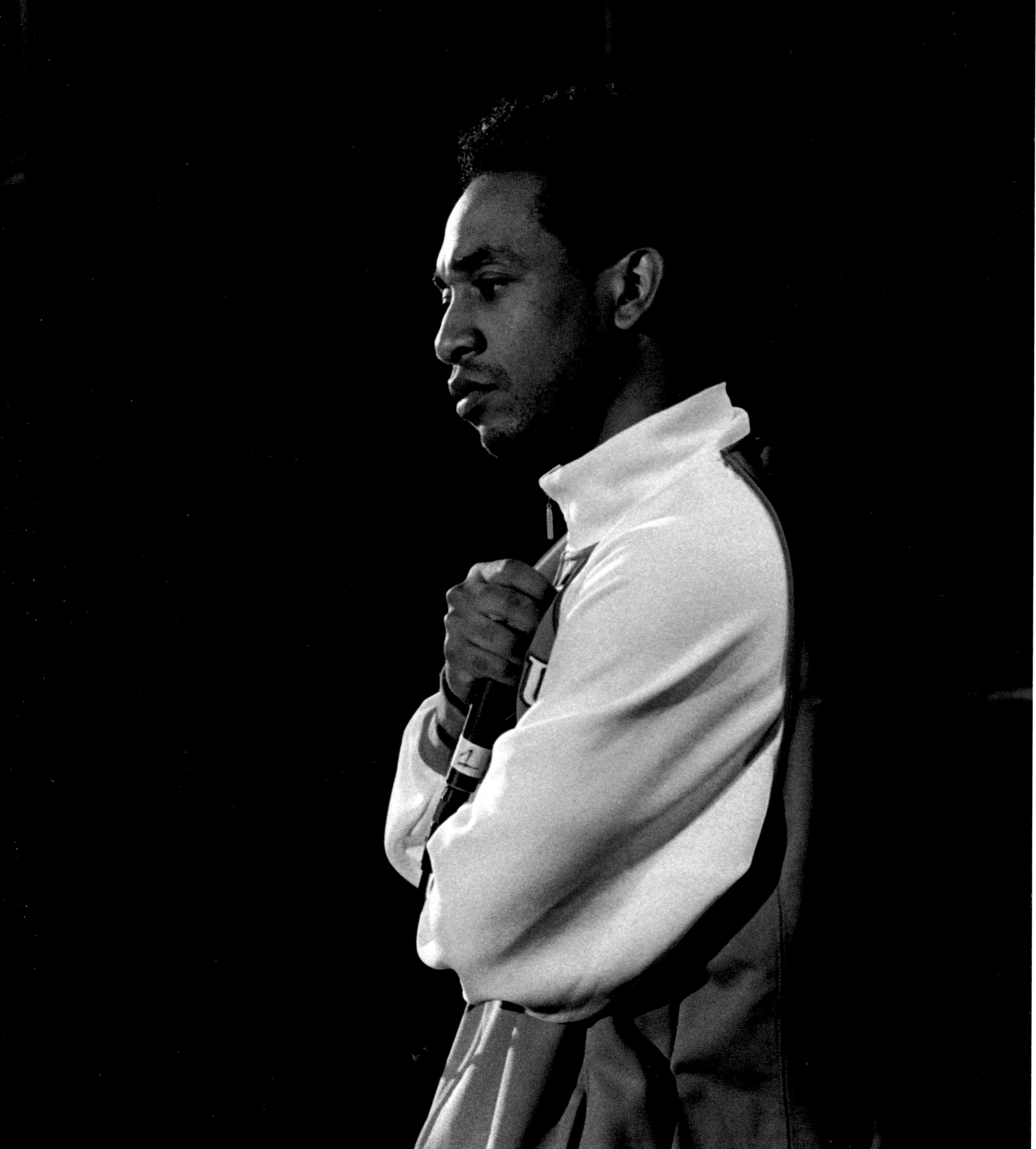

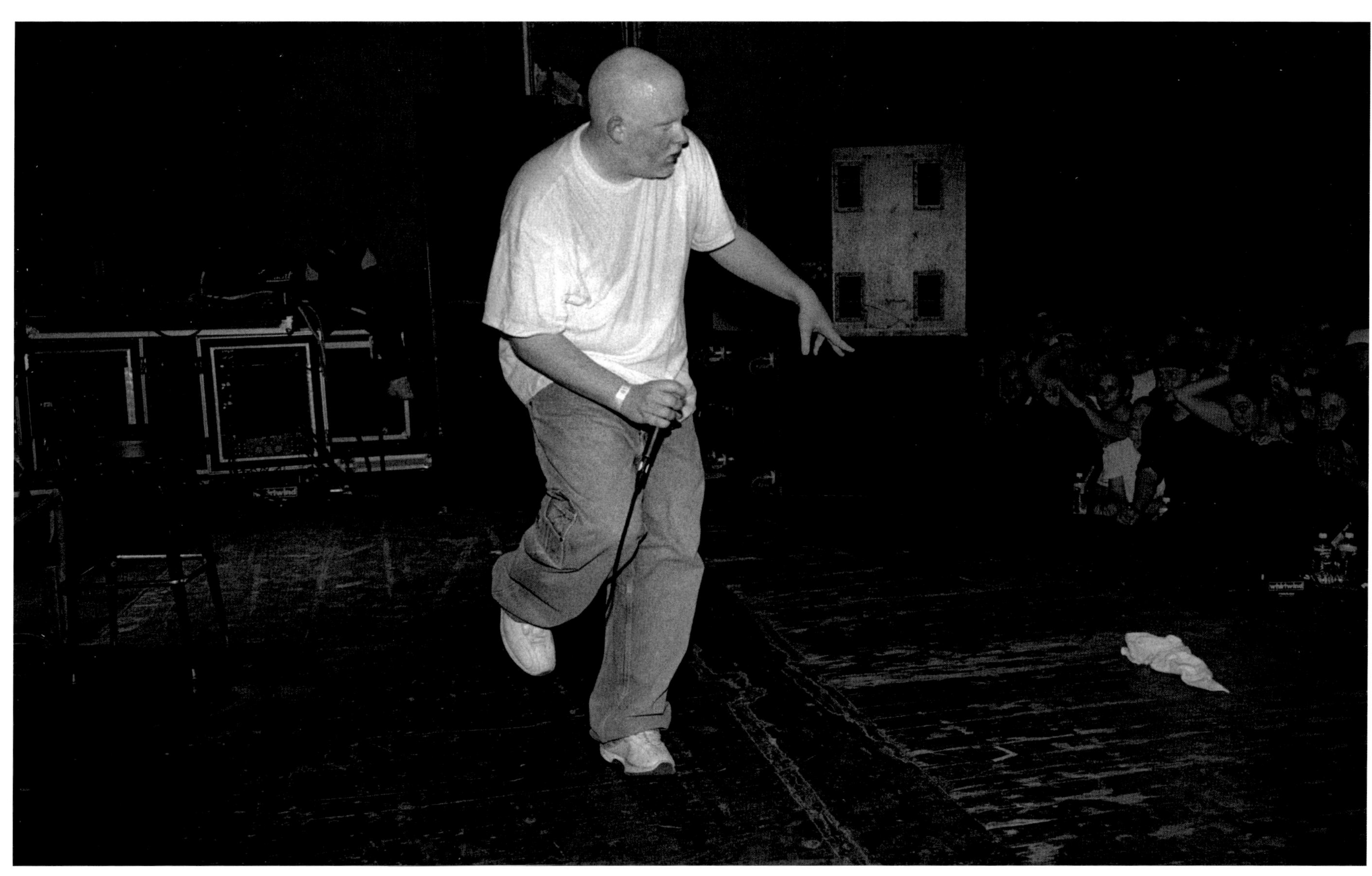

BROTHER ALI, 2002

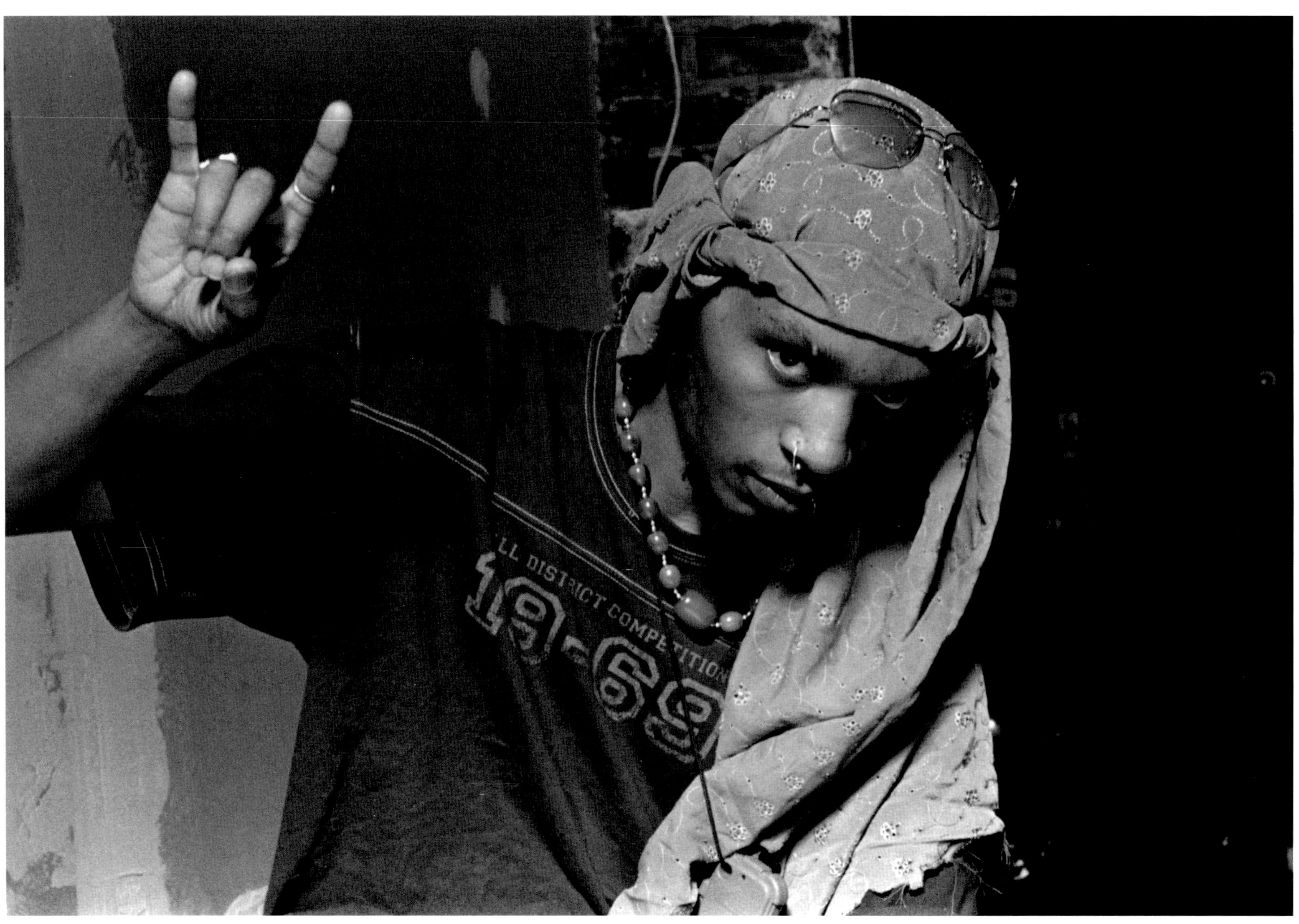

 DEL THA FUNKY HOMOSAPIEN, 2002; Opposite: DEL THA FUNKY HOMOSAPIEN, 2009

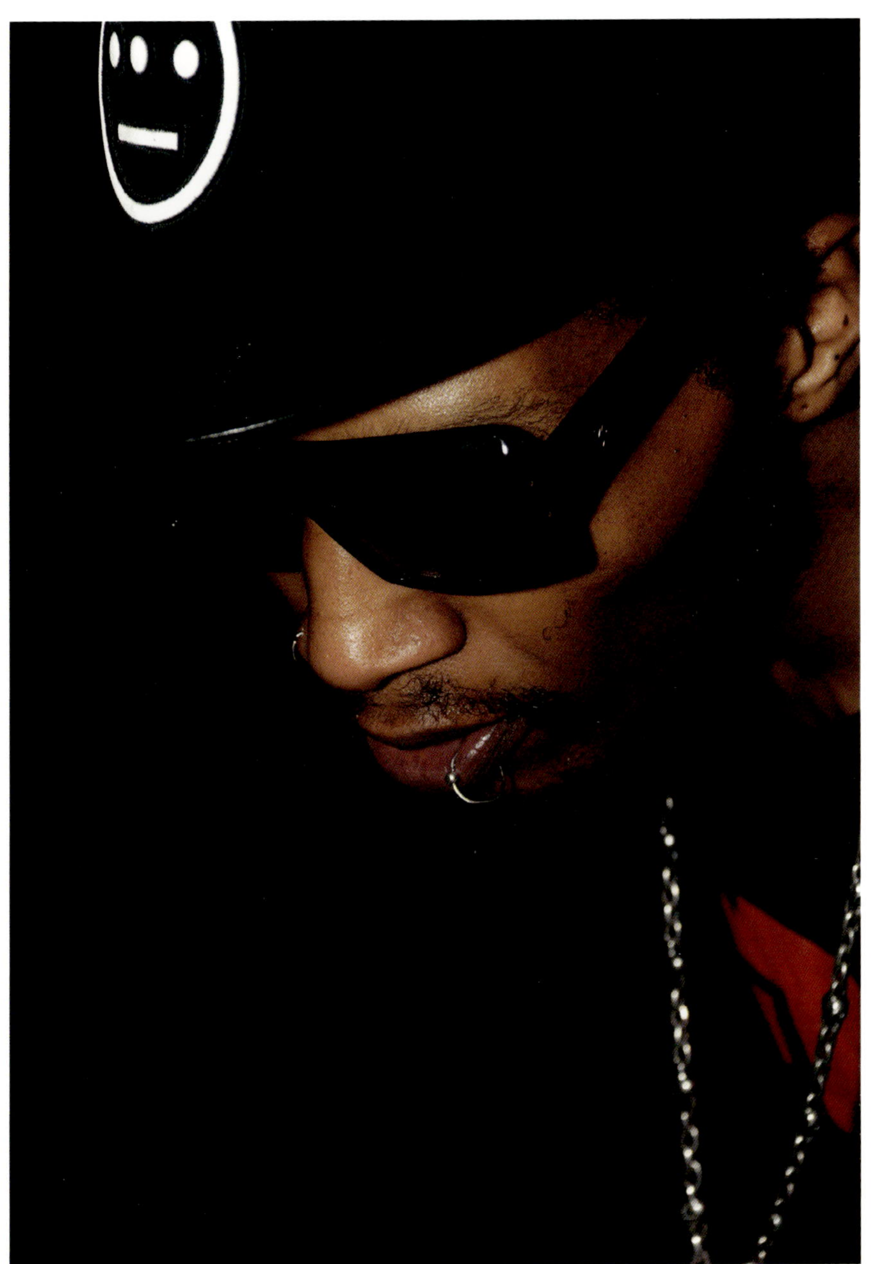

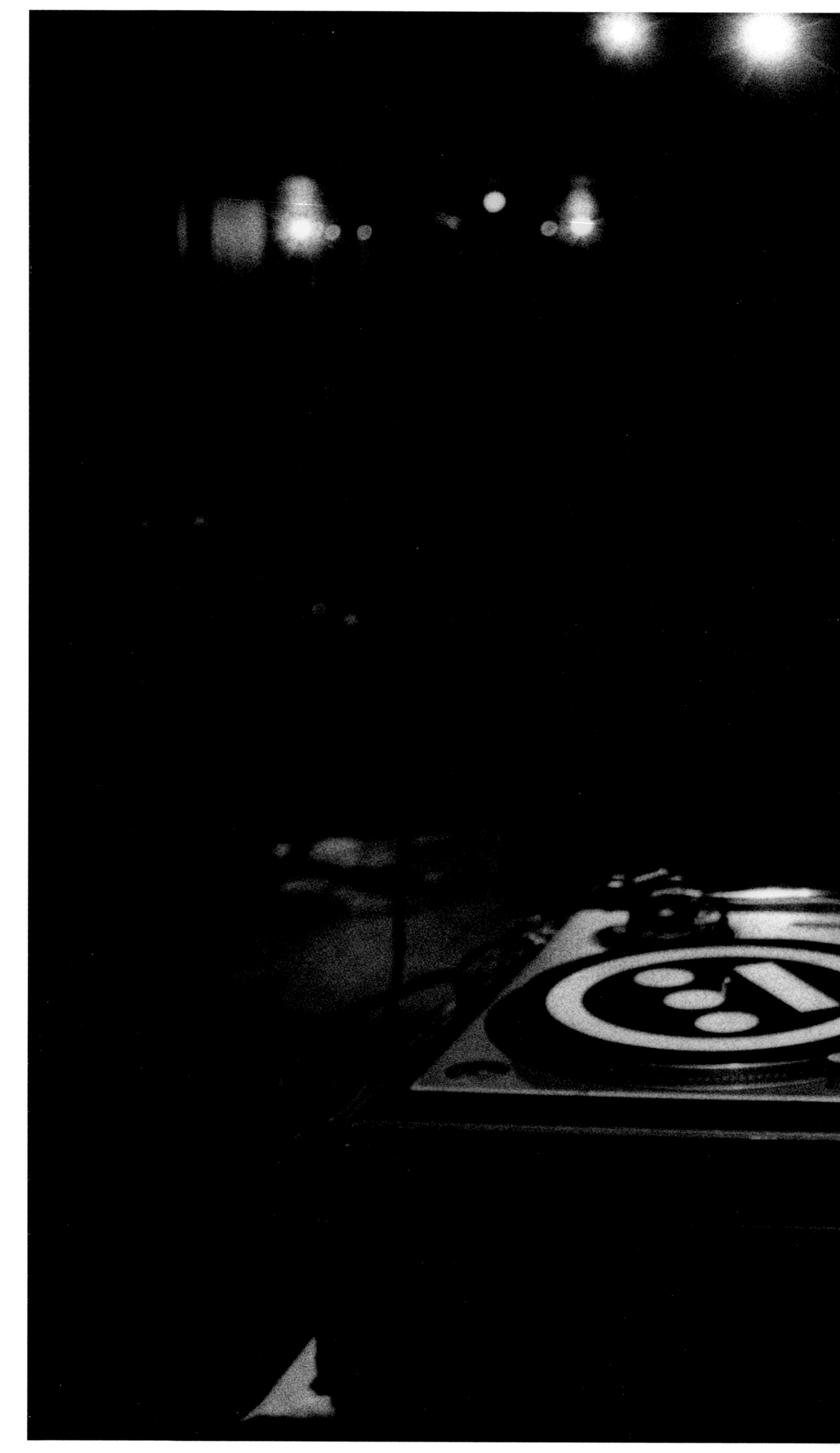

 HIEROGLYPHICS, TURNTABLES, 2001

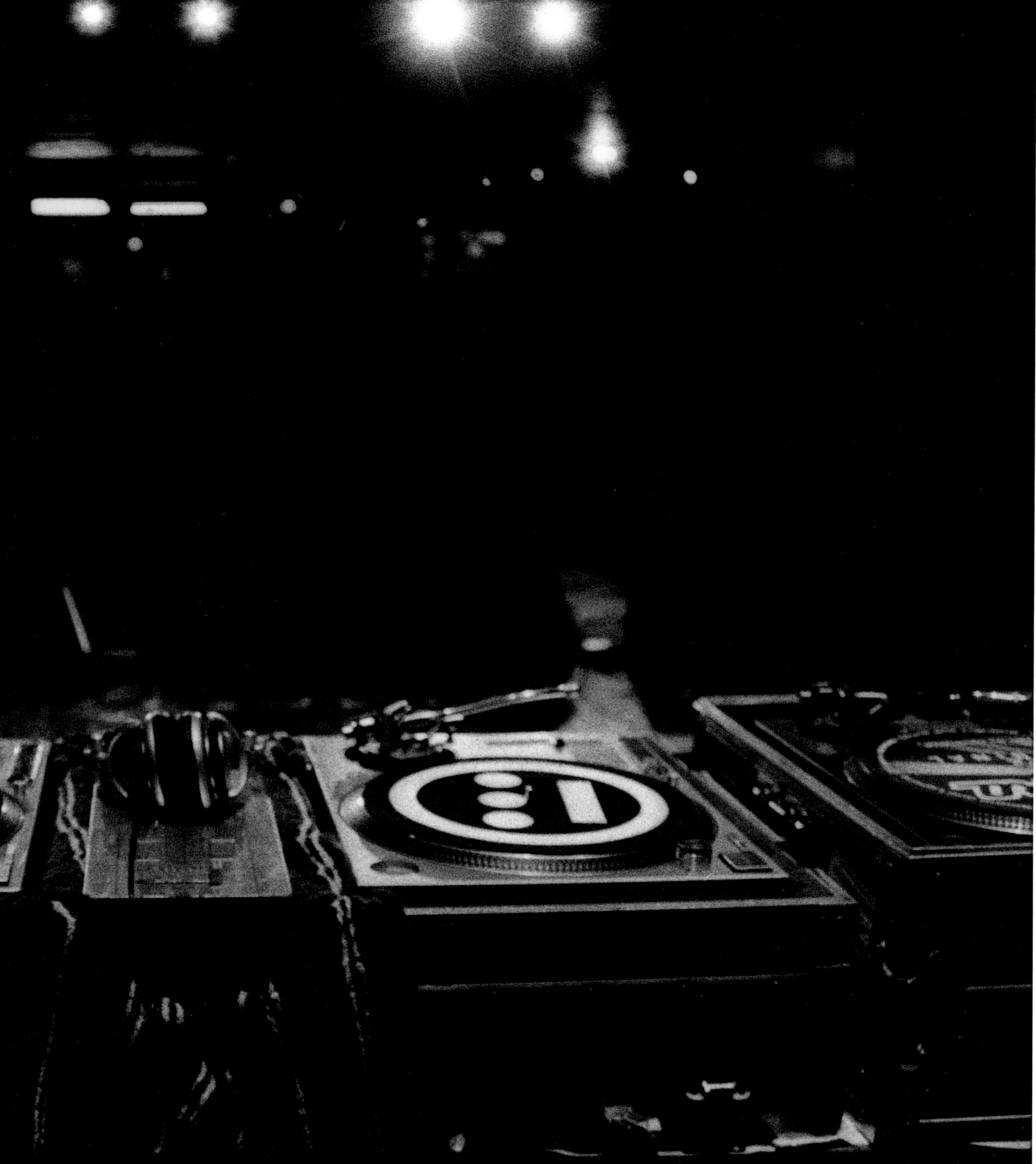

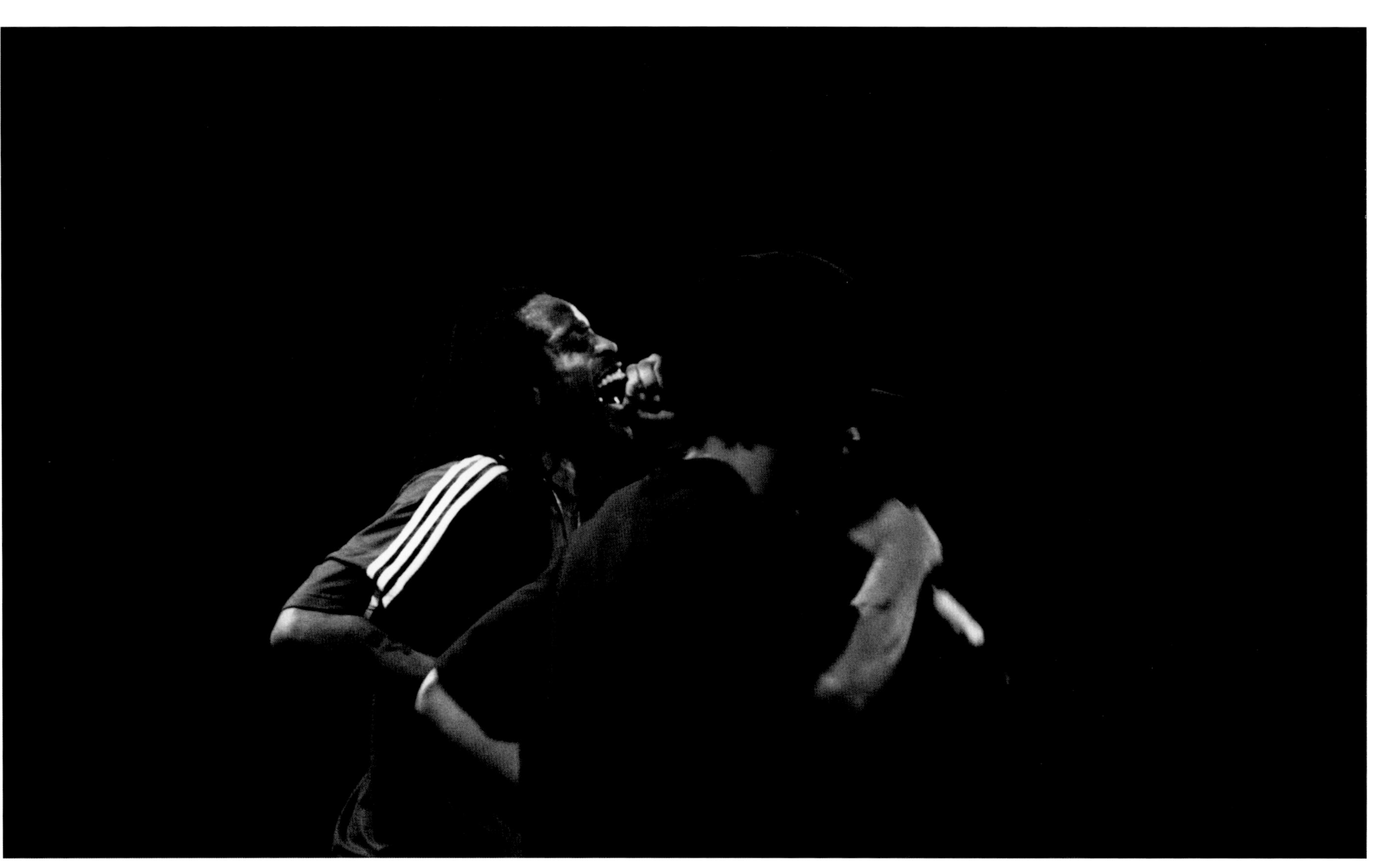

 THE PHARCYDE, 2001

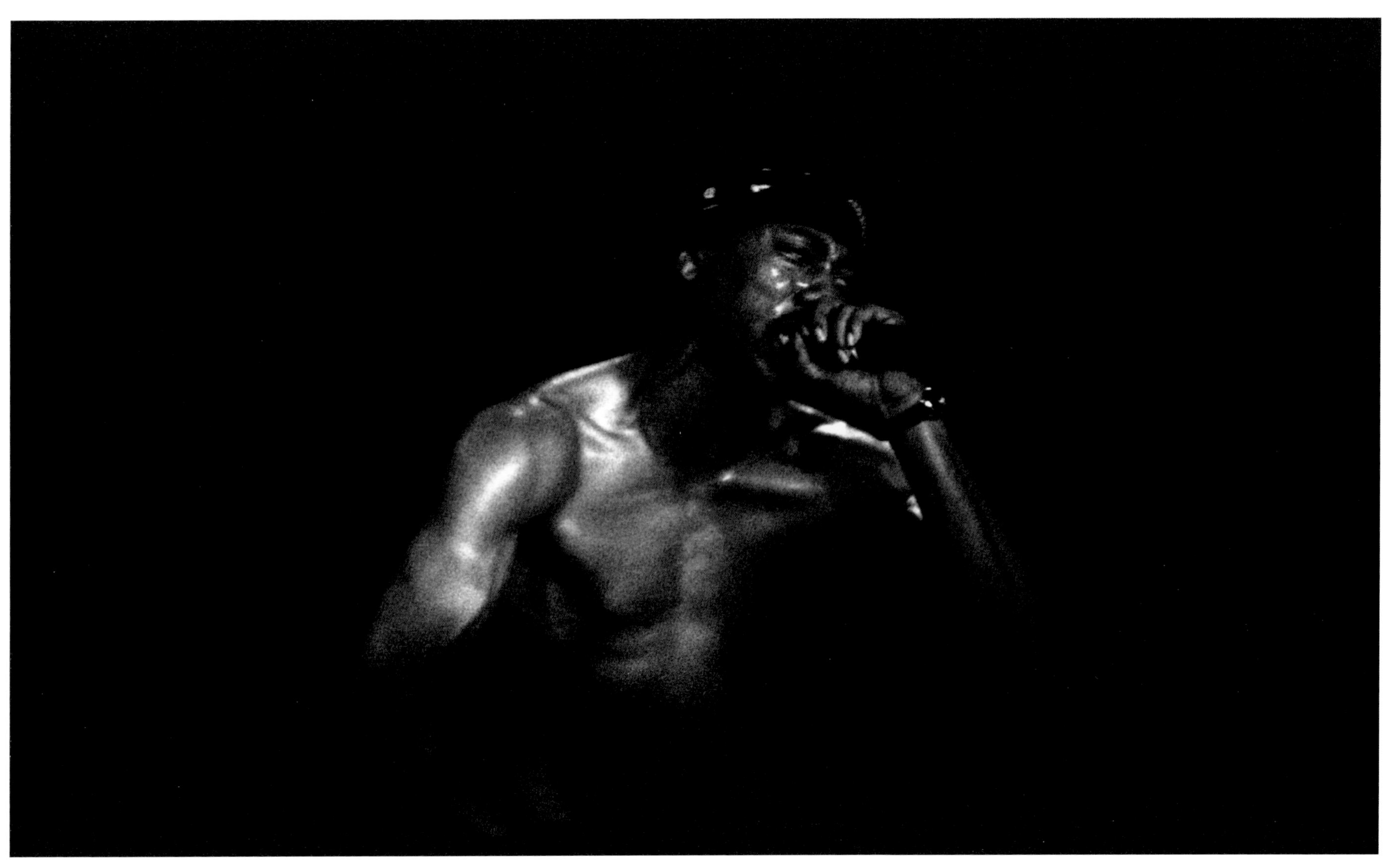

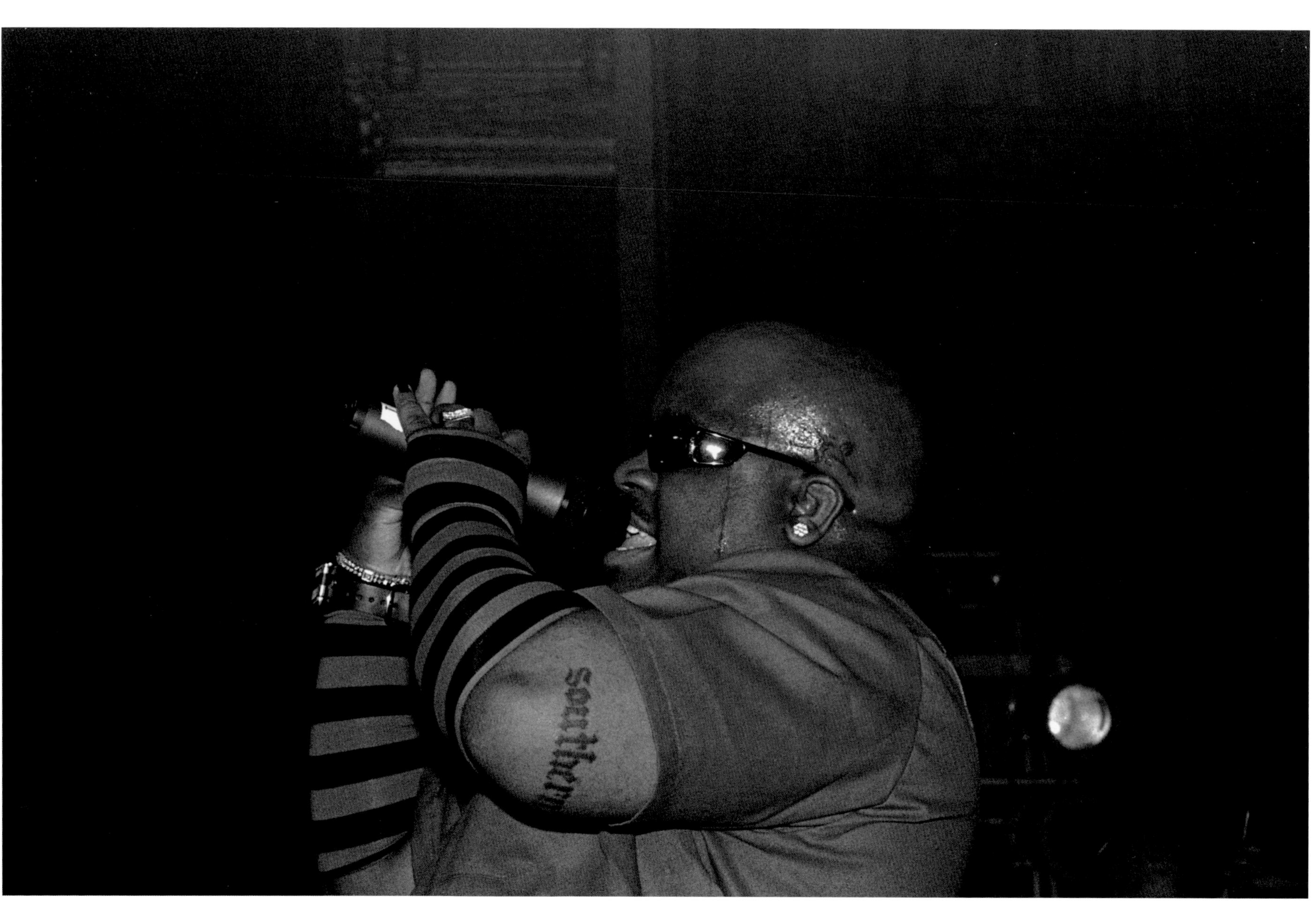

 CEELO GREEN, 2002

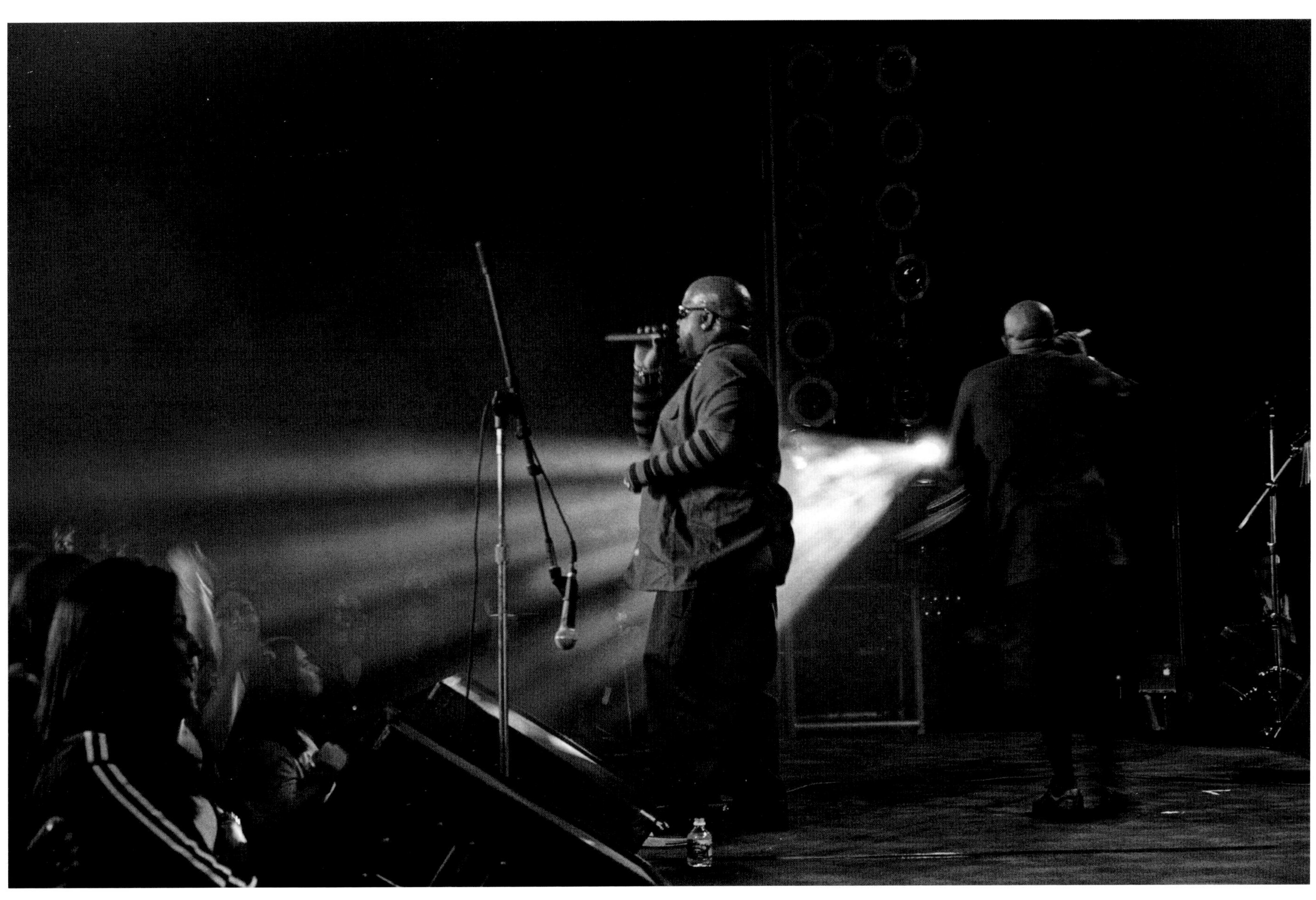

CEELO GREEN, 2002

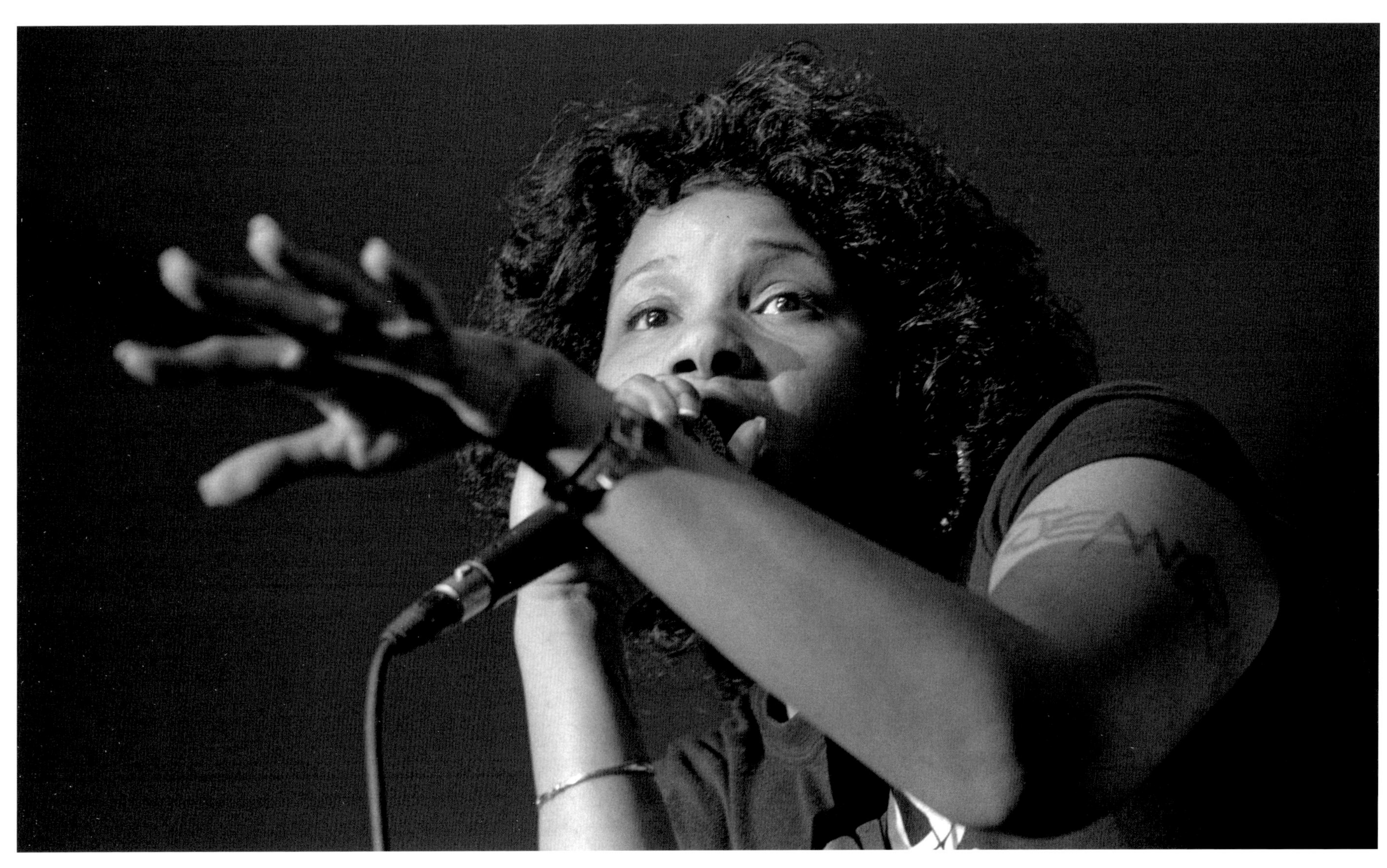

JEAN GRAE, 2005

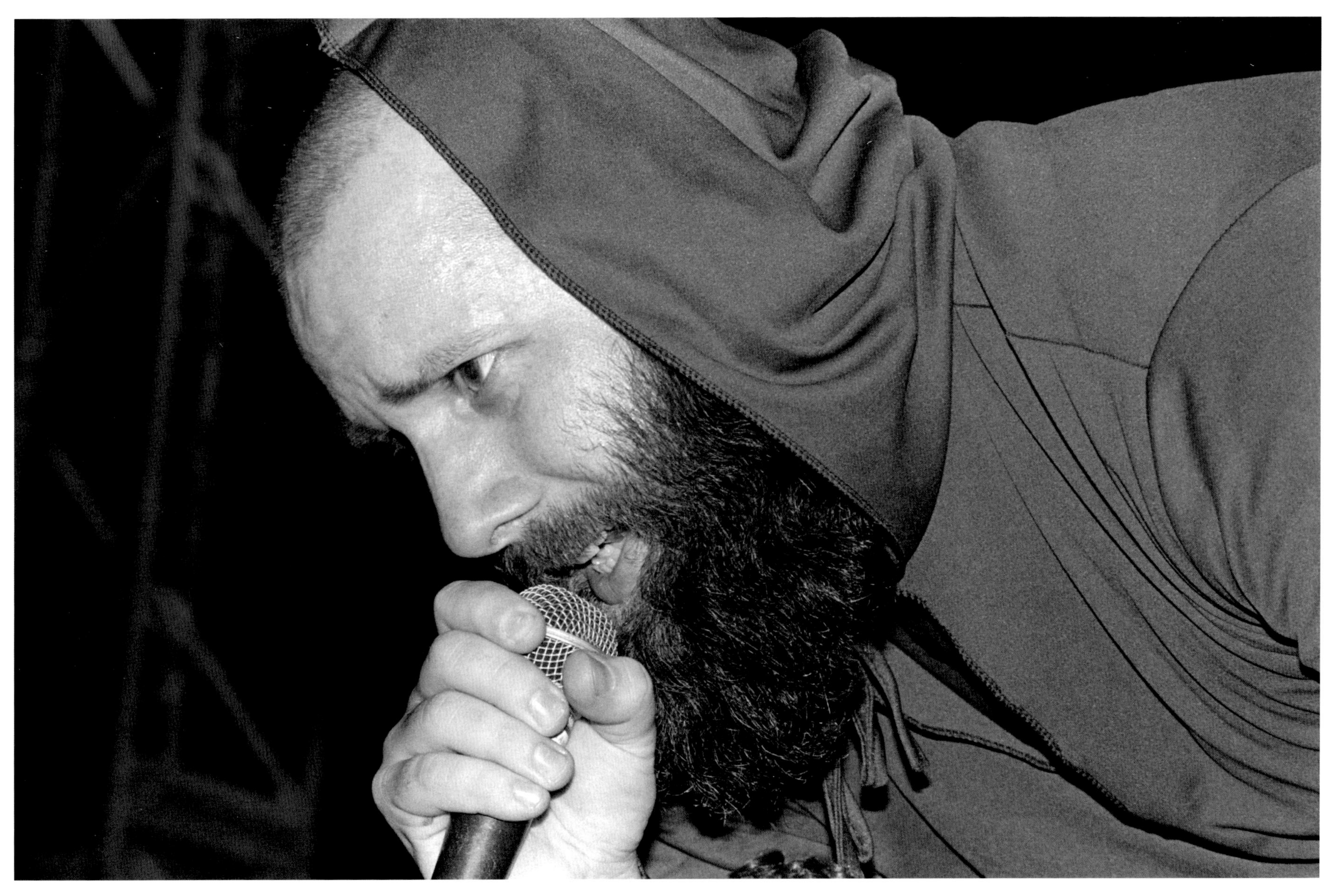

SAGE FRANCIS, 2005

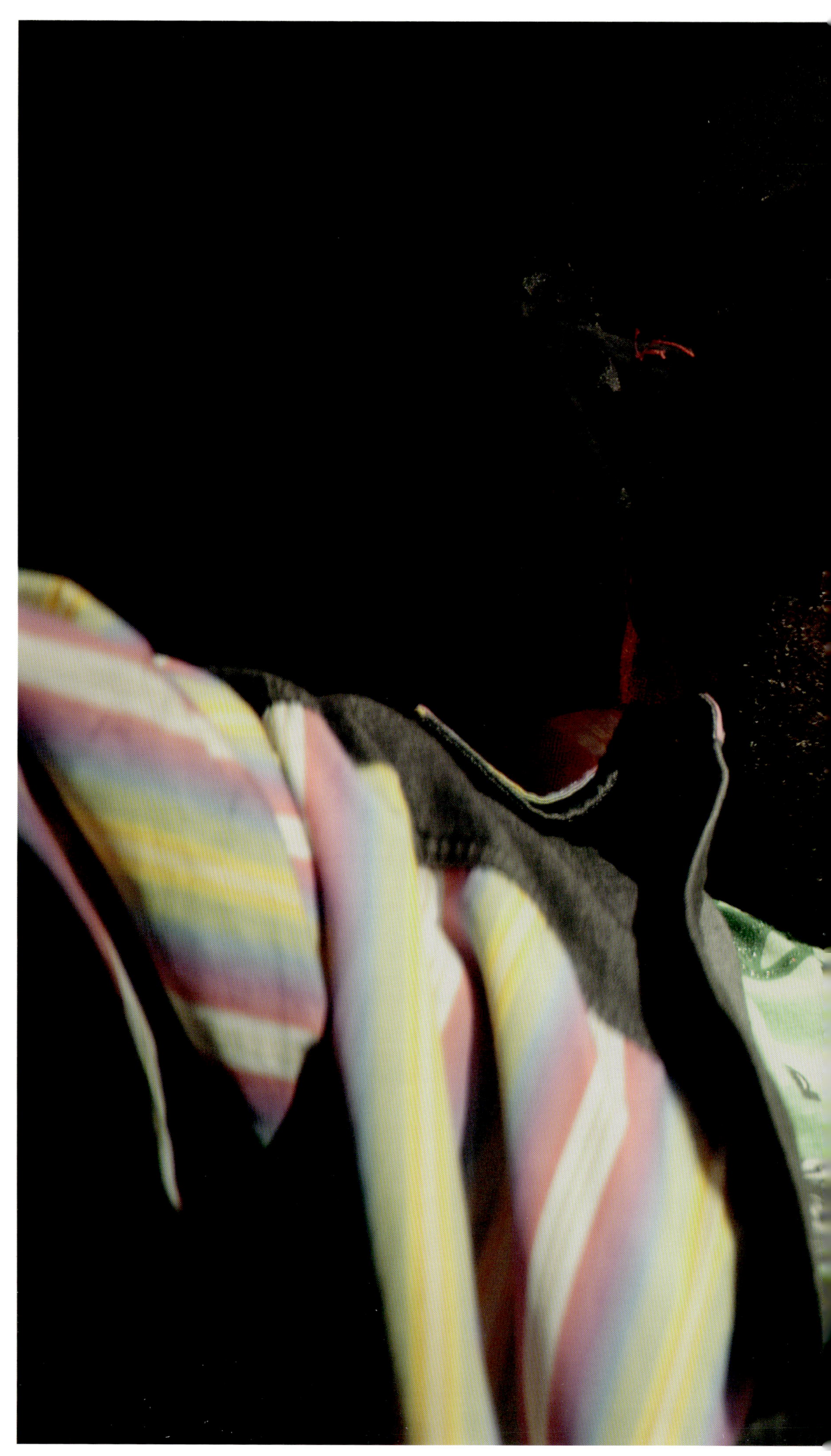

 GEORGE CLINTON, PARLIAMENT FUNKADELIC, 2010

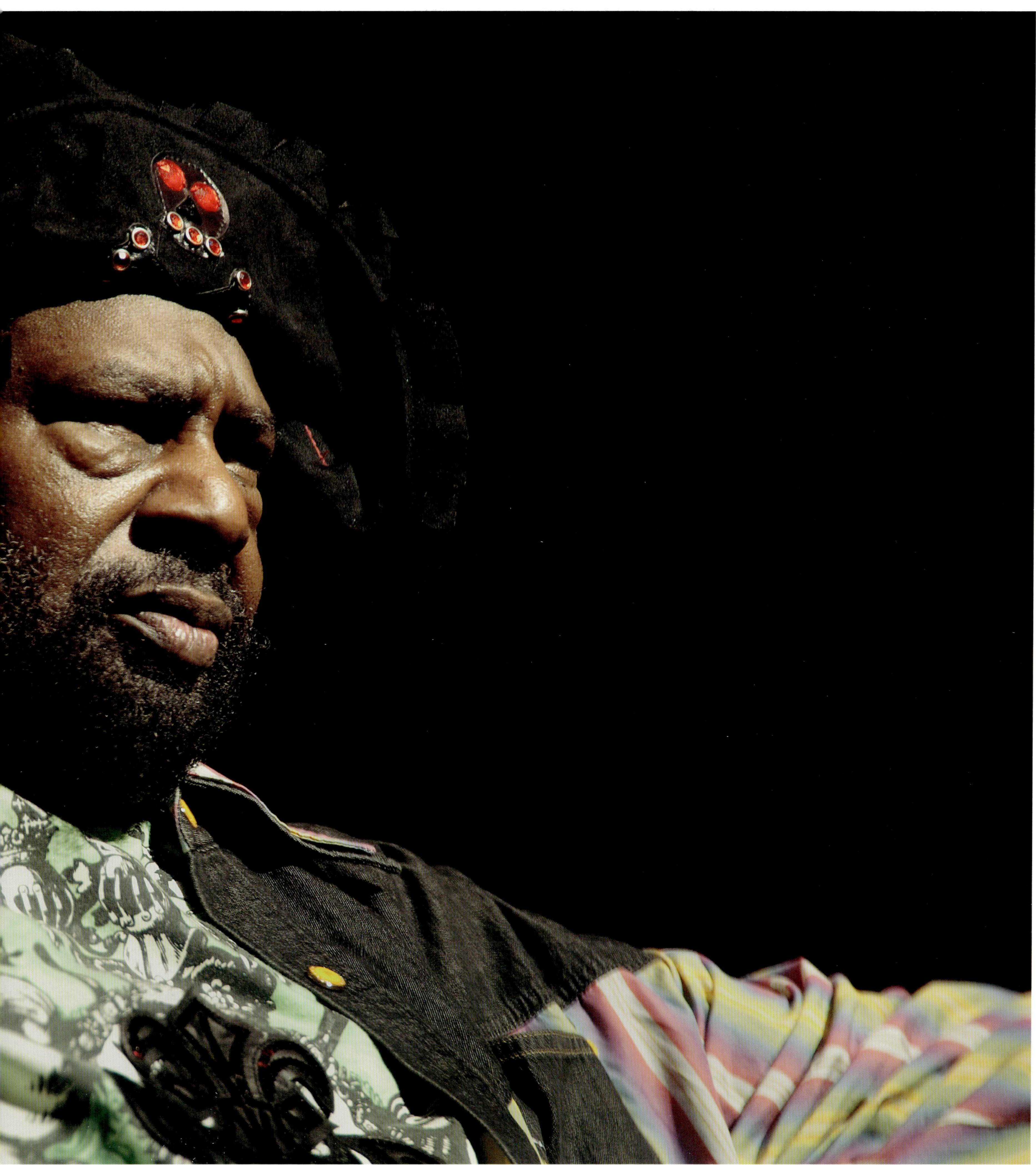

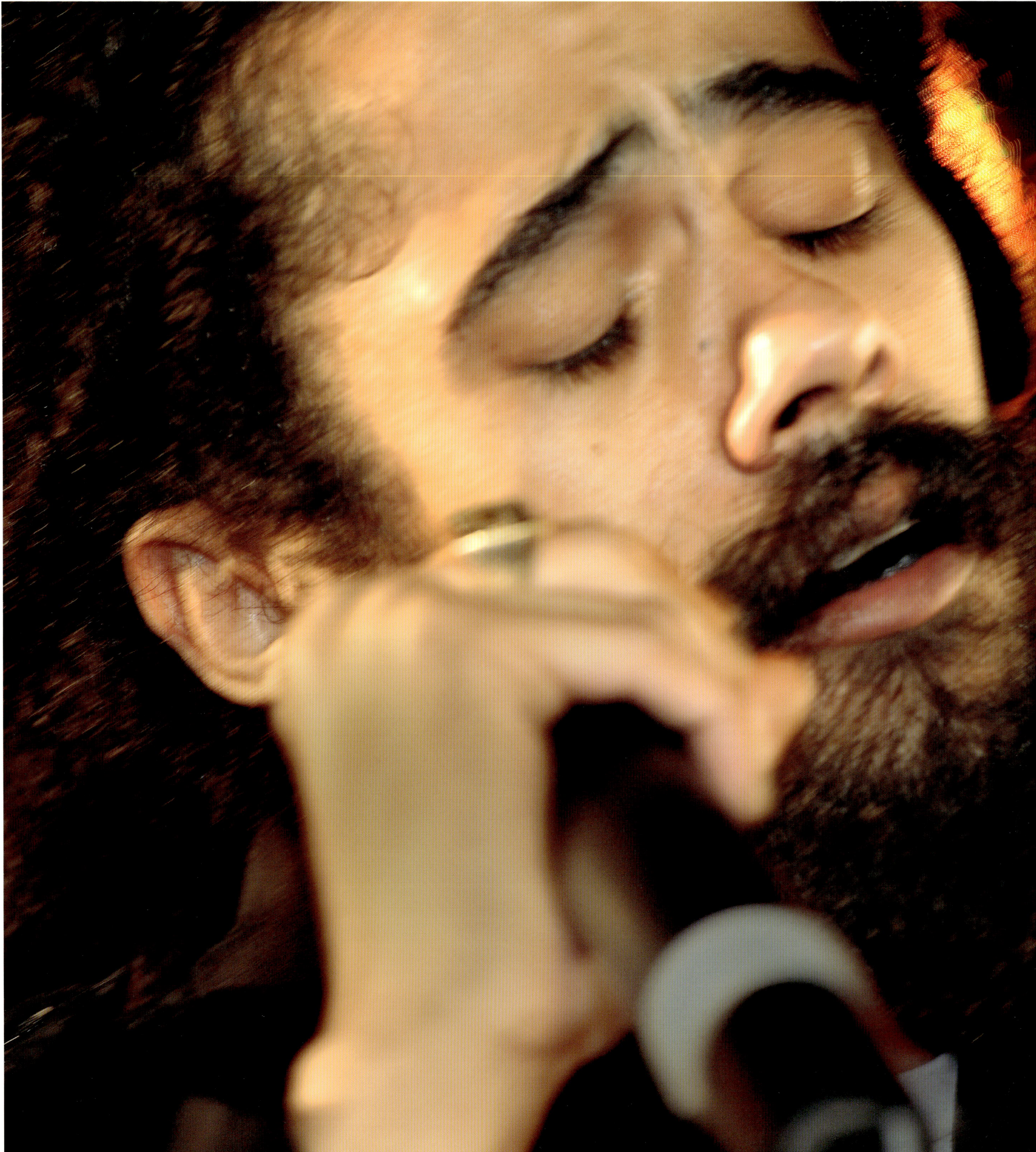

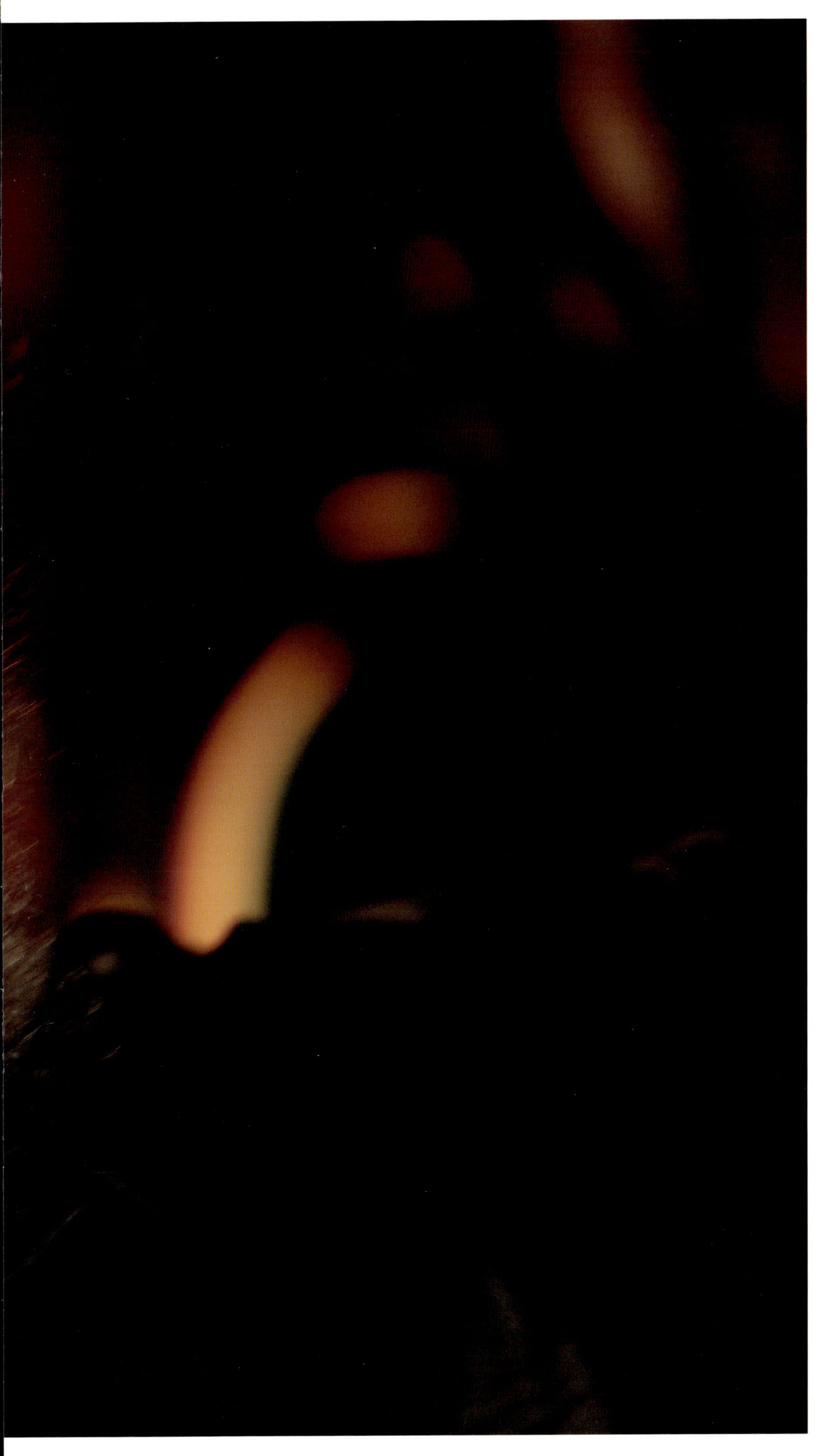

DAMIAN MARLEY, 2010

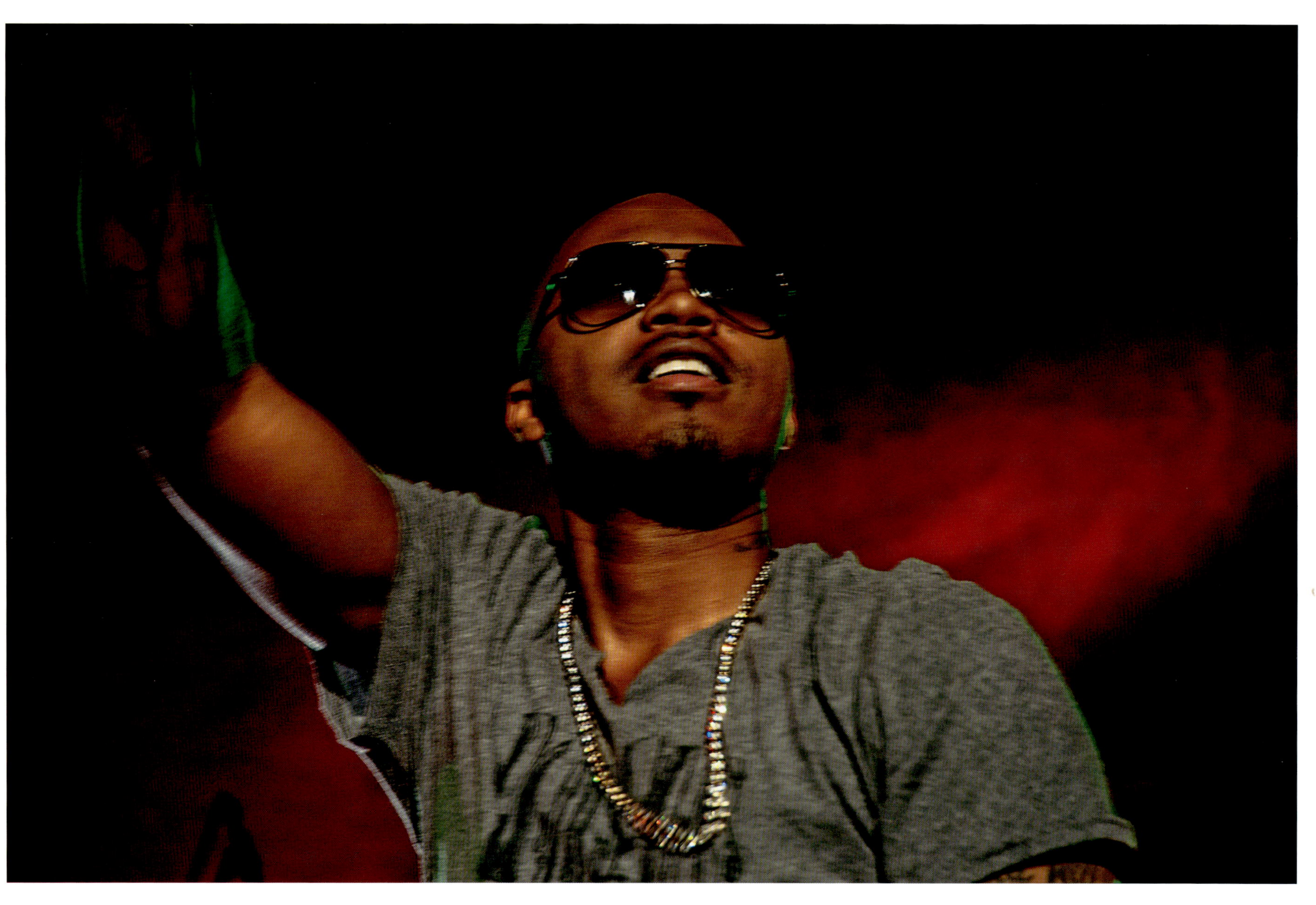

 NAS, 2010

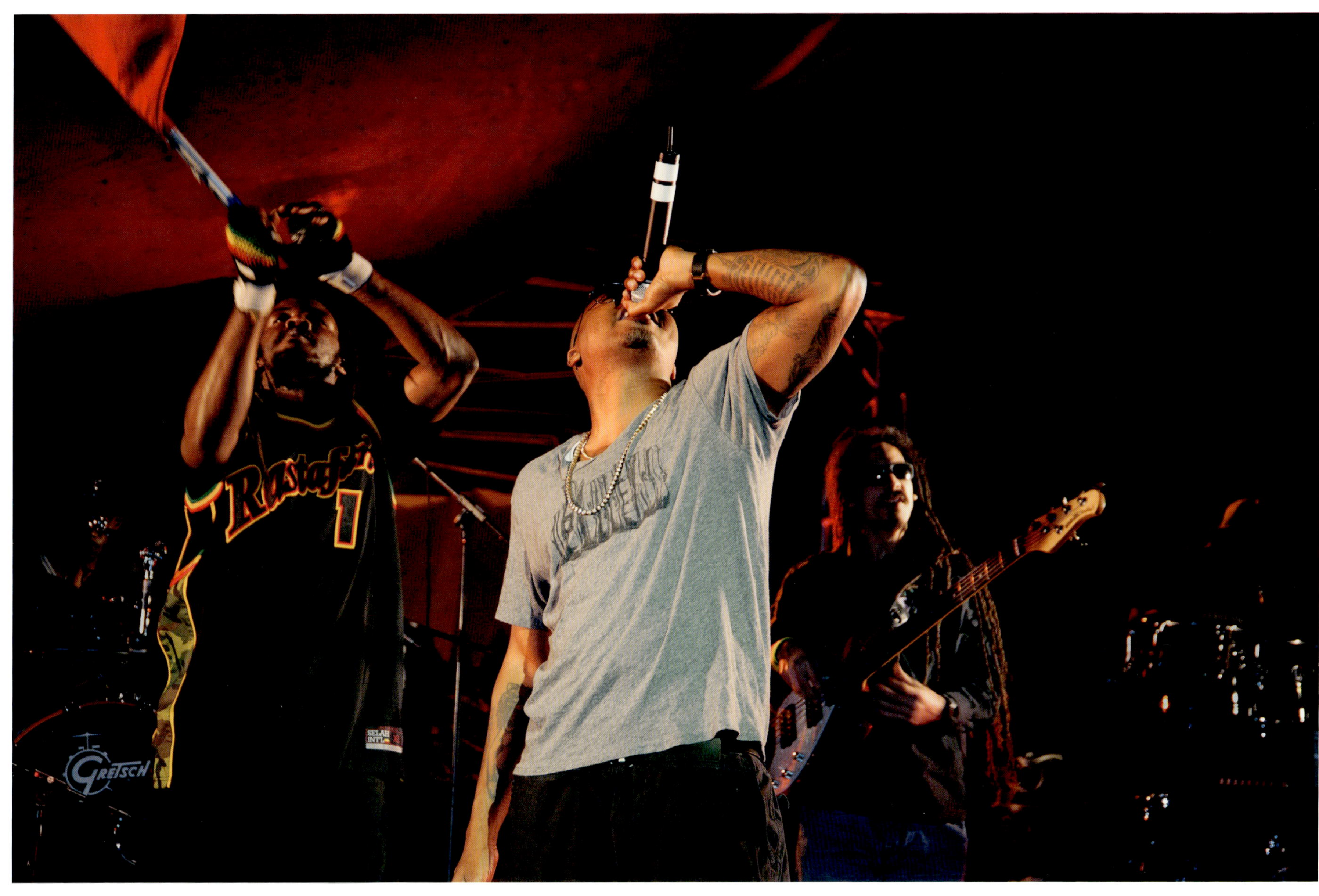

NAS, 2010

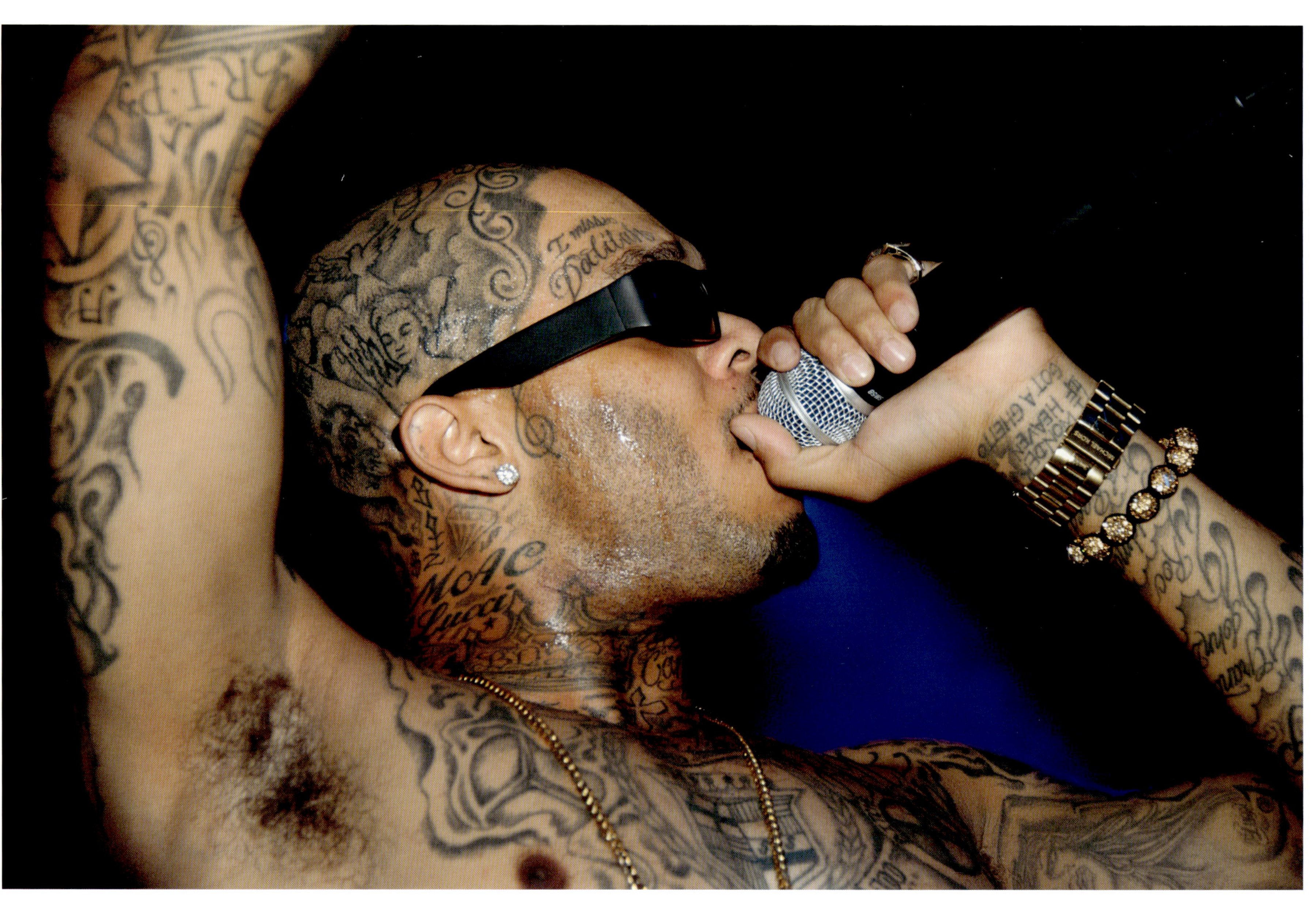

 MAC LUCCI, 2011

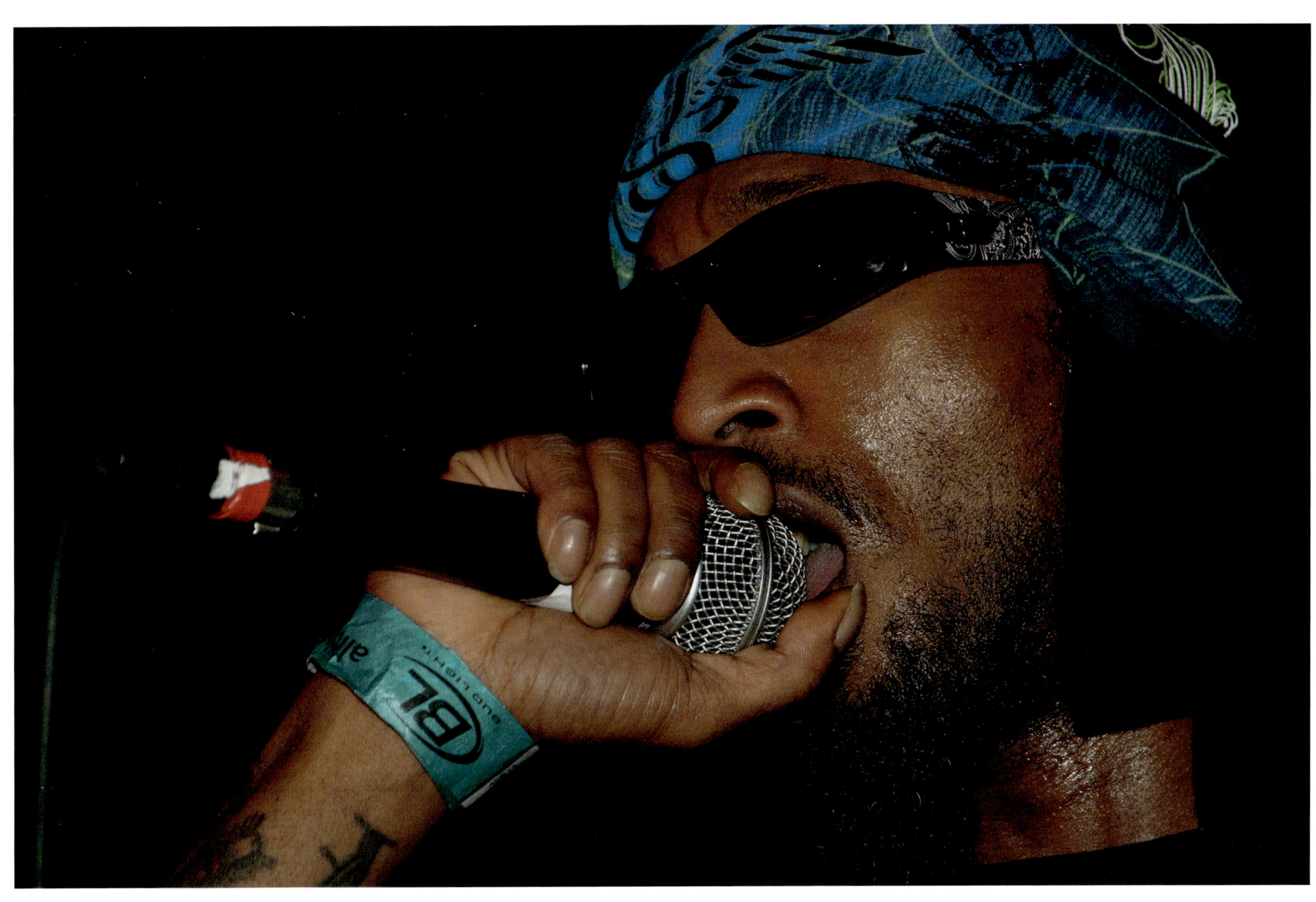

A-PLUS, SOULS OF MISCHIEF, 2007

114 EL-P, 2007

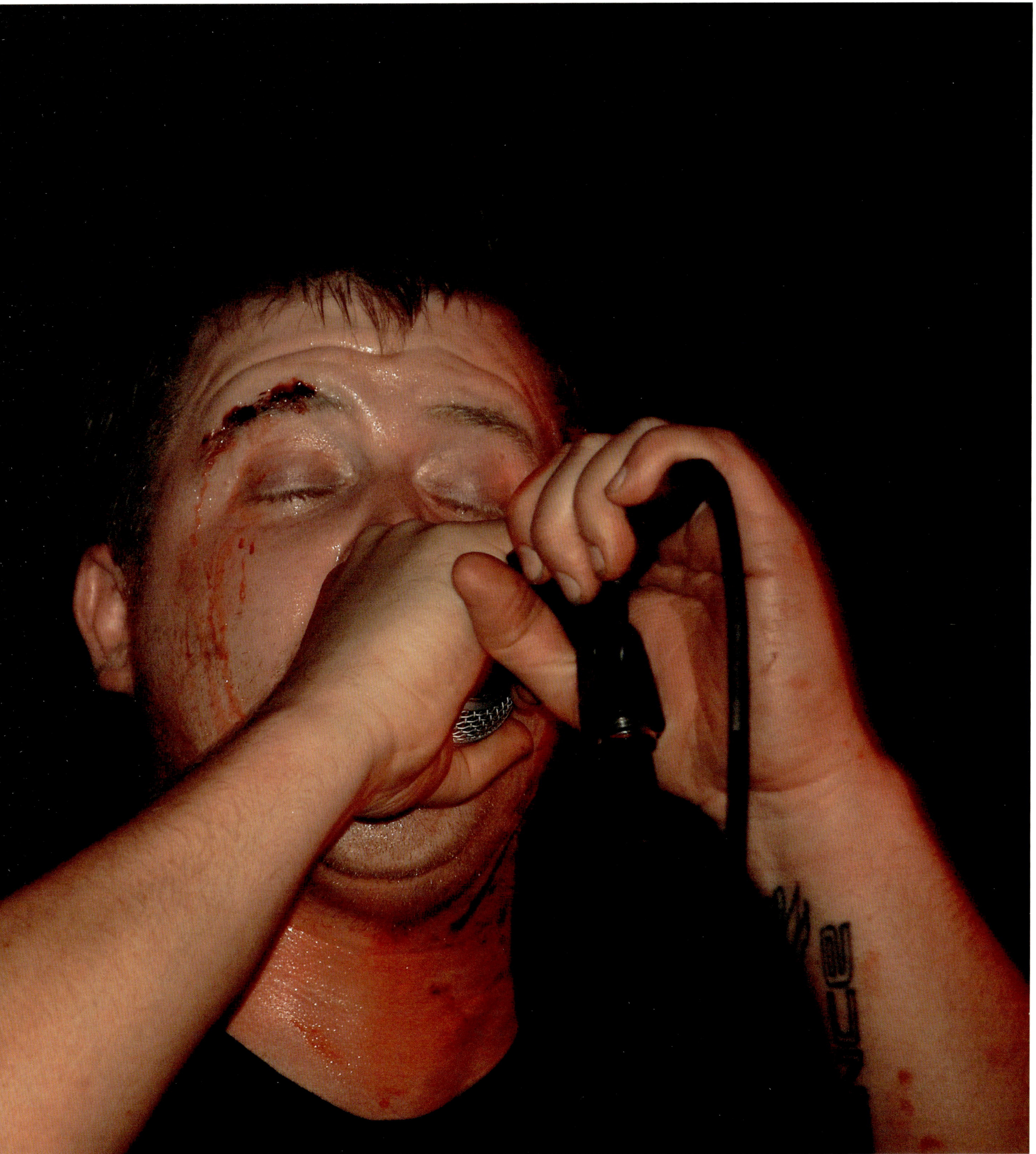

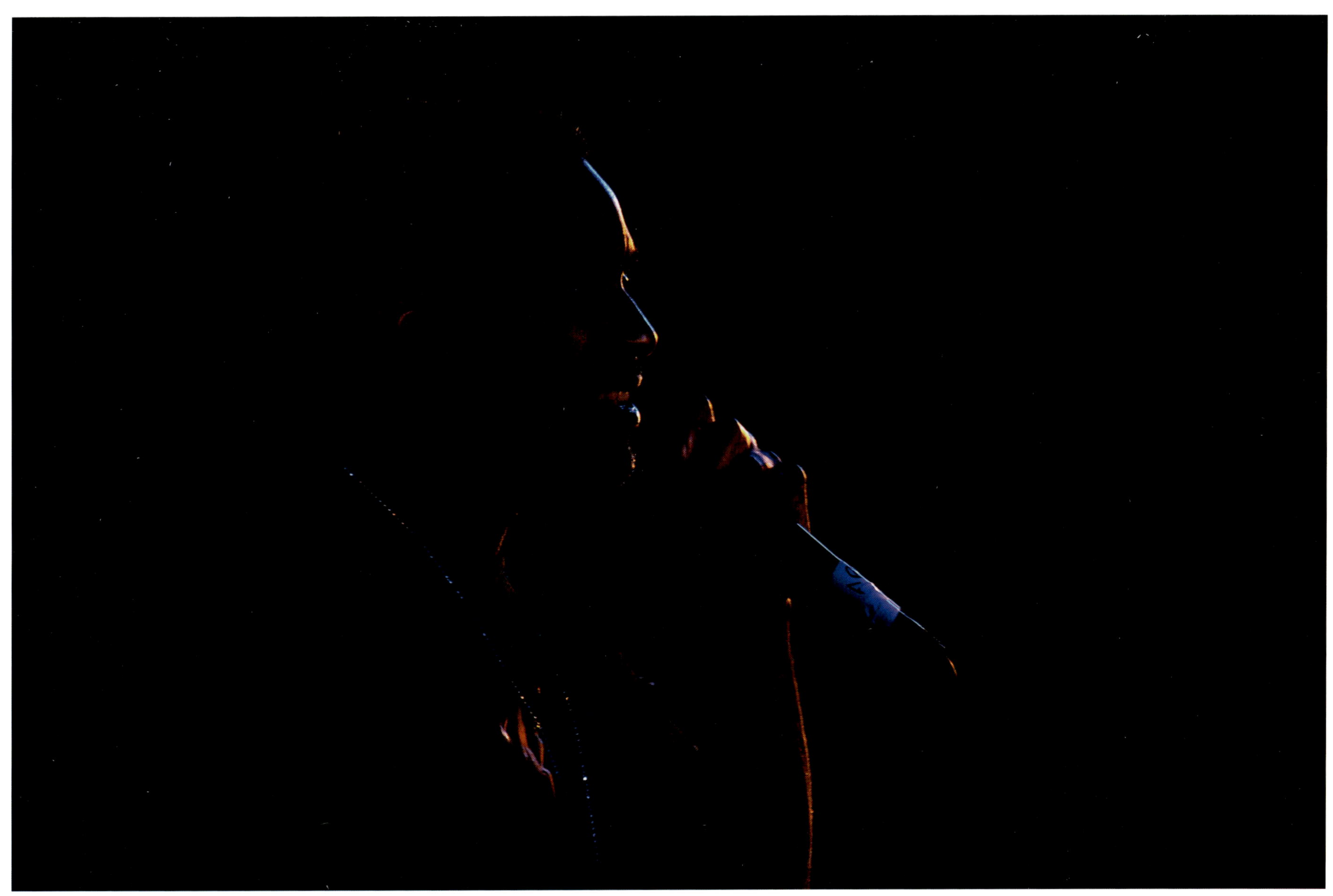

ACEYALONE, 2007

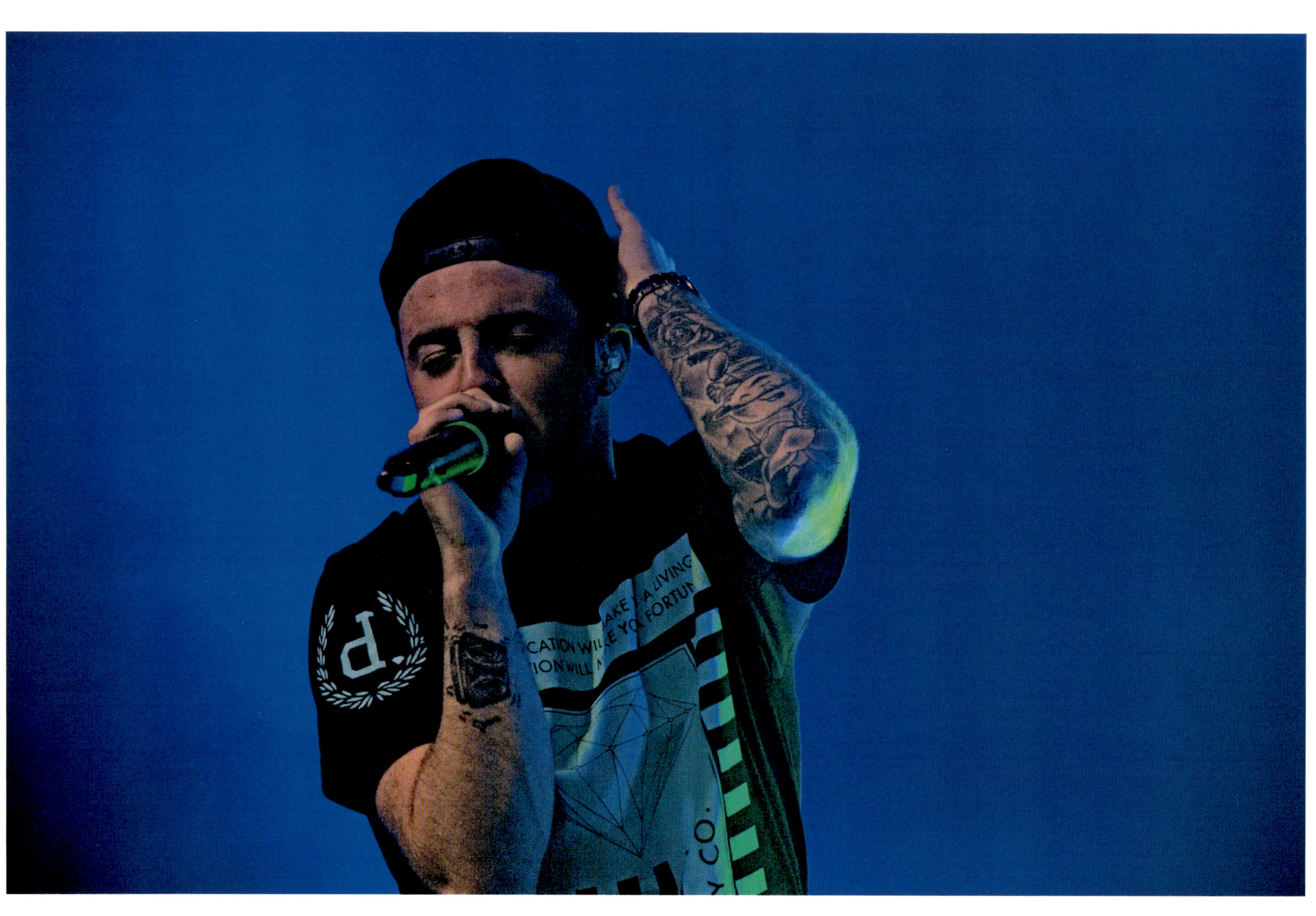

 MAC MILLER, 2011

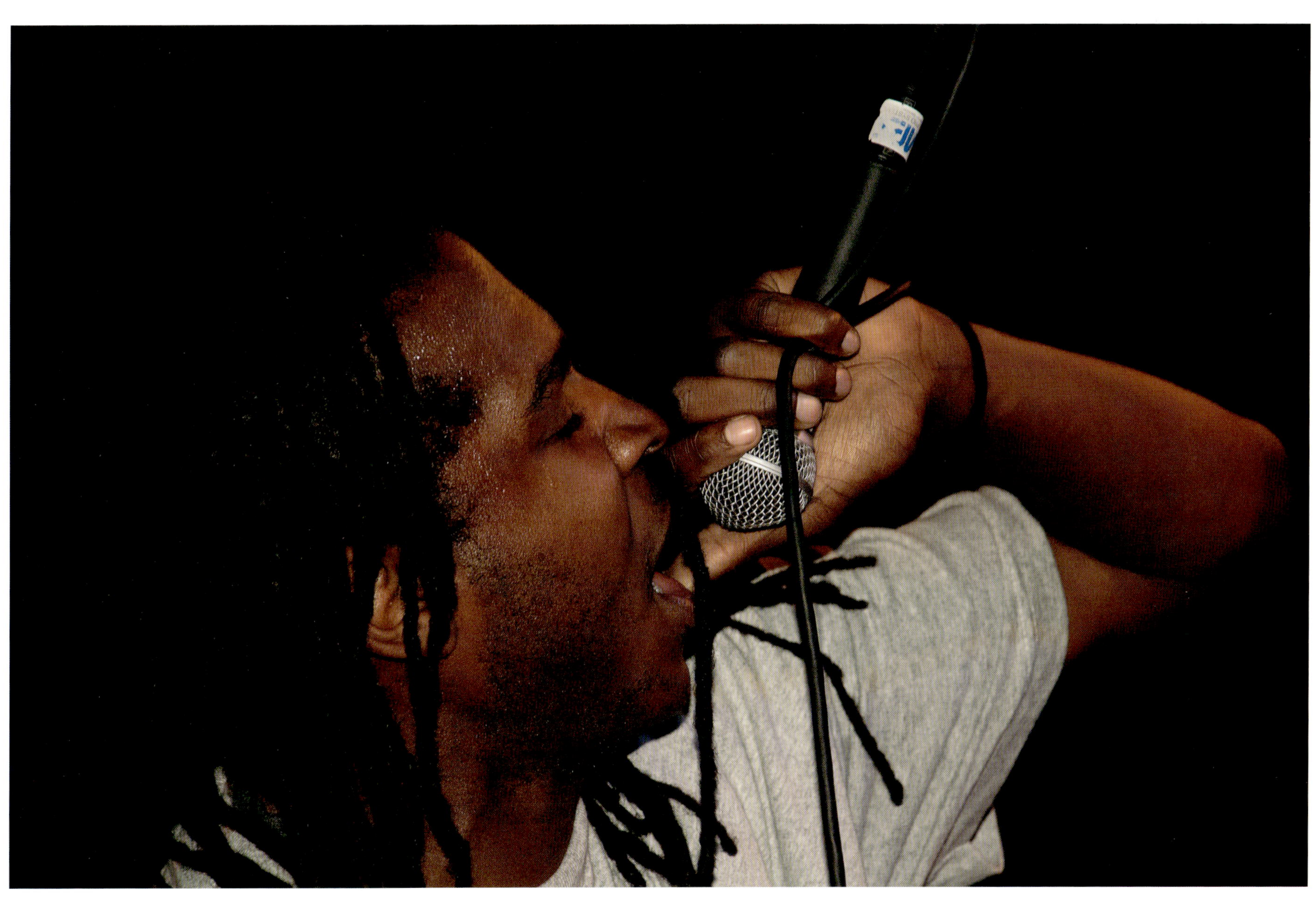

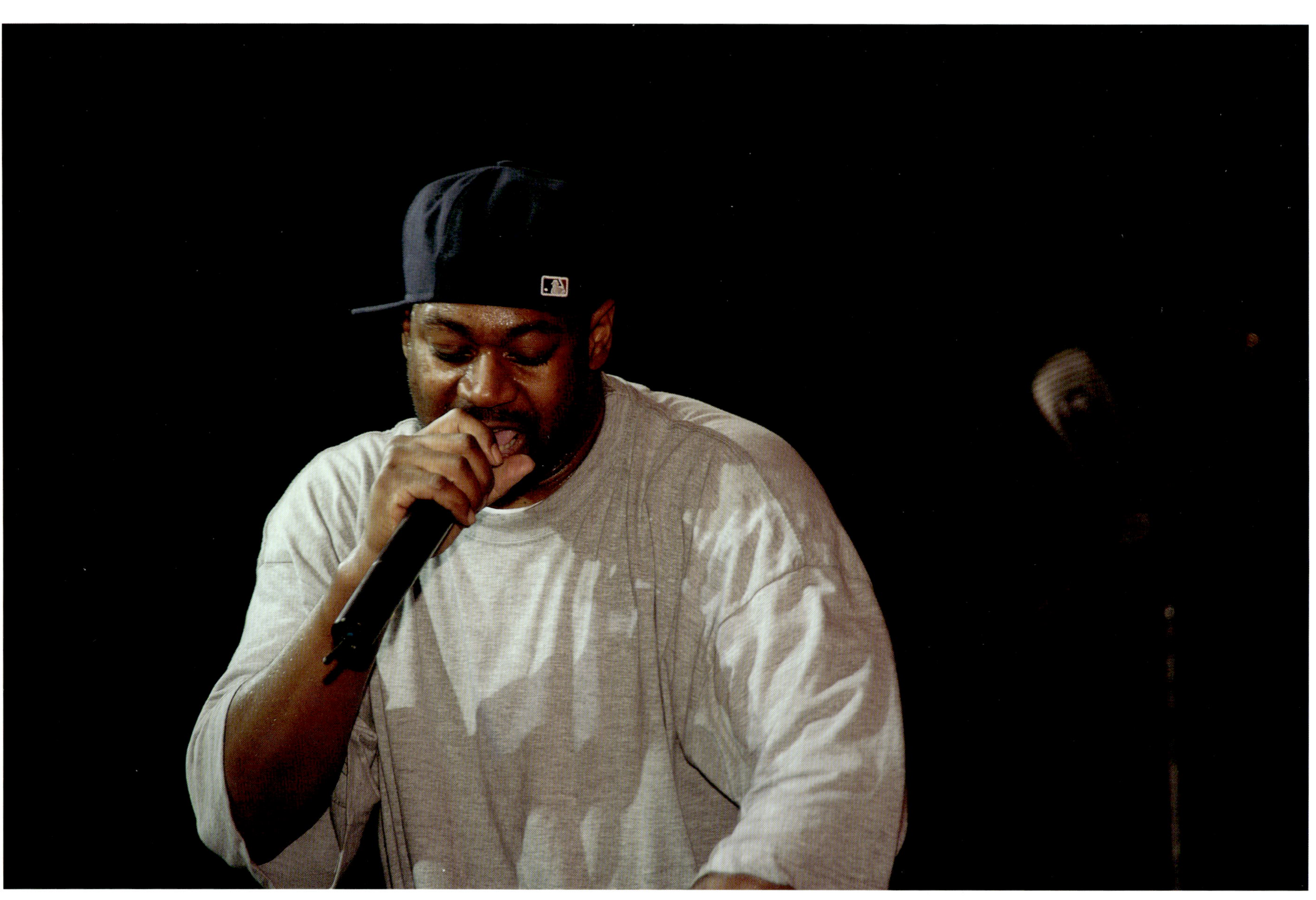

 GHOSTFACE KILLAH, 2009

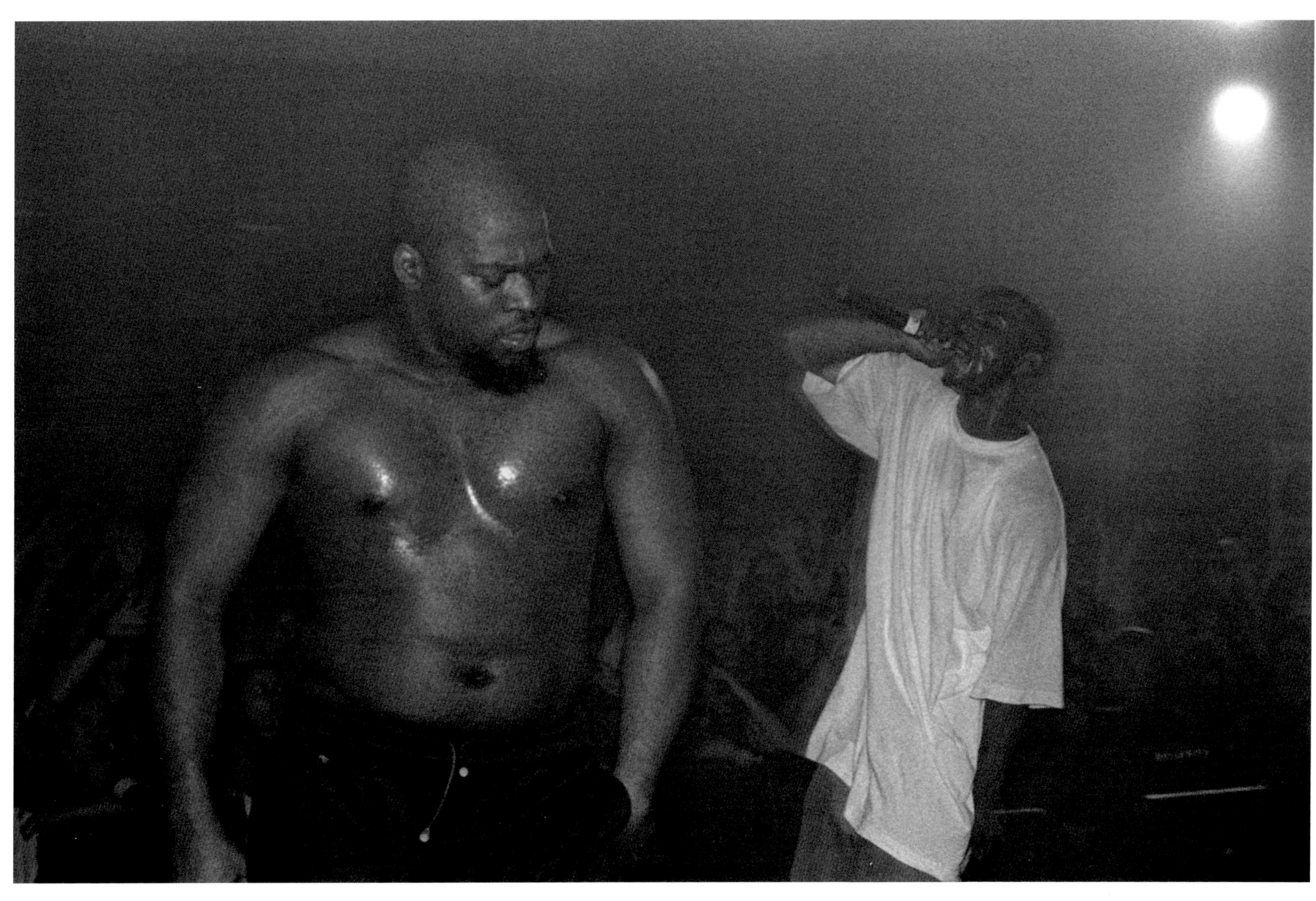

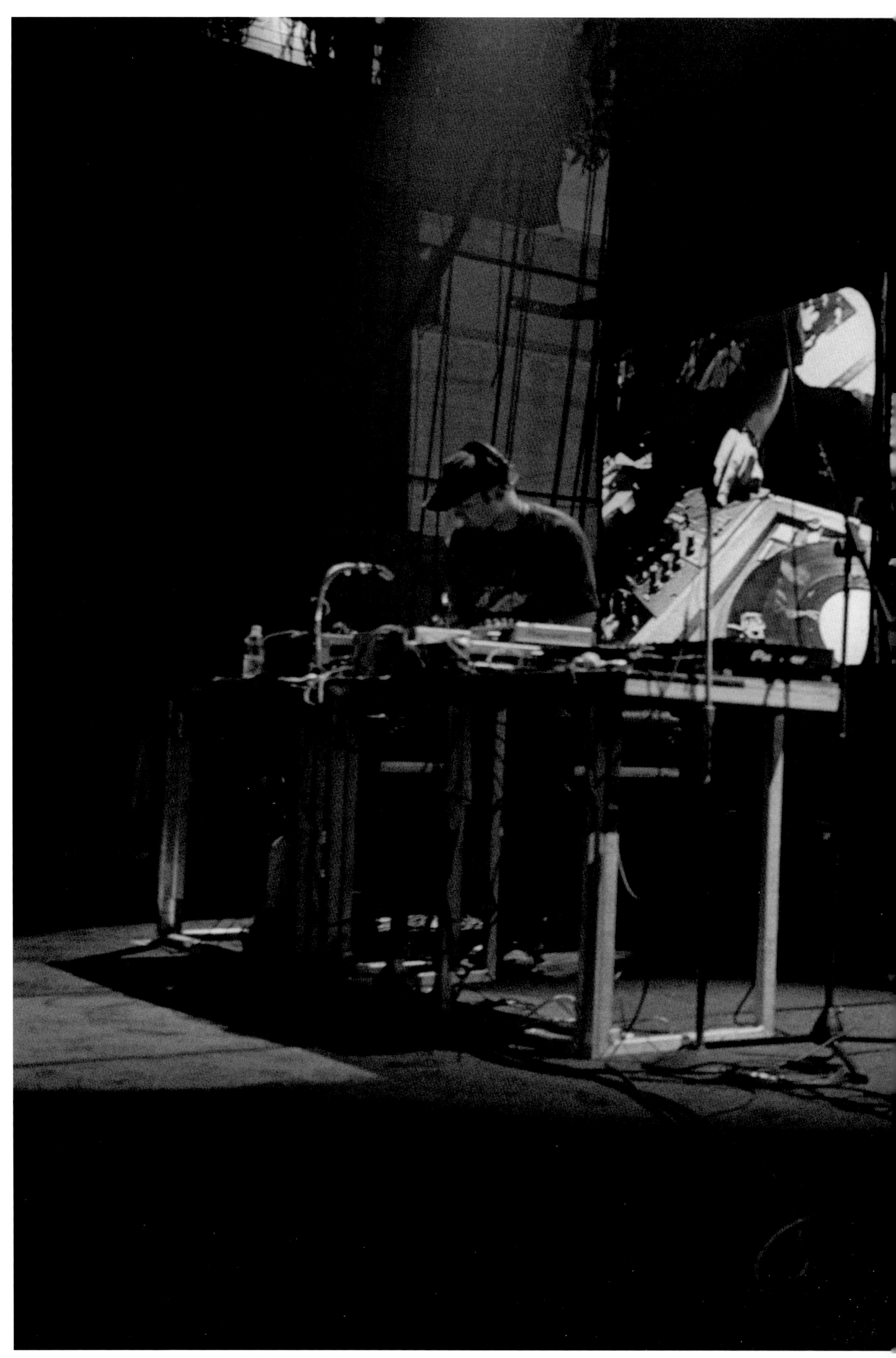

 DJ SHADOW, 2002

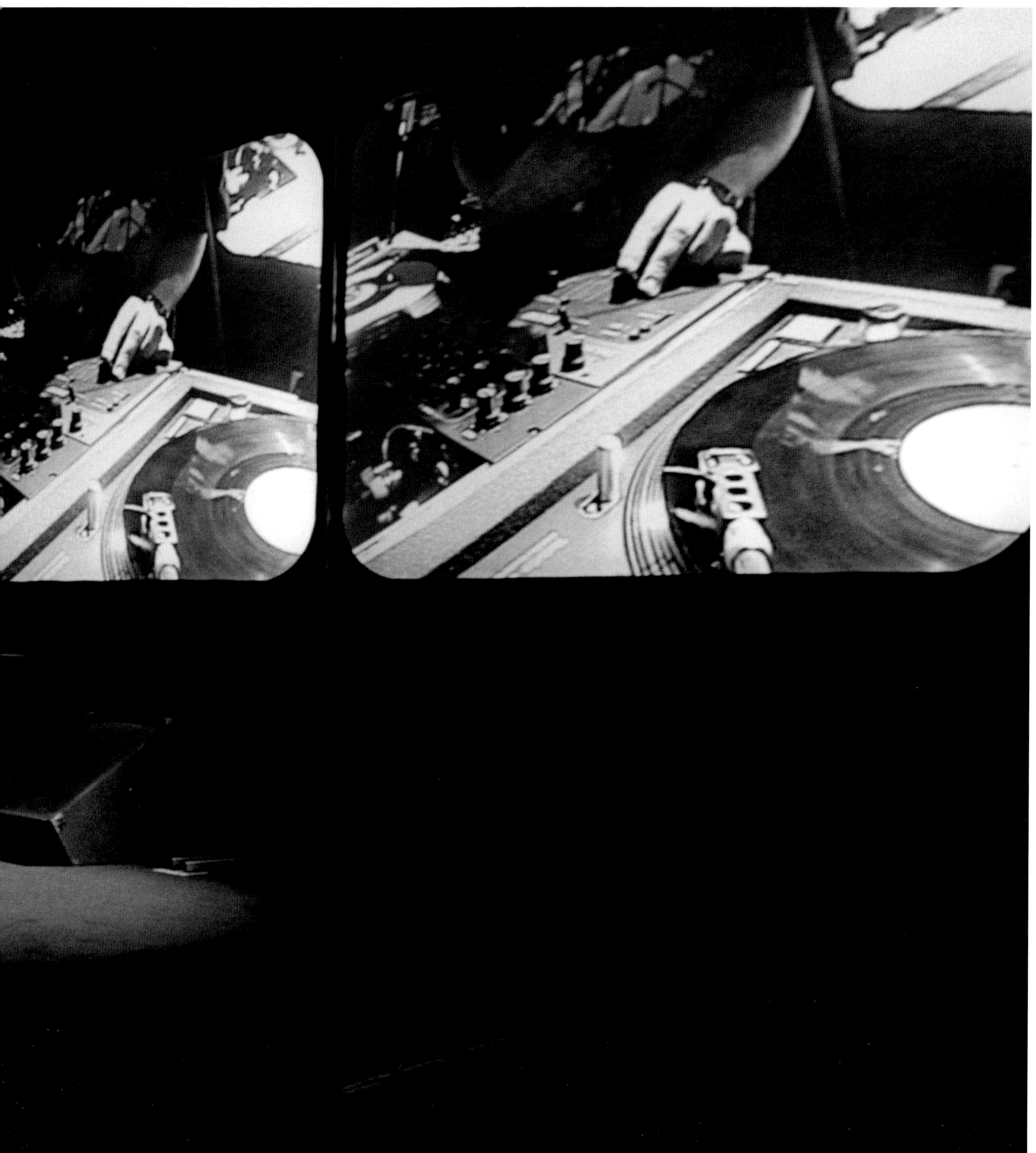

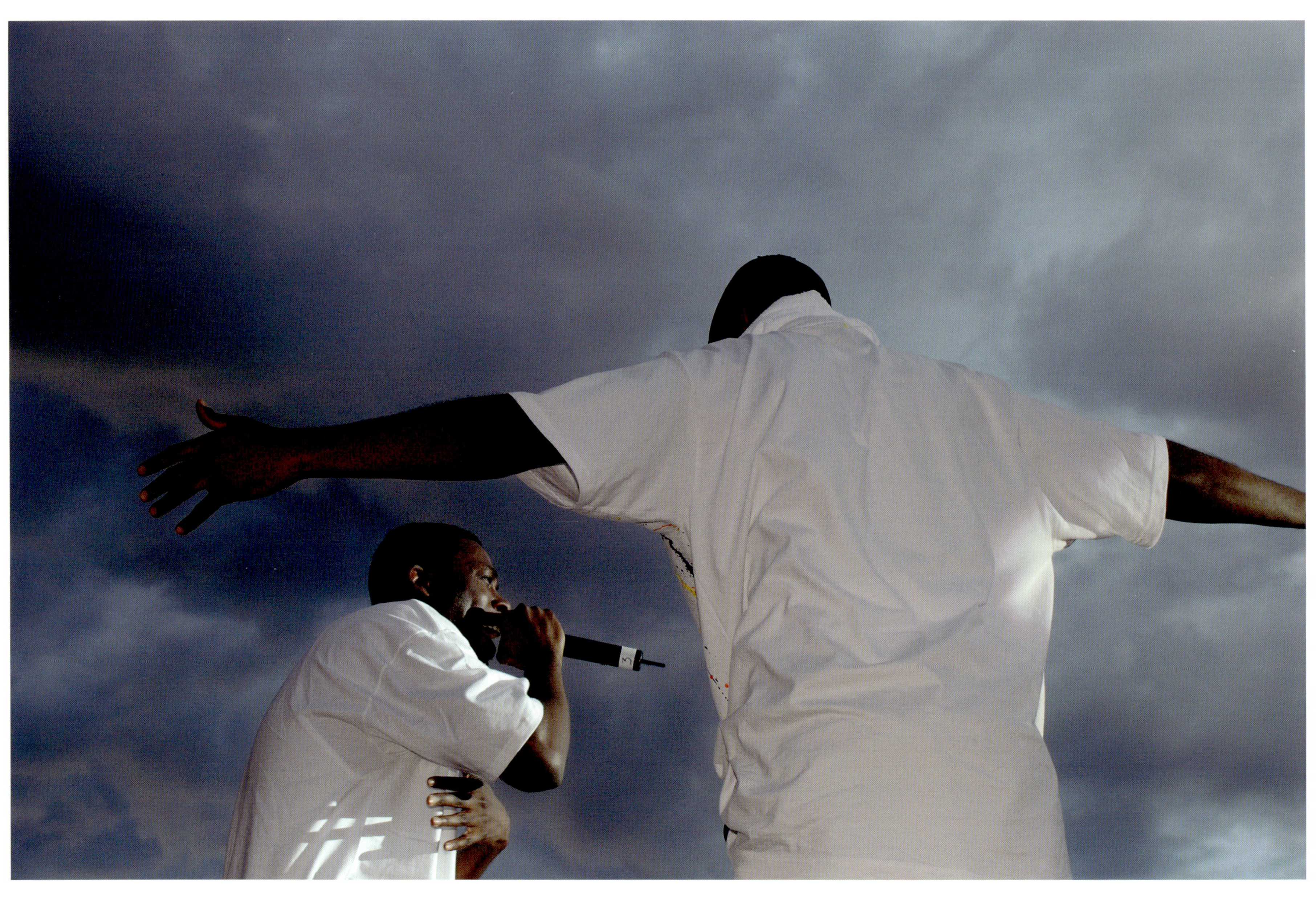

Above: GZA (left) AND RZA (right), WU TANG CLAN, 2007

Opposite, top to bottom:

MASTA KILLA, WU TANG CLAN

GHOSTFACE KILLAH, WU TANG CLAN, 2007

WU TANG CLAN, 2007

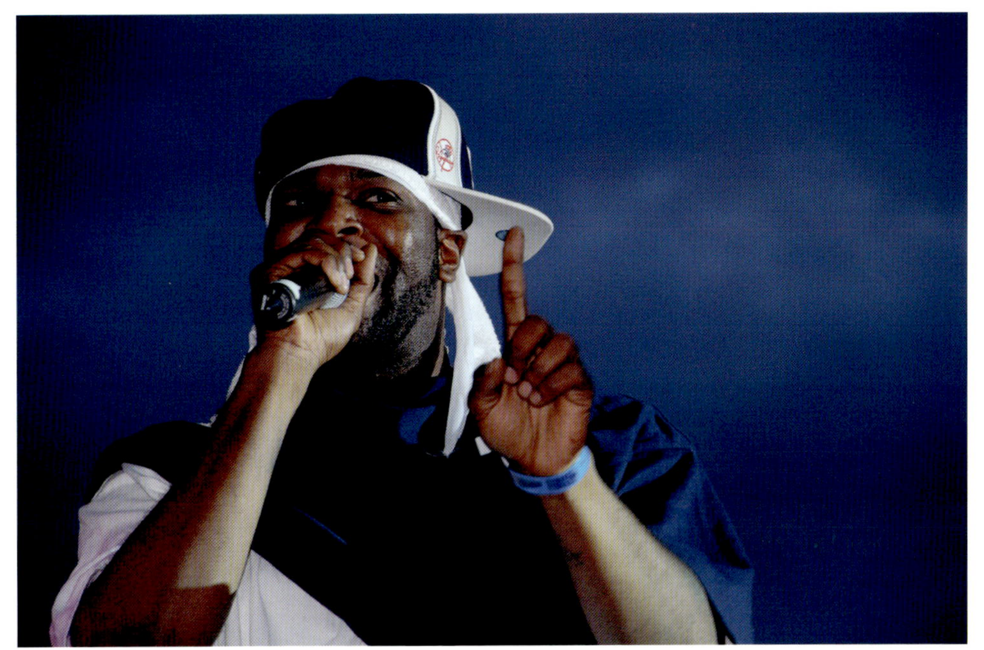

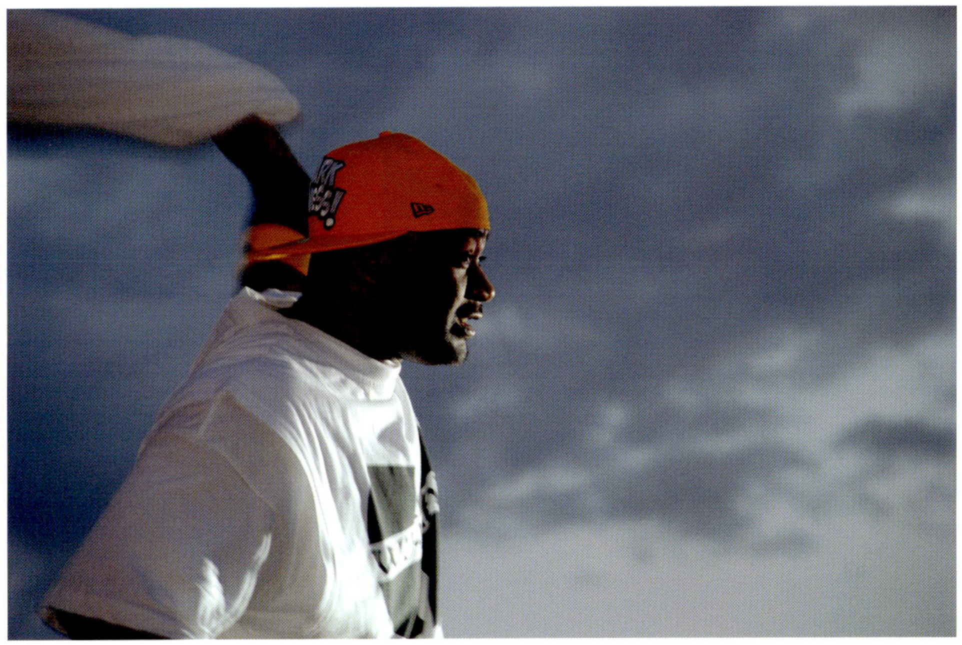

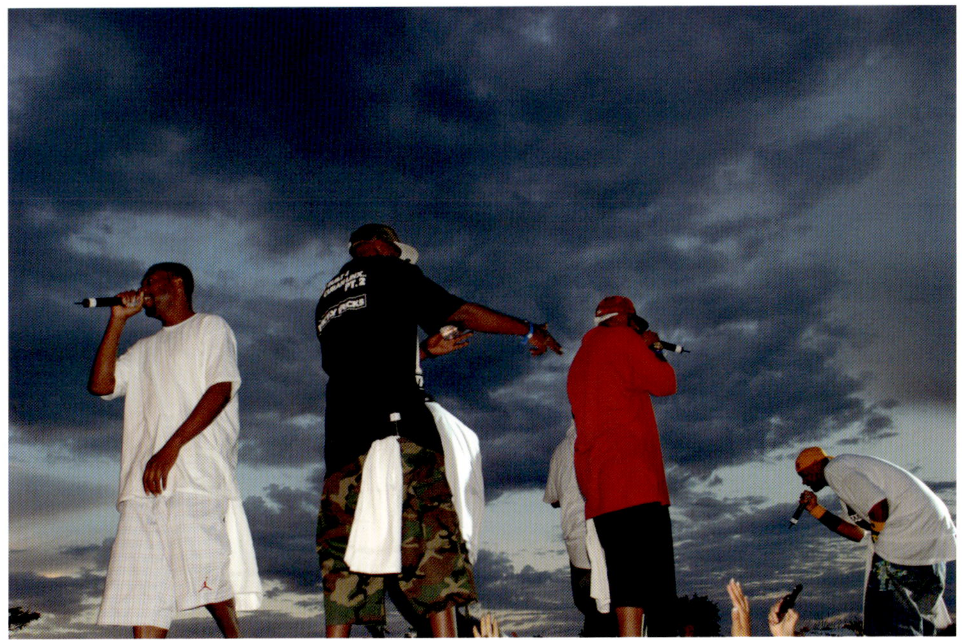

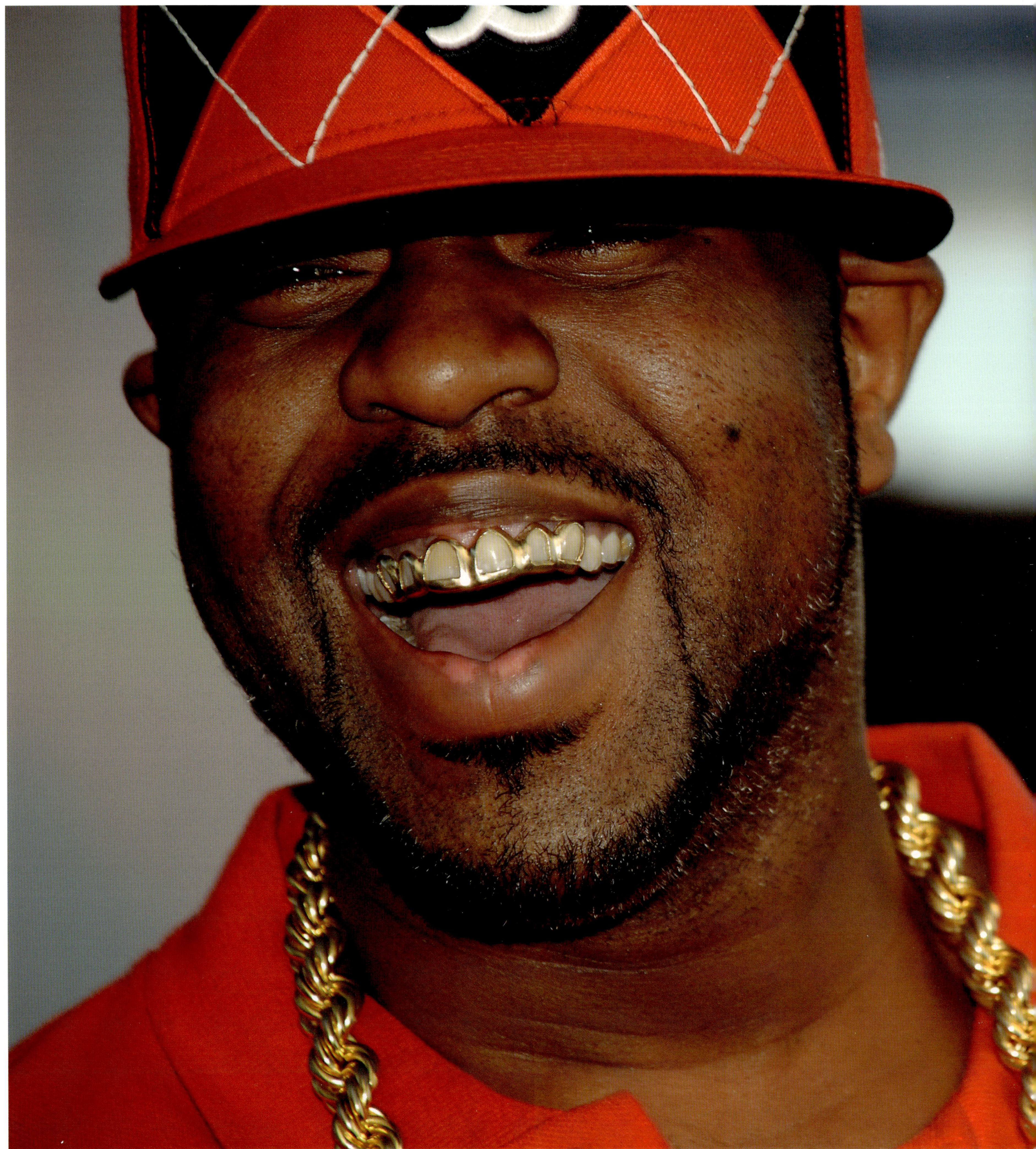

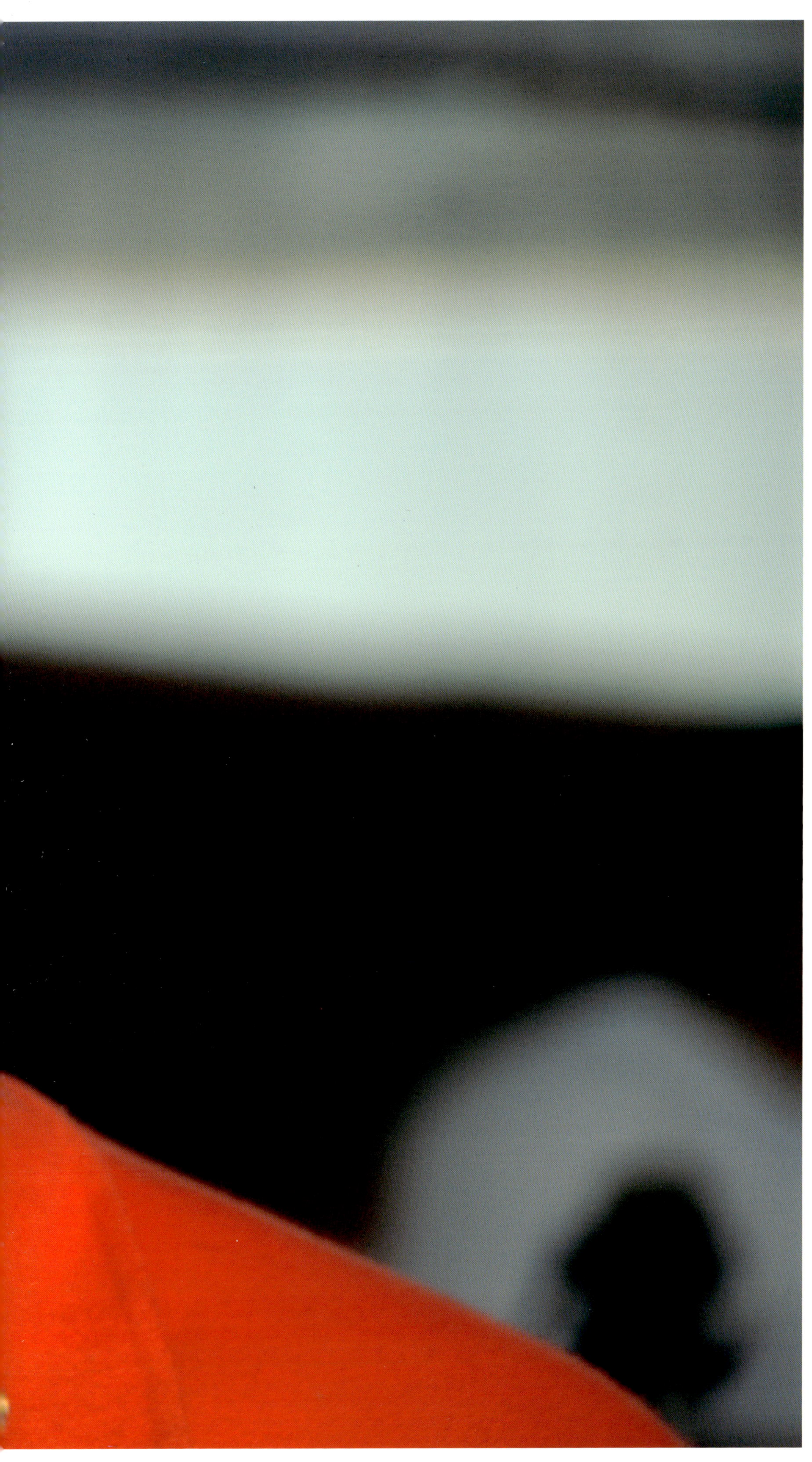

CAPPADONNA, WU TANG CLAN, 2007

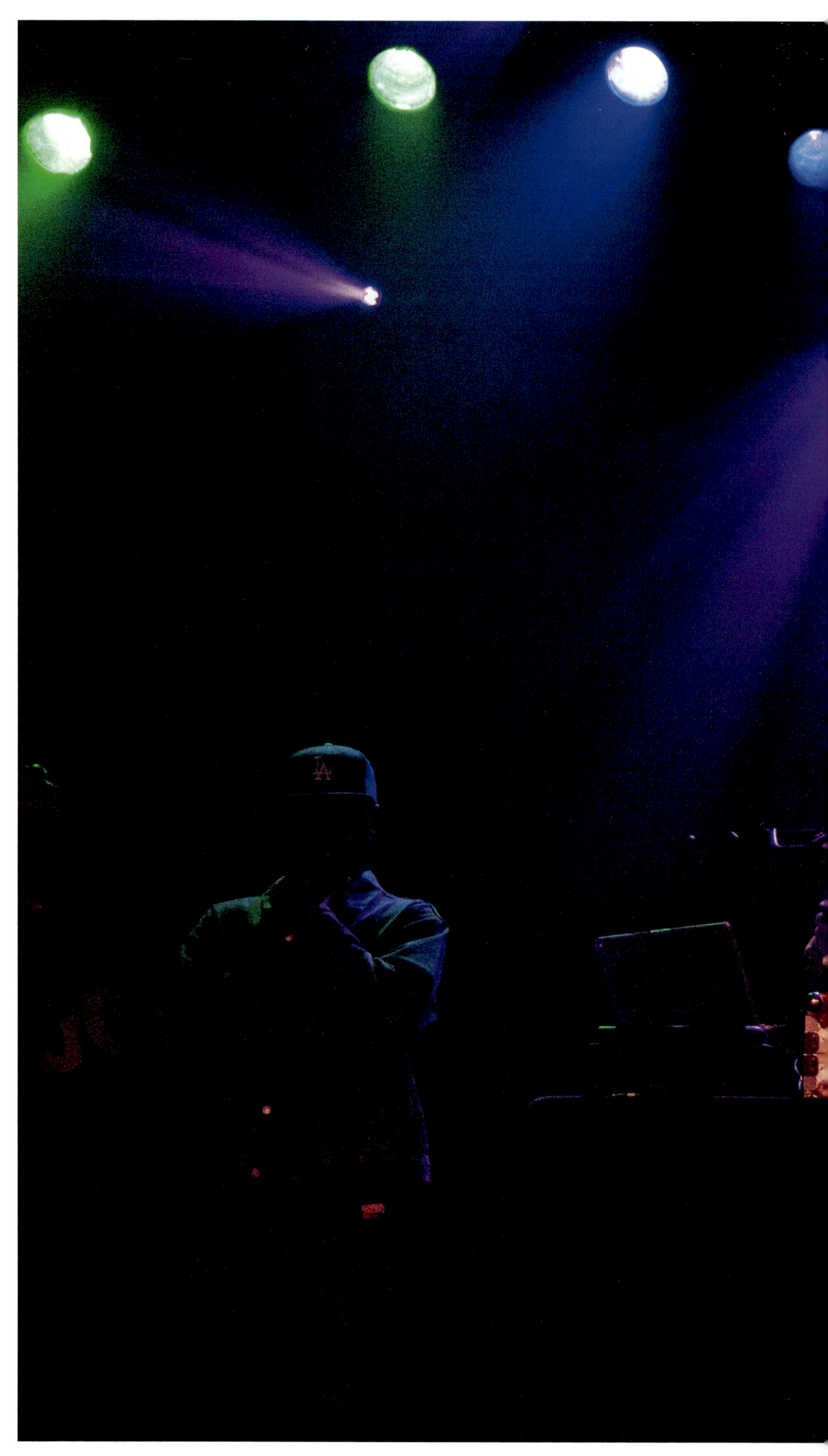

 WIZ KHALIFA, 2010

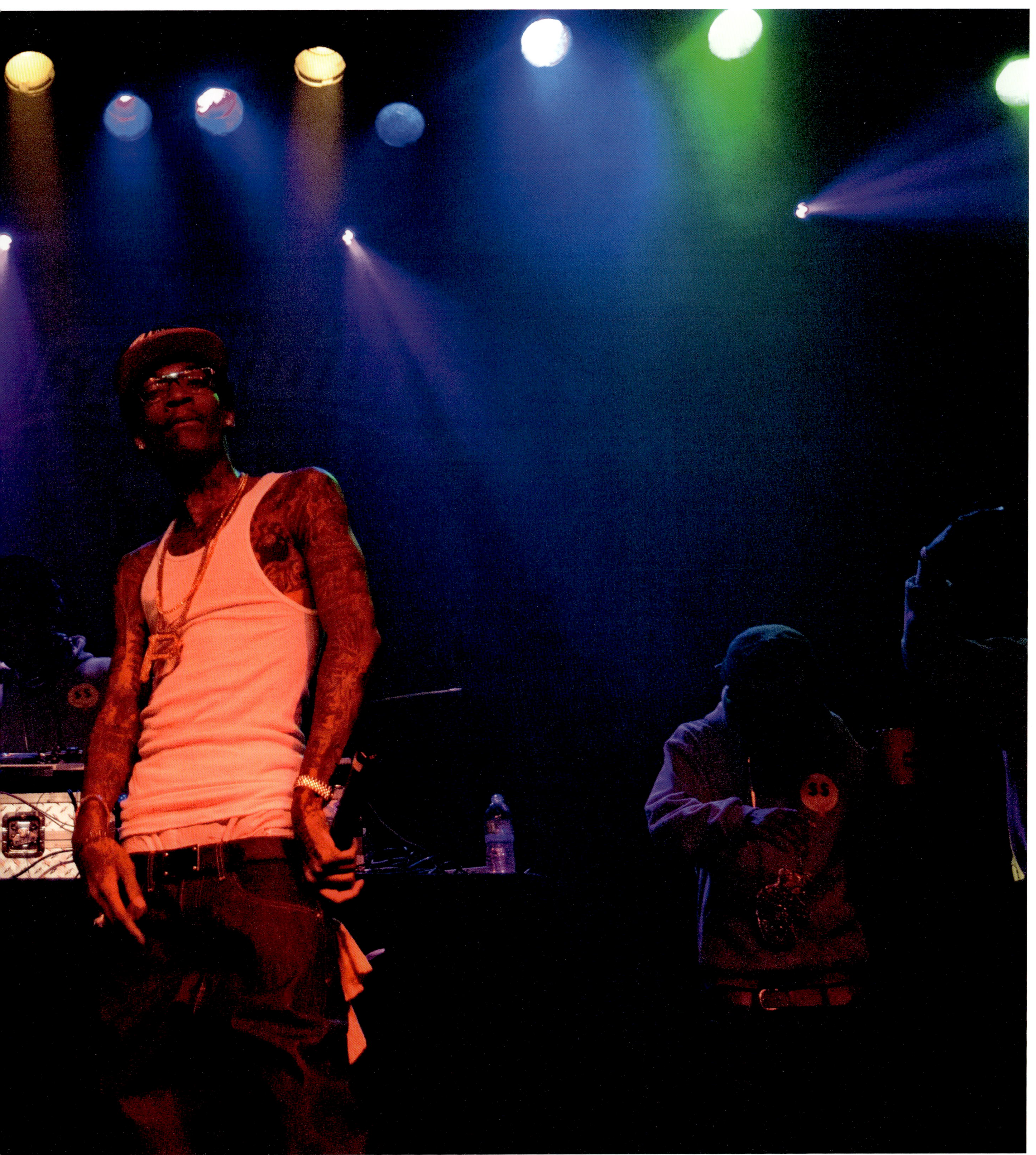

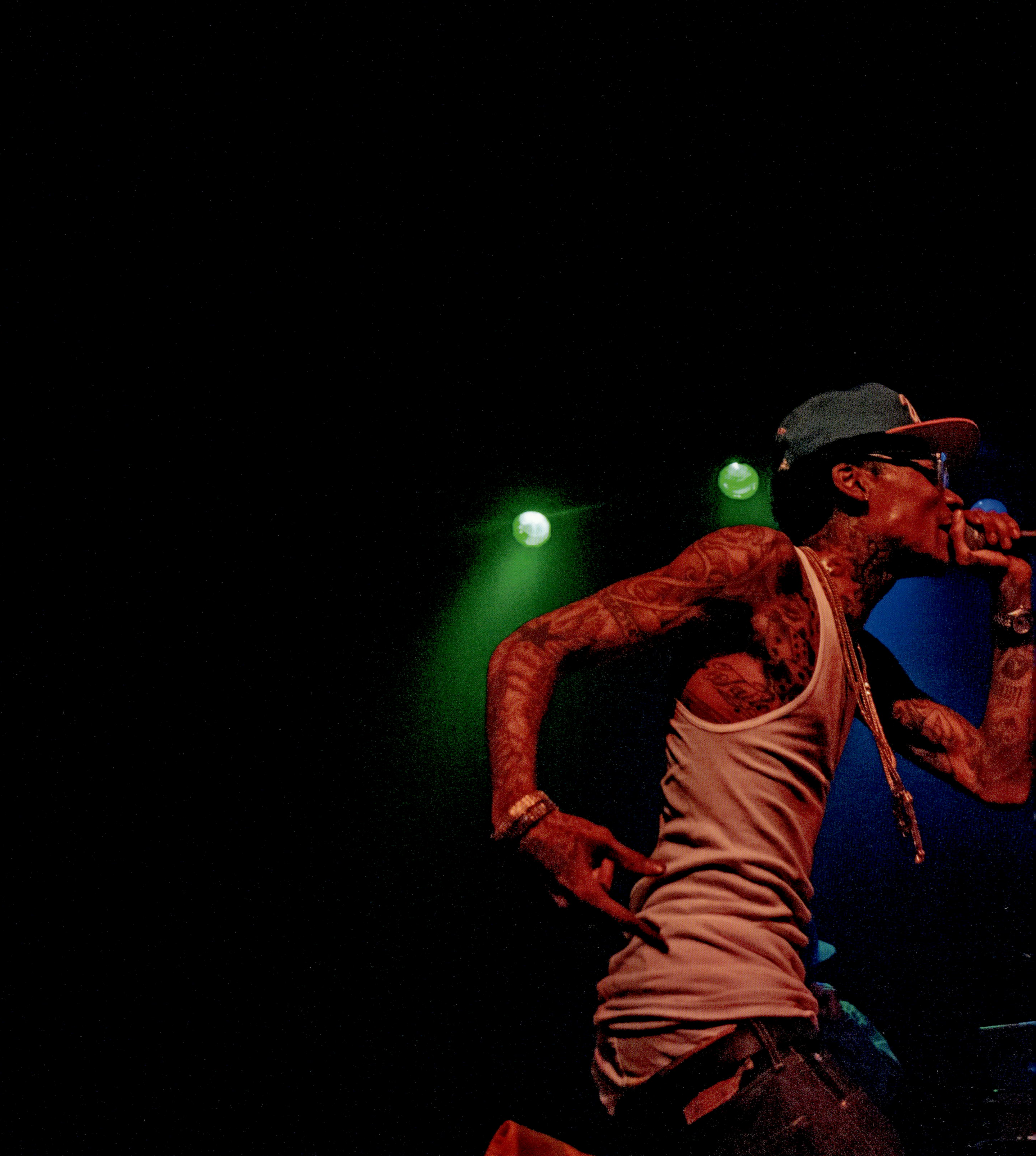

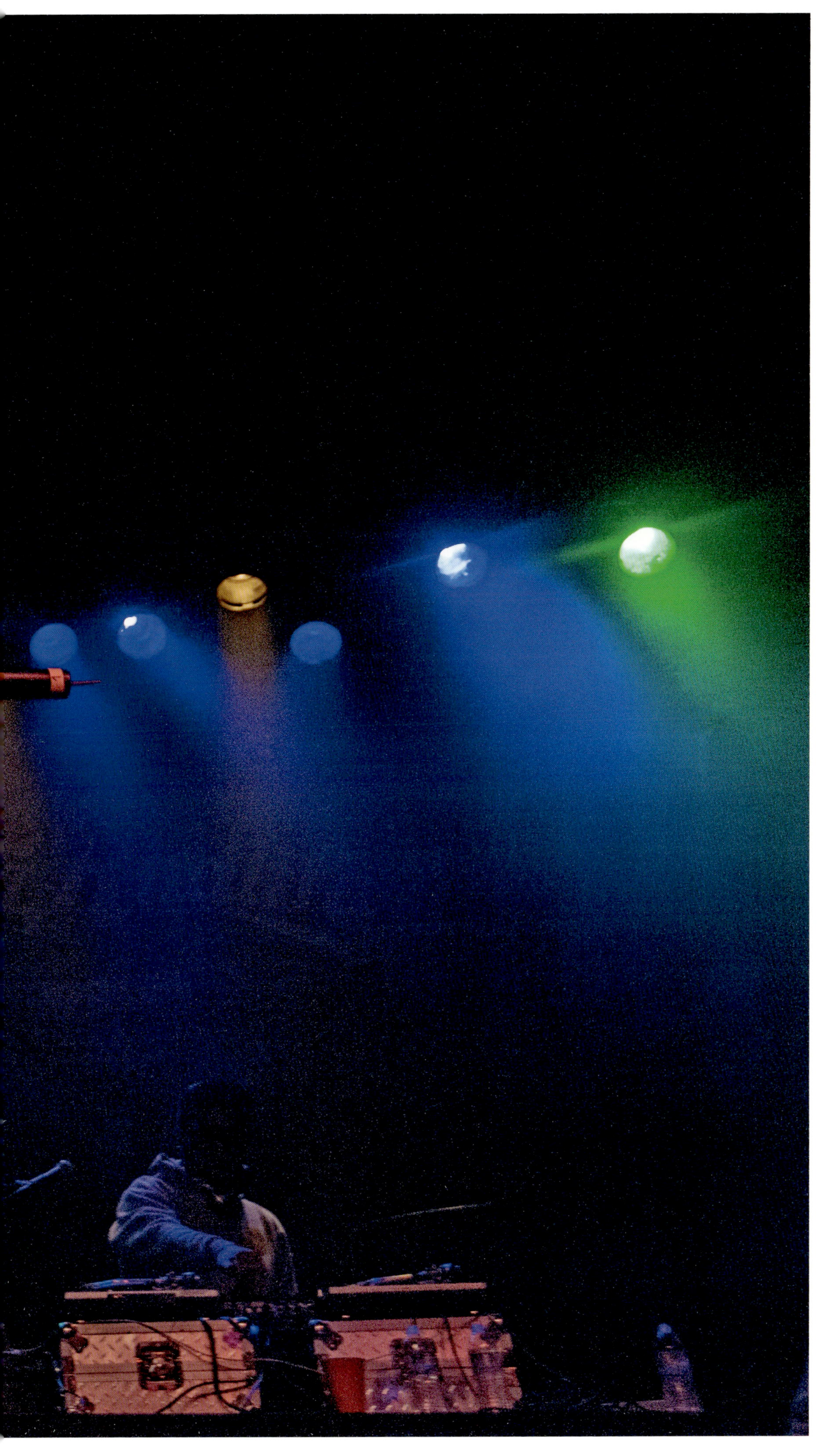

WIZ KHALIFA, 2010

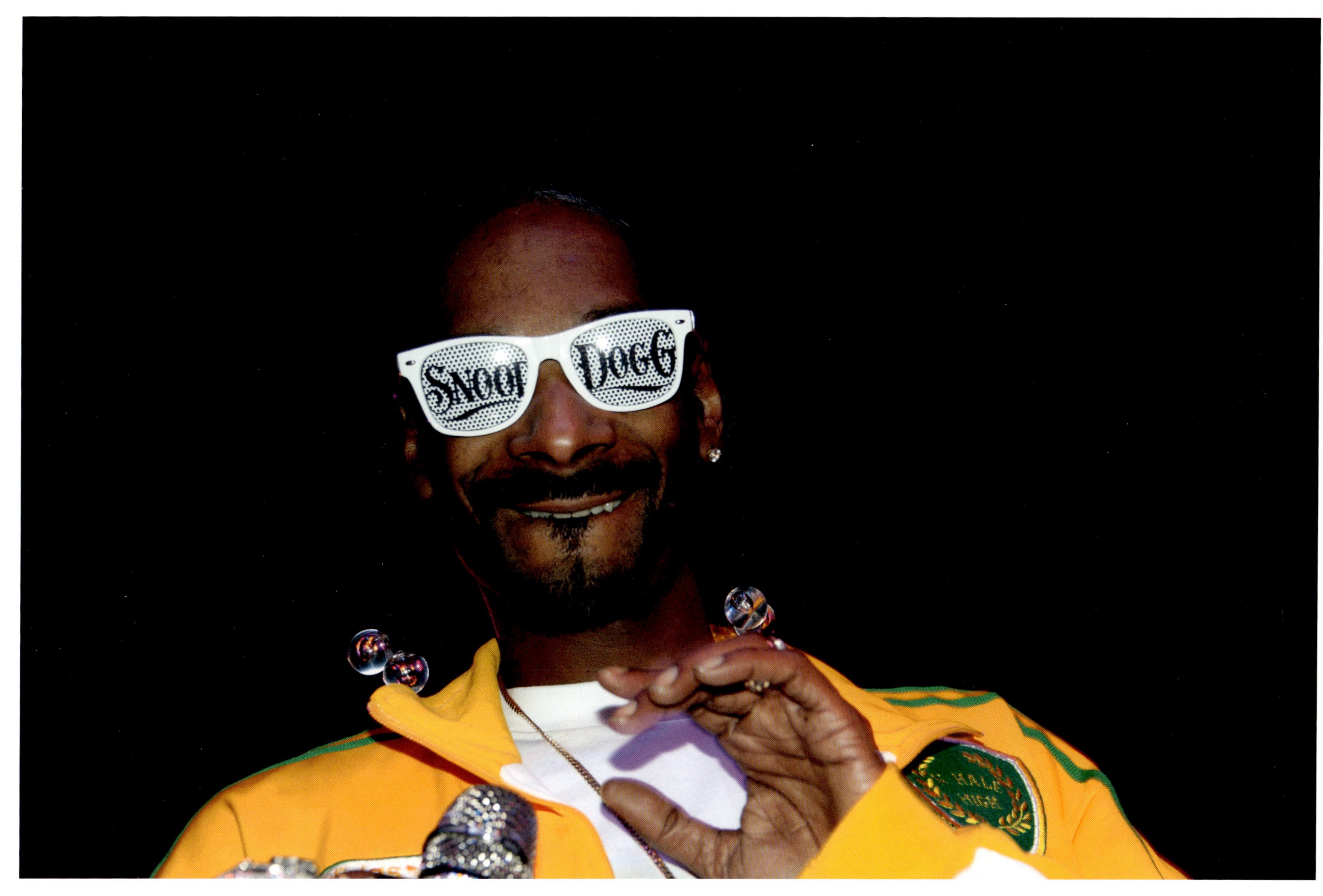

SNOOP DOGG (SNOOP LION), 2011

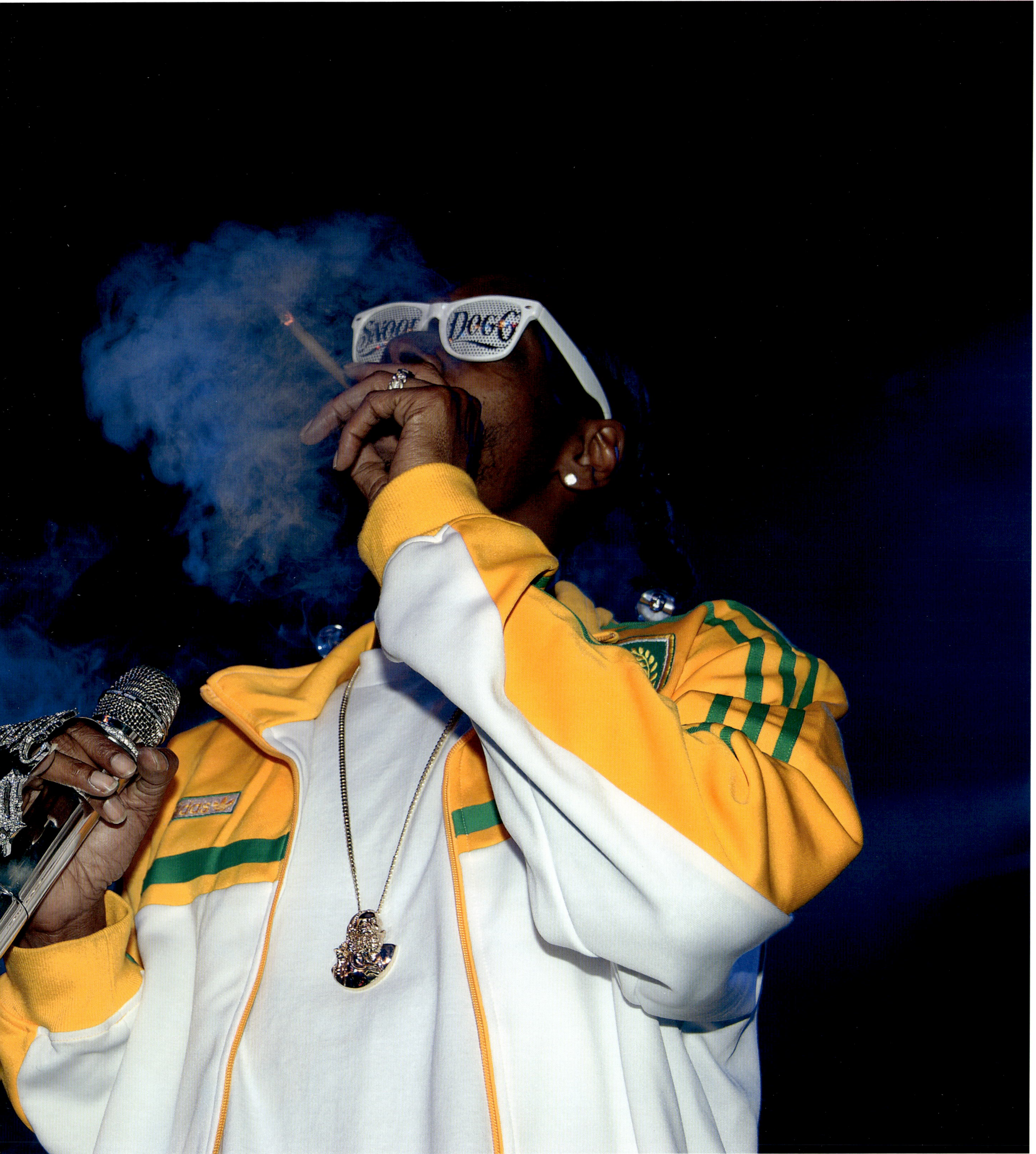
DOGG

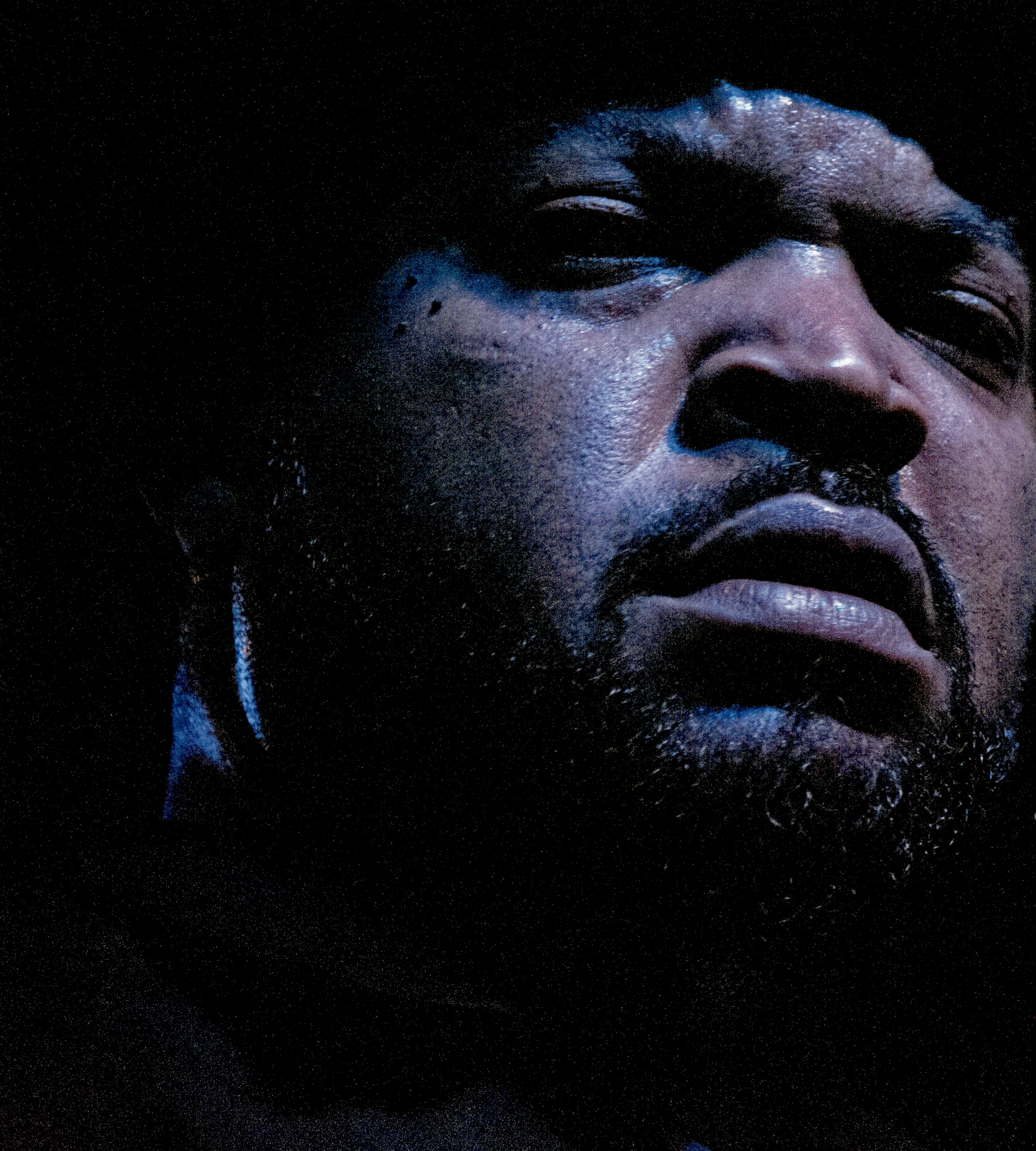

ICE CUBE, 2011

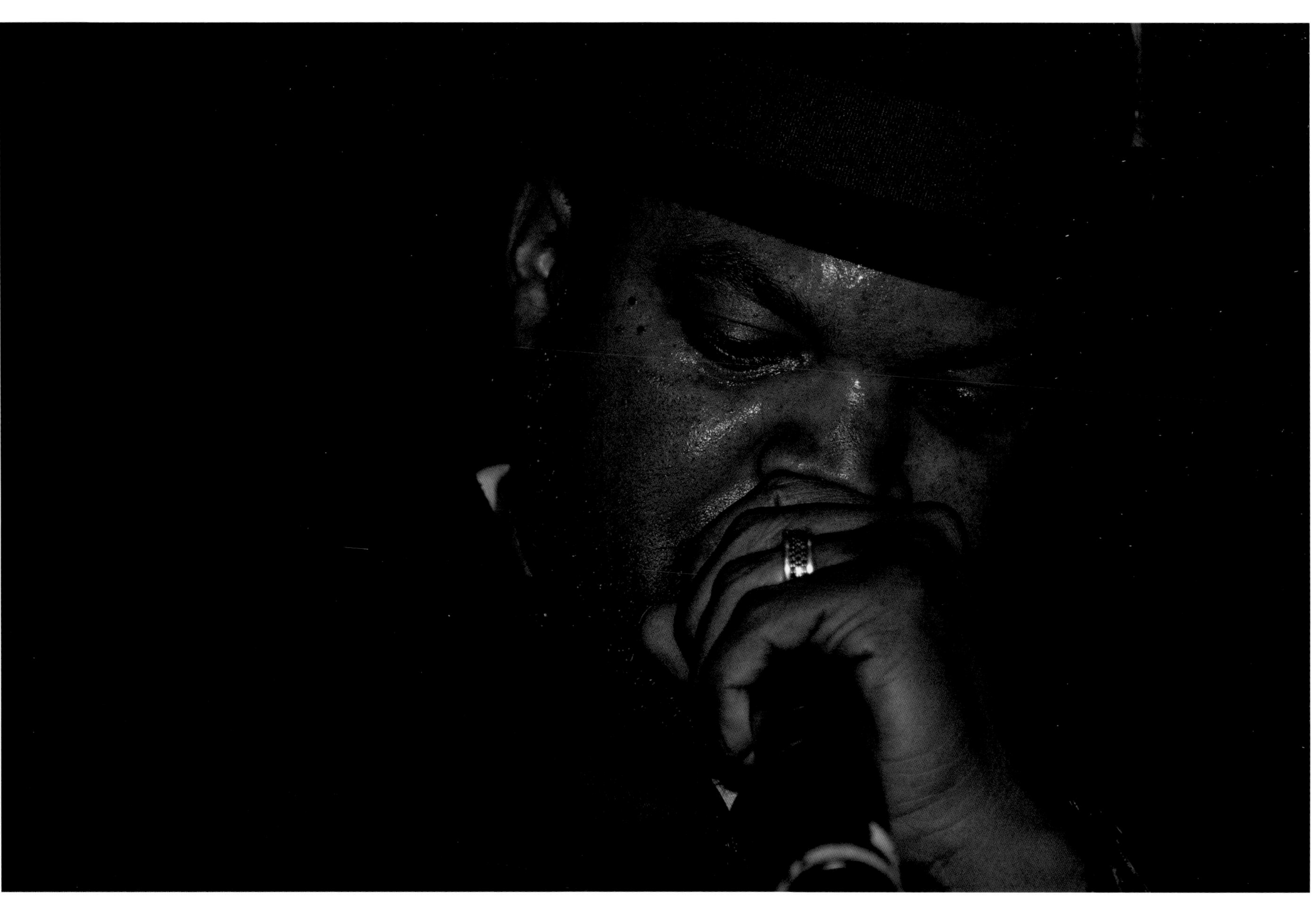

 ICE CUBE, 2011

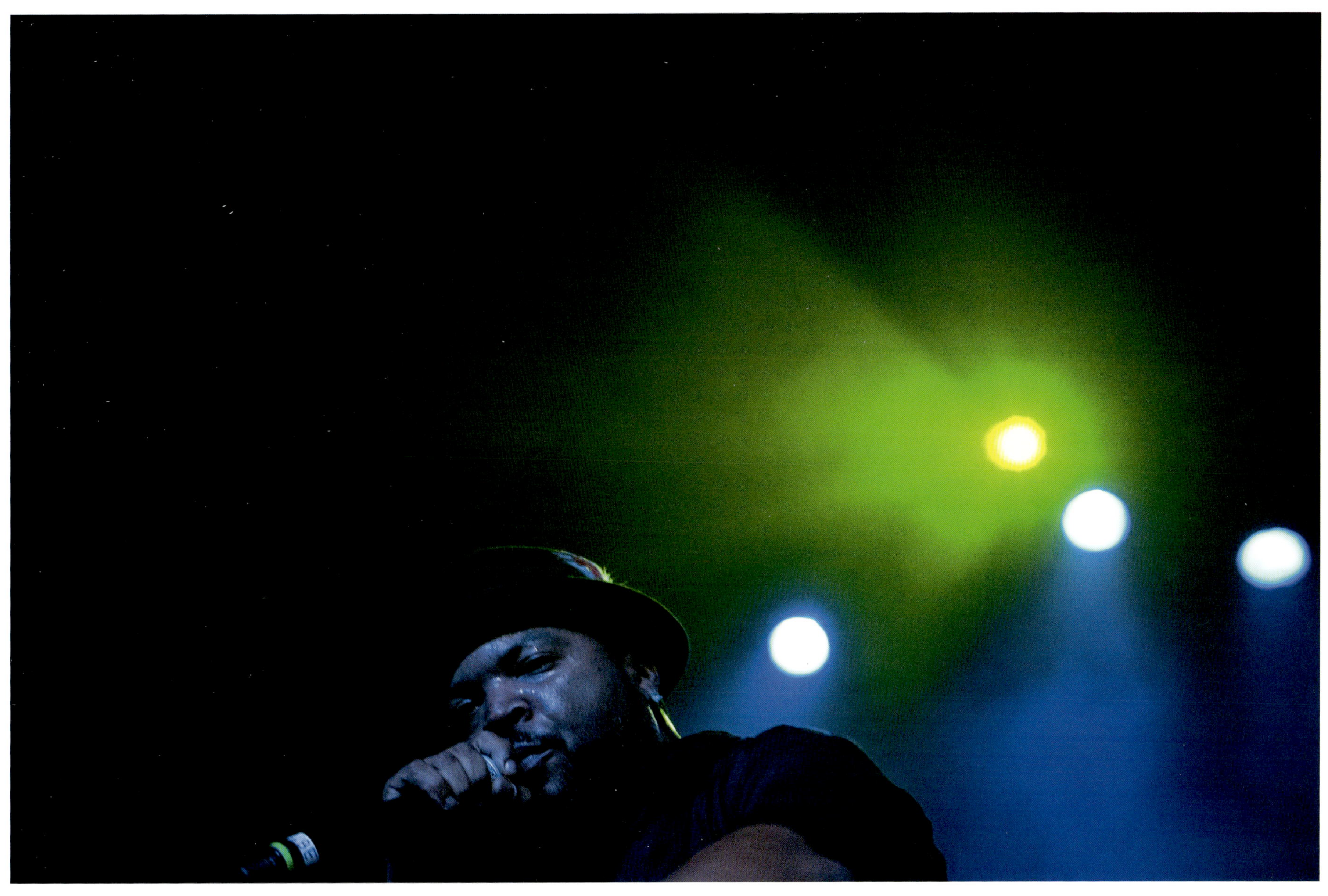

ICE CUBE, 2011

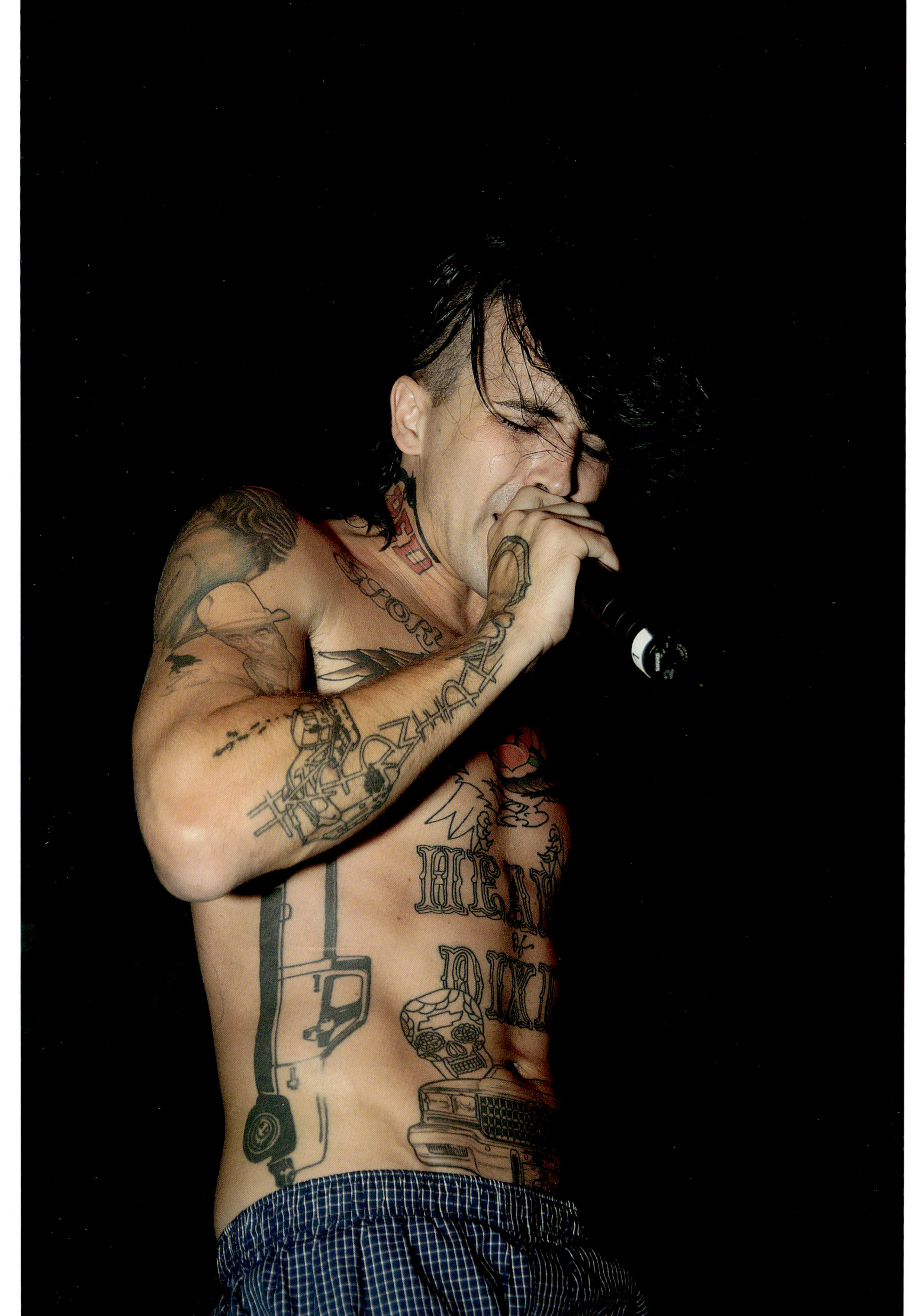

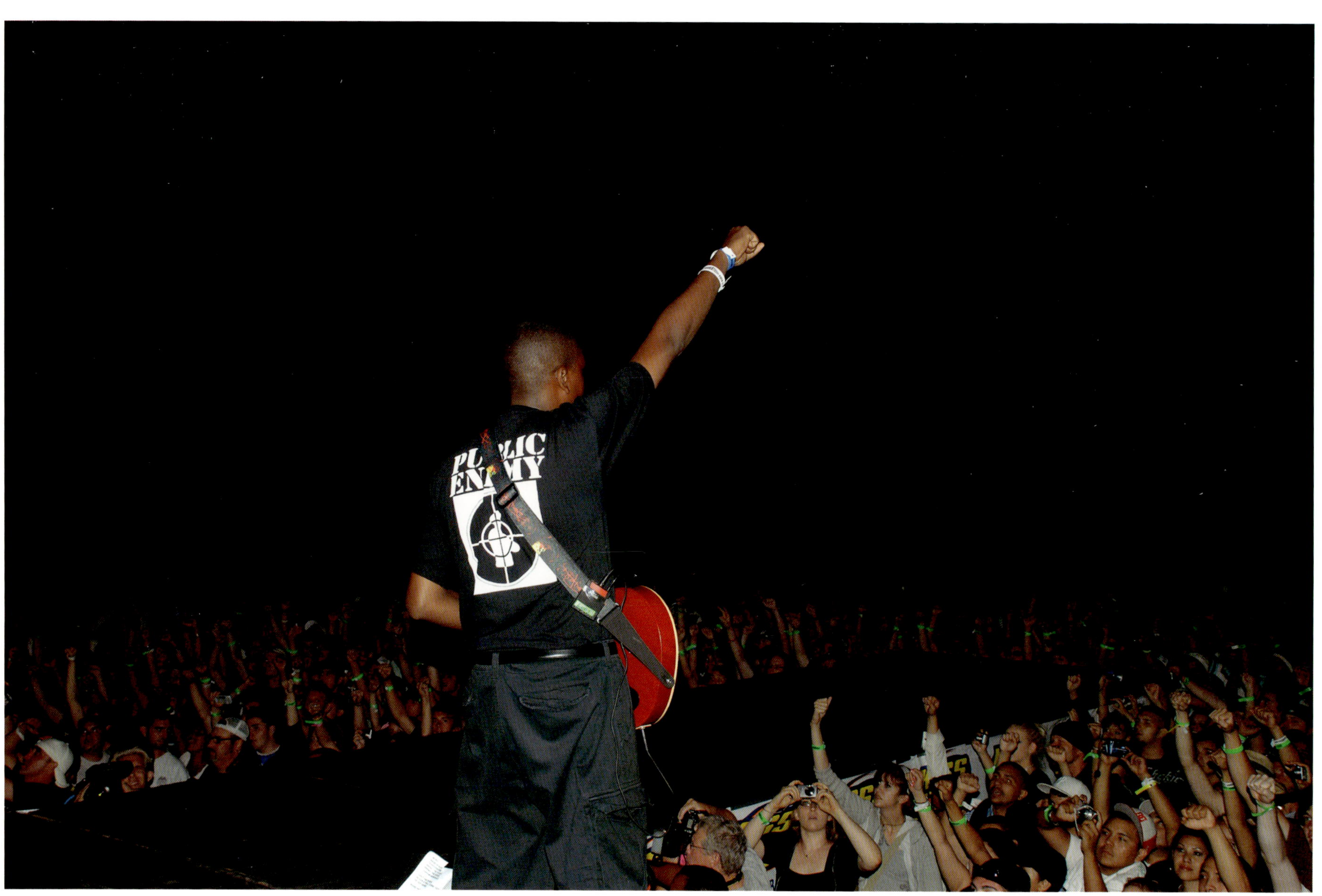

 KHARI WYNN, PUBLIC ENEMY, 2007

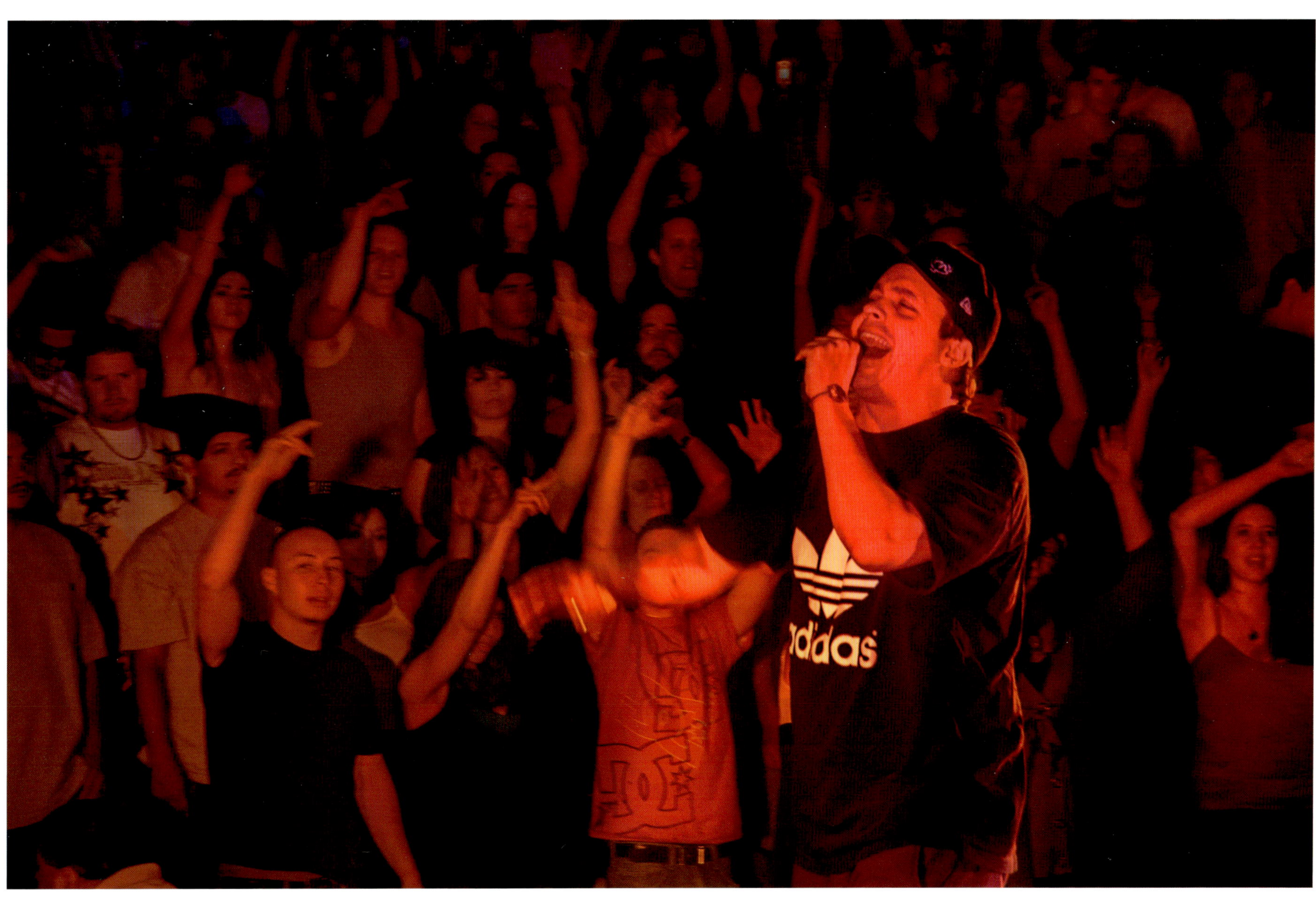

SLUG, ATMOSPHERE, 2009

144 YELAWOLF, 2010

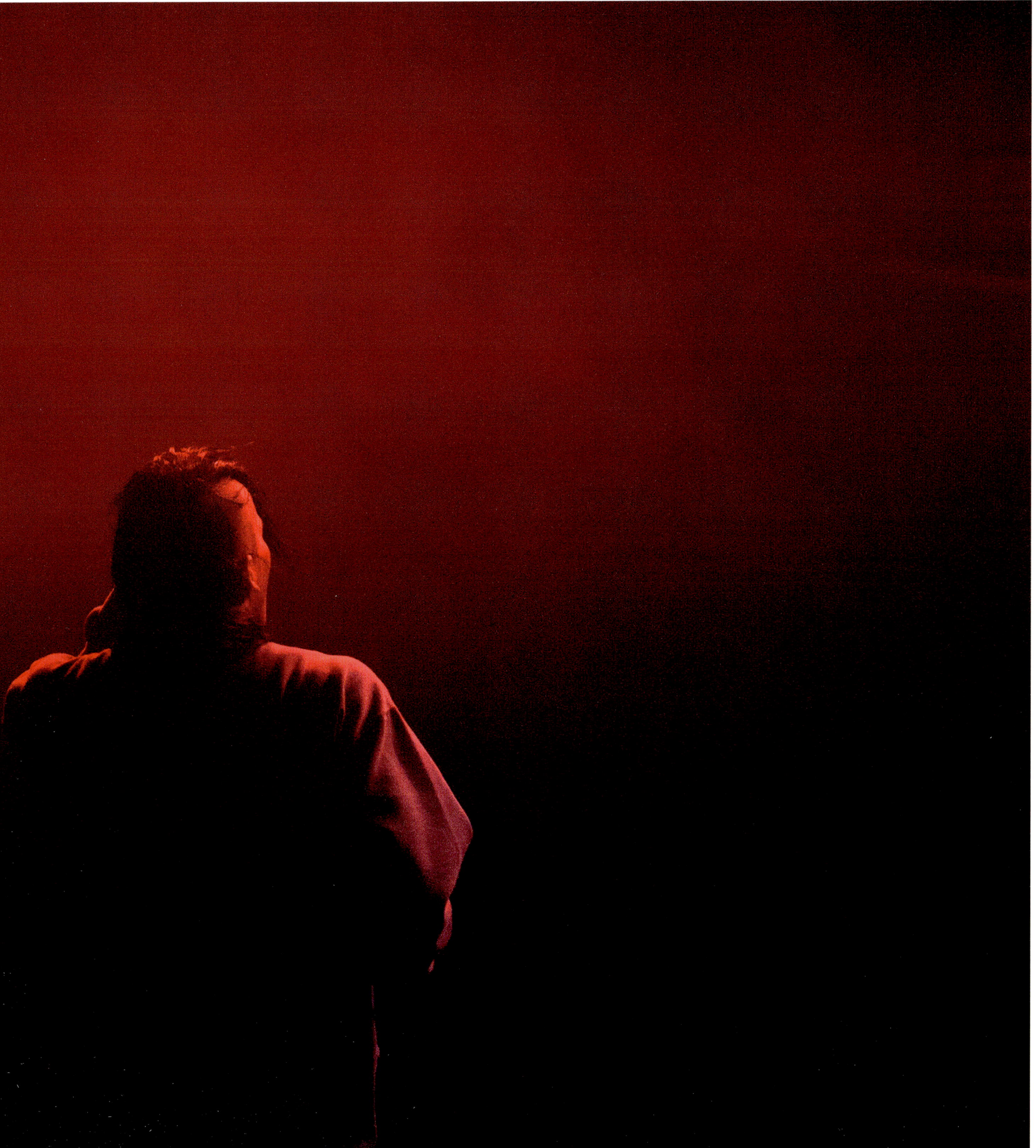

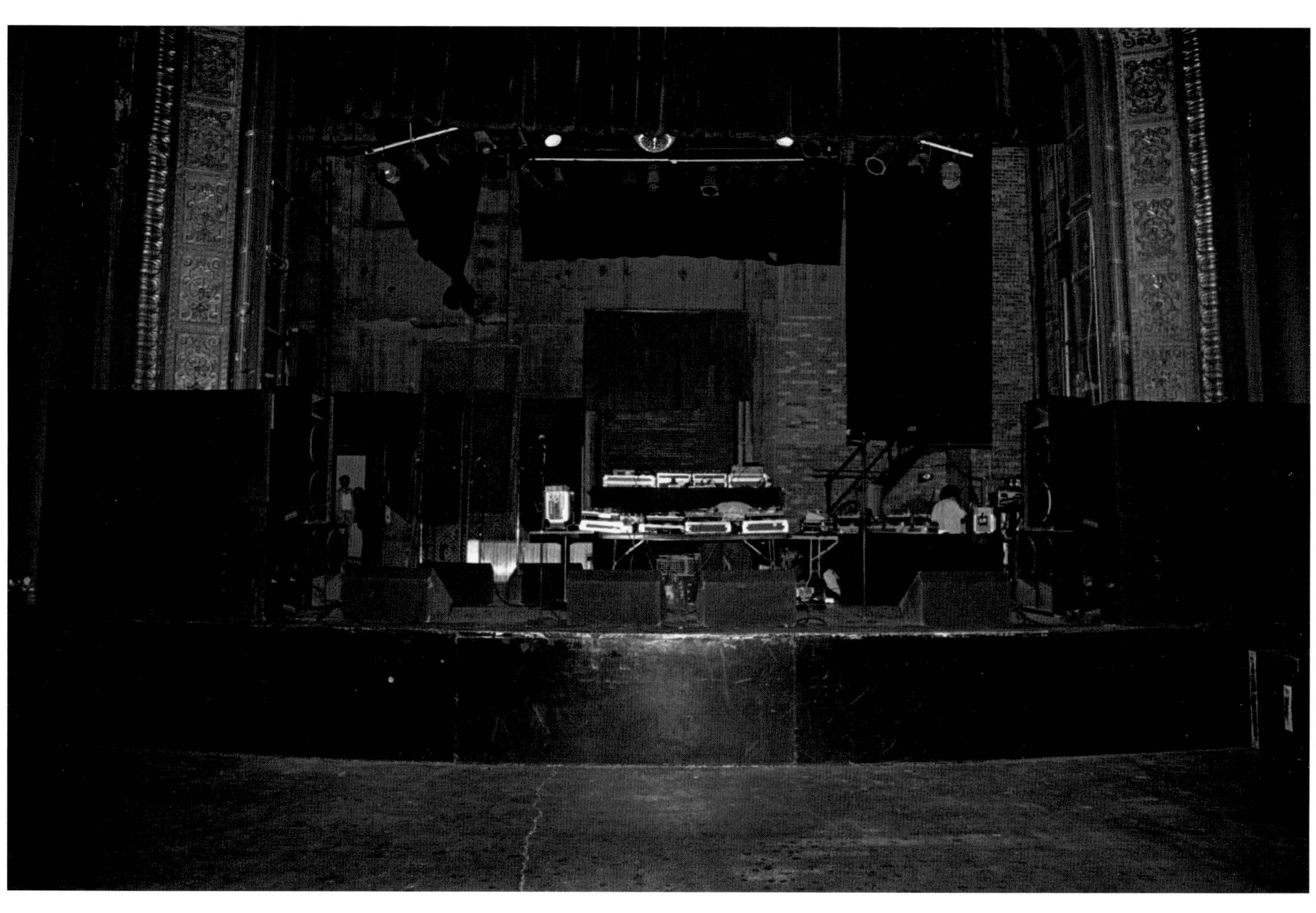

146 SUNSHINE THEATER, 2005

INTERVIEW

November 4, 2012

Frank H. Goodyear III [FG]: David, let me begin by asking you how the series began. I know the story of your attending shows with your son Zac, but what prompted you to bring a camera to these performances, beginning in 1999?

David Scheinbaum [DS]: You know, the story with Zac is really key. Inspired by a teacher who was originally from the South Bronx, he and a number of his friends got involved with break dancing and hip-hop music and culture here in Santa Fe. Of course, that led to them wanting to go to concerts, and it turned out that I was the only parent who was willing to drive them. As this was a group of twelve-year-old kids, I felt that I had to stay, in part because I knew so little about hip hop. What I did know I had learned from the mass media, which at the time generally presented a negative image of hip hop in terms of violence and gang activity and shootings and stabbings and such. So I stayed, and I sat in the back of the venue that night watching. Everything I saw that evening was positive, as well as my interactions with the other young people who were at the concert. Once the word got out that I was going to be taking them again, a few parents called with concerns. "Is this safe? Are you going to stay with them? Isn't there violence there? Aren't there drugs? Isn't there, you know, bad language?" My answer to most of those questions was basically, "Yeah, I guess." Photographing these performances didn't occur to me at first. But after a couple shows I realized that if I was going to be attending concerts with these kids for a while perhaps I could use my camera to try to show people what really goes on. Being put in the position of being a spokesperson for something that clearly I was not qualified to be a spokesperson about fascinated me. I didn't consider at first what it would take to photograph there. Certainly it wasn't as easy as bringing my camera and just starting to photograph, because there were many barriers to that. Once I decided to bring my camera, it took close to a year before I was able to position myself to where I wanted to be as a photographer in terms of access.

FG: Were there specific things that you saw at shows that interested you as a photographer? Was it the musicians, the crowd, or was it the whole ambience of the scene?

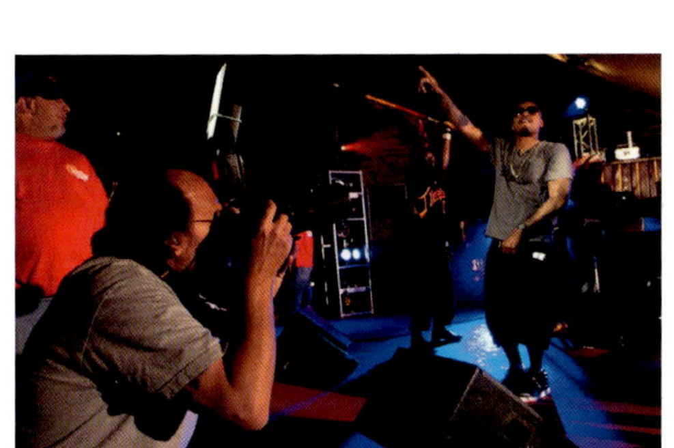

PHOTO: COLLEEN HAYES

DS: It was the whole scene, though I need to add that what led me to do this work was driven by a lot of things in my past. Music in my youth was not just a form of entertainment; it was very much my social group. The way I looked, the way I dressed was very much in line with the performers we were listening to. It was through music that I received my news, formed my politics. It drove so much of my experiences as a teenager in terms of experimenting with various things and lifestyles. It's what we all rallied around. I experienced that same youth revel at that first hip-hop concert with Zac. There was a social code there. There was a dress; there was a look; there was a style; there was a handshake. There was joy and love and an incredible positive enthusiasm in this crowd. And there were artists who, before or after their performances, would talk about politics and what was going on. Whether it was George

Bush or Obama, or whether they were talking about educating yourselves or taking care of each other and watching each other's back, there was this incredible rapport that the performers had. Before and after the show the musicians would walk through the crowd and be part of the venue. It wasn't like they were hiding backstage. There was this relationship between the concertgoers and the performers, and it reminded me a lot of my youth. Back in the 1960s the music became a voice for a generation, and so here it was all again, and I was thrilled to see it. At first I was shocked and surprised that I was even permitted to make photographs. They didn't make me sit in the back or stand in a corner. They totally welcomed me. It got to the point where I was allowed not only to photograph, but I was welcomed onstage, backstage, which is where I wanted to be. And as much as it took a lot of time and patience with permissions and personalities, the bottom line was that I was accepted into this culture as a total outsider. I found it to be a remarkable and very positive experience.

FG: You mention that there were barriers you encountered. What were the specific challenges associated with doing photography in these spaces?

DS: The initial challenge was getting permission and access, and that took a long time. When I first met Thomas, the person who promoted the shows at the Sunshine Theater in Albuquerque, where I did most of my work, he was supportive, as he had seen me there before with these young kids from Santa Fe. After initially meeting it took close to a year of writing emails, letters, phone calls, and tracking him down in Albuquerque to get to the point of me explaining to him what I hoped to do with my camera and to secure his permission and support. This journey ended with Thomas and me meeting at a Starbucks in Albuquerque with me pulling prints out of a portfolio approximately the size of the table we were sitting at. But this only got me into the theater with my camera. The big part of that first year, the big barrier, was actually getting permission to photograph the various artists, because each travels with an entourage, a show manager, a stage manager. Some people don't want you photographing at all. Some people only want you photographing the first few songs. Some people won't allow you onstage. But many were very supportive from the start. It took a good part of a year until I was able to create the kind of network to support this project. Another person who was a great help to me was Tom Sarig, who I originally met as the husband of a friend. Upon finding out that he was an A&R man for MCA records who was working very closely with both Blackalicious and The Roots, as well as with many other hip-hop groups, it was through his support and generosity that I was able to get connected with a number of managers, record labels, and PR firms who were also instrumental in my ability to photograph. Another very important aspect was having the support of two local newspaper editors—Rob Dean from the *Santa Fe New Mexican* and Julia Goldberg from the *Santa Fe Reporter*—both helped me with press credentials and access to some of the other venues where I photographed. In terms of photographic challenges, the big problem was that I had never used an automatic camera with autofocus. At the first two shows that I went to with my 35 mm camera, I found out quickly that there was

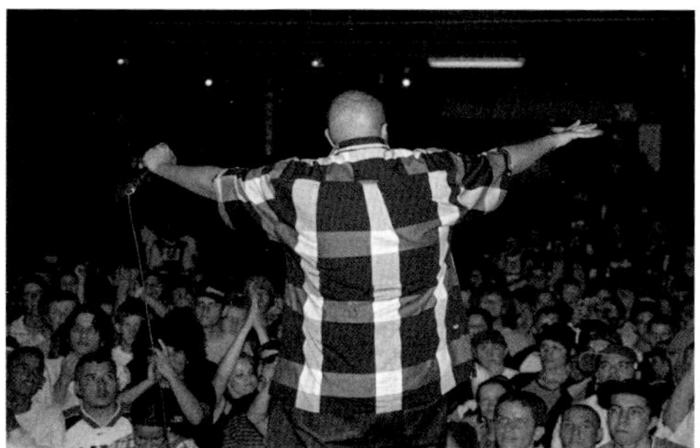

GIFT OF GAB, BLACKALICIOUS, 2005

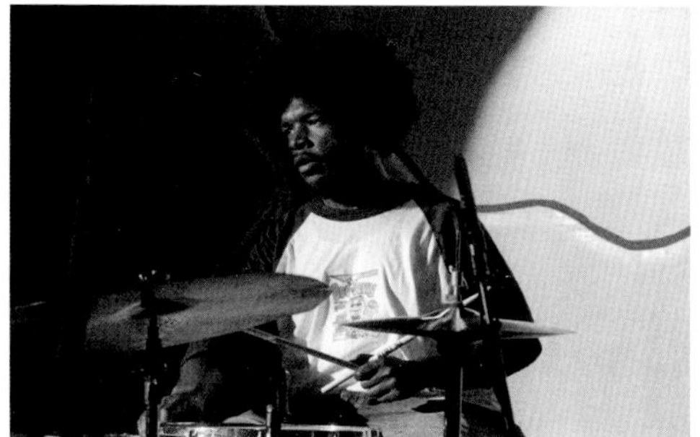

?UESTLOVE, THE ROOTS, 2003

no time to focus. By the time I had the camera focused, the shot was over. Like a lot of street photographers I learned to shoot from the hip, taking pictures without really looking in the camera. In this new situation, literally and figuratively I was shooting in the dark. I was guessing at exposure; I was guessing at focus. Things were moving fast. But from those first few rolls of film, there turned out to be a few photographs that I'm very attached to, especially images of a crew from Oakland, California, called Hieroglyphics. By the third time I went to photograph I borrowed a camera from Wendy Young, a former student of mine who was also teaching at the College of Santa Fe. It was an autofocus Canon. I had never used autofocus before, but it made all the difference in the world. It was good in low light, and it focused really well. Afterwards, I purchased a Contax 35 mm camera to use for this hip-hop work. I bought it because I believe it had at the time the fastest autofocus in low-light settings. You could be in a totally darkened room and the camera would actually focus on what you were pointing it at. That became the camera that ninety-five percent of my black and white was shot with.

FG: Regarding the long history of photographers documenting musical performance or creating artistic work that responds to music, were there specific photographers who were influential to you?

DS: In terms of music photography, the only photographer I was really aware of and still primarily the only one who inspires me is Roy DeCarava, though I didn't study with him. When I went to Brooklyn College, my teachers Barney Cole, Walter Rosenblum, and Murray Weiss were former members of the Photo League and later the Photographer's Forum. Every few months Roy DeCarava would visit as a guest artist to do critiques with our class. I was able to learn from him and talk with him and have him comment on my work when I was a student. And it was probably through meeting him at that time that I attained a serious interest in his work, especially the jazz images that ended up being published in his book *The Sound I Saw*. Those photographs are very gutsy. He's pushing his film, increasing the speed and compensating for that in the darkroom. By the time I began photographing hip-hop shows in the late nineties, you could buy film like 3200 and I was pushing Tri-X to 1600. The photographs from my first group of concerts were very much modeled after the look and the feeling that I admired in those DeCarava photographs. You feel there's spontaneity in those photographs, and the framing is a little off kilter. They're taken looking up, looking down, looking to the side. They're low light. They're grainy. The look of the photograph corresponds with the feel of the club and the feel of the music. Julia Margaret Cameron was another photographer who gave me the confidence to proceed along this new path. In her day many criticized her portraits for being out of focus and misunderstood her technique for a lack of talent. In correspondence with Sir John Herschel, she wrote, "What is focus, and who has a right to say what correct focus is?" I don't know if that's exactly right, but it's the way I remember it. That was one of Beaumont Newhall's favorite quotes. When I make pictures that are blurry or they move or they're fuzzy, I think of Cameron and the sheer emotional strength of her photographs. That's what gets me through my darkroom sessions when I'm printing these images that are not so sharp. She and her work have probably given me more artistic license than anyone besides Roy DeCarava.

FG: David, let's transition to the tradition of concert films. You have told me in the past about your admiration for films like Martin Scorsese's *The Last Waltz,* which was released in 1978. I don't know whether you've seen Mel Stuart's *Wattstax* about the famous 1972 music festival at the L.A. Coliseum, but it shares much in common with Scorsese's film. To what degree has film shaped your thinking about how to portray your subjects and to document these performances?

DS: *The Last Waltz* is a favorite film of mine. Because of my love for The Band and their music, I have seen it many times. I can't say that I was consciously aware of how it was shot, at least at first. When I saw it later on DVD and watched an interview with Scorsese, he spoke about how important it was to have cameras set up onstage behind and to the side of the performers. As a filmmaker he was trying to document the music and the performance. It made sense that one needs to be up there with the performers. The whole notion of looking toward the audience, instead of being in the audience looking at the stage, this was all an epiphany for me. When I watched the film again, I looked at the camera shots and the camera angle. One of the beauties of that film is that you feel like you're there. You're right there in it, and it's because of the point of view of the camera. I don't know how many shows I had photographed when I became aware of this, but from that point on I decided that I needed to shoot from the stage. Though I try to stay in the wings so the audience doesn't see me, being onstage and being a few feet behind or next to the musicians is where I want to be. Of course, the performers move around a lot. That said, once they see me photographing they'll often come my direction and help to make sure I'm getting shots. They have helped me in their own way, knowing what I'm trying to do with my work.

FG: Let's continue with you being onstage. What are you looking for during a performance? Are you concentrating on a particular individual? Are you looking for a variety of details among different people? Or is it a process of discovery—that you don't know exactly what you're looking for when you get onstage and begin your work?

DS: I want to see their eyes, their faces, and to capture how they perform. This emphasis grows out of what I'm trying to achieve. I want to create portraits that counter the whole gangster image of rappers and hip-hop artists. It's important to me to photograph these performers as human beings. To do so, you need to see their eyes and their faces. Of course, there's a lot happening onstage, and at times I'm interested in capturing the movement—the hand movements, the foot movements, the body movements. Those pictures are part of trying to get a feel for the music. To depict sound visually is not an easy thing to do. Alfred Stieglitz talked about hearing the music of Ernst Bloch in your mind when you looked at his "Equivalents." But to capture music in a still photograph that doesn't have a soundtrack, you end up one way or another concerned about motion, lighting, and other things. But again, I'm always trying to capture their eyes, because if you can't access a person through their eyes, they remain, to me, anonymous. They're just a figure. For example, with photographs of workers from the Farm Security Administration archives you'll see many images where people's faces are hidden in shadow and the picture becomes simply an example of a "farm worker." But when you see a picture of a person in the fields with a hoe in his hand and you see the sweat on his brow and the glint in his eye, you begin to see into his soul. It's no longer a "farm worker." It's now a picture of a person.

FG: At the same time, as you well know, performers tend to wear different masks. They have a stage mask, a public face that they wear to the world, and then they have a more private self, or even multiple private selves. To what degree is your work interested in exploring these different personas? For instance, in a photograph such as your portrait of Daniel Dumile, aka MF Doom, he literally wears a mask onstage. This alternate persona is an important part of his act. And then there are more intimate likenesses, such as your tender portrait of Mos Def taken close up backstage.

DS: I tend to photograph people with their mask on. That's what I am more likely to have the opportunity to do. The Mos Def image is different because it was made after a performance. Things were relaxed. We were in a party-type room, and I said, "Hey, do you mind—can I take a few photographs?" It was just him and me. I find that photograph so compelling and so beautiful and so open. But the truth is that I don't have that opportunity often. Most of my photographs are taken during the performance, so everyone is in their persona. They're dressed for the show.

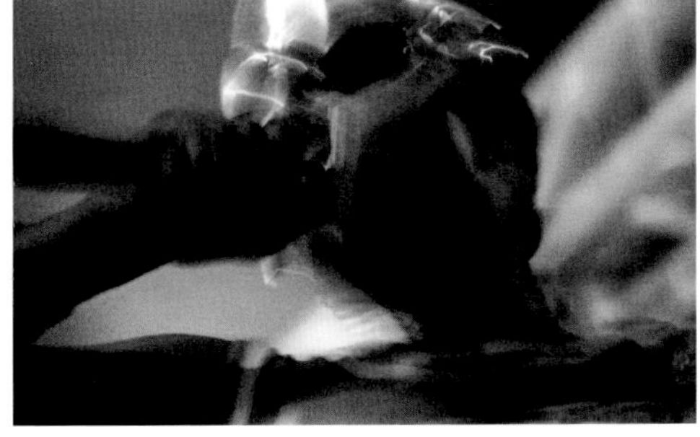

MF DOOM, 2005

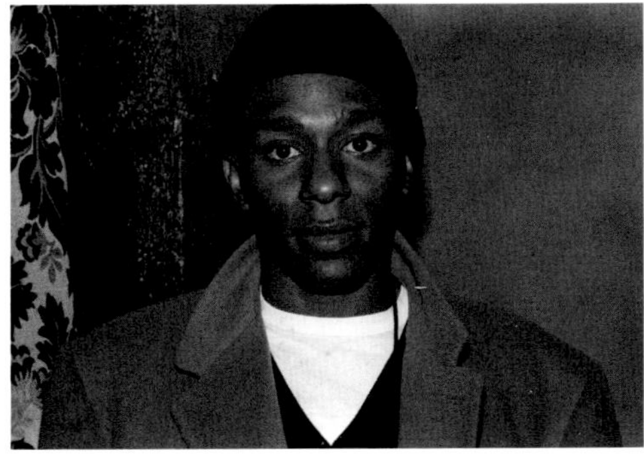

MOS DEF (YASIIN BEY), 2002

FG: There are certain groups and individual performers whom you've seen many times over a long time period. Can you speak a little about your relationship with those groups?

DS: There are several performers whom I've photographed many times. The crew from Hieroglyphics, some of the members of Souls of Mischief, Del—I've seen them many times. It's been twelve years now. There's another artist named Bukue One who's been a great friend and help to me. ?uestlove and The Roots—I have photographed them five or six times. When I see them, it is personal, and they often ask me, "How's the project going?" But it's not a friendship thing where I can simply call them up. Given my age, I'm way out of this demographic. Yet, when I go to these shows and I walk into the theater now after all these years, there's so much love and so much feeling. It's really become a family. Everyone—even the kids from the shows—I don't know them, but they know me, because they see me show after show. It's terrific to walk in and have all the security guys always come over to me. They ask me about my pictures. They ask me what's going on. All the stage guys, all the sound guys—it's kind of crazy. I don't know how this all happened, but these are my friends, and it's really quite wonderful.

FG: You've anticipated where I wanted to go next. Can you tell me more about the Sunshine Theater, and it being a kind of home for you? What's unique about the experience of photographing in Albuquerque—the type of audiences it draws and the dynamic in the crowd? It's not Brooklyn.

DS: It's not, and not many people have ever seen hip-hop shows and crowds that are not filled with black people. There's not a large black population in New Mexico. Thomas, from the Sunshine Theater, has shown a remarkable commitment to the youth of New Mexico through his TooZany and his ZanyLyfe initiatives. Rather than the youth of Albuquerque having or maintaining gang associations, Thomas has created a ZanyLyfe association for youth of all races, backgrounds, and classes to rally around. He has created numerous opportunities for the youth to meet performing artists and to attend shows for free, and has basically made the Sunshine Theater and a few other venues throughout New Mexico safe havens for all these hip-hop kids. In terms of the hip-hop community, it's primarily—like the population itself—Anglo, Hispanic, and Native American. The Sunshine Theater is made up of the youth of Albuquerque, yet, traditionally, hip-hop music and culture have been driven by the black community with its roots in the South Bronx. Hip hop has often shed light on adverse conditions that affect certain ethnic groups in this country. The music has given voice to the social and political issues and focuses on the ills and inconsistencies of our culture of these times—whether it addresses housing or social services or medical facilities or living conditions or jobs, or outright racism. The largest hip-hop demographic is in New York, Chicago, Atlanta, Detroit, Los Angeles, and Oakland. The music is principally about the black experience in these cities. However, of course there are large numbers of serious and extremely talented artists of all ethnicities. So, again, Albuquerque's kind of off that map, but it, too, has a serious core of artists and a consistent fan base.

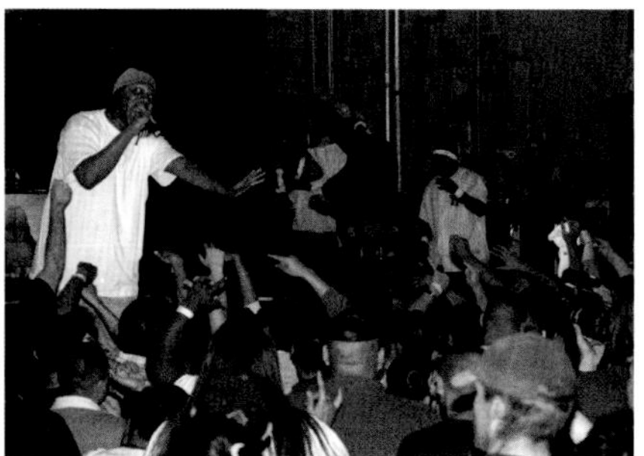

KRS-ONE, 2002

FG: That said, you have photographed in other venues, in big cities in California and elsewhere. What's different about photographing away from the Sunshine Theater? What is it like to work at a venue like Coachella, in which you've got a much larger audience and a more urban audience?

DS: In terms of the audience and the vibe around the music, these are all the same wherever I have photographed. I've photographed in New York and L.A., and I've photographed at the Coachella festival with tens of thousands of people. However, the real difference comes down to access. When I'm photographing outside of the

Sunshine Theater, no one knows who I am. It's harder to move around. It's harder to photograph. When I went to Coachella to photograph, I was one of probably a hundred other photographers, and we were restricted to this one area in front of the stage. Fortunately, I knew some of the artists who were performing, so I was able to get a slightly better vantage point from which to photograph. If I didn't have the support of Thomas and the TooZany crew in Albuquerque, I could not have done the work that I've done. I feel there is an intimacy, an immediacy to the pictures that I'm able to make there that I couldn't make when I was at a place like Coachella. There it's a very different experience, and it's no longer the type of personal work that I like to do. It's just taking pictures. Whereas, when I'm at the Sunshine I have that same feeling in my body as when I have my 8 x10 camera set up. I feel like it's my work. I'm doing it for me. I can think. I'm not under any pressure. I'm not under any time pressure. I can do whatever I want. And those are the conditions that I need for that creative impulse.

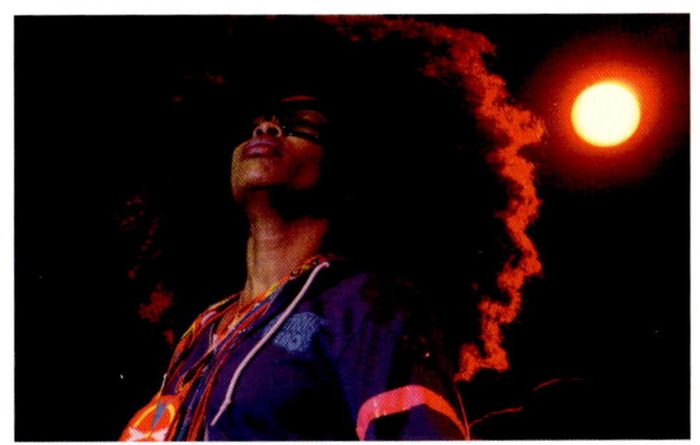

ERYKAH BADU, 2009

FG: Let's move on to the color work that you've recently completed. After the exhibition "RECOGNIZE! Hip Hop and Contemporary Portraiture" at the National Portrait Gallery in 2008, you began to work in color. What prompted this change, and what were your thoughts about the resulting pictures? Are you working exclusively in color now in terms of this series?

DS: The show we did together was a real highlight for me as an artist. It was an important opportunity not just for me as an artist but specifically for this work. These photographs are quite different from most of the other work that I've done and that I continue to do. I'm not known as a hip-hop photographer. The show motivated and empowered me. At the same time, after I came to Washington and I experienced the show, I returned home kind of in turmoil. I came back with more questions than I went with, and rather than feel more secure, I came back feeling that it wasn't right, or perhaps that it wasn't done. The biggest part of the experience in Washington was seeing Kehinde Wiley's work. I watched people walking into Kehinde's gallery with these giant, incredible paintings—the sheer size and the power and the color. Everyone in those rooms was animated. They were talking louder. They were laughing. There was an energy in those rooms. My work was different, and there was something that I had to acknowledge about size and color, something that I had avoided in my own work to date. I must admit that I come from a very conservative training. There's a great story that Beaumont used to tell. The students are looking at a group of mediocre color photographs, and the comment is made, "Well, if you can't make it good, make it red." The twenty-first-century version of that remark is: "If you can't make it good, make it big." The truth is that I've always avoided big, red things. I never wanted to fall into this notion that you had to rely on color or size. I was a straight black-and-white photographer. That's my training. The most precious, most beautiful photographic experiences that I've ever had have probably been viewing contact prints. Walker Evans's 35 mm contact prints or a Paul Strand 4 x 5 contact print or an Ansel Adams 8 x10 or an Edward Weston 8 x10—these are beautiful things. But then you go stand in front of a Kehinde Wiley painting, and it just put me in turmoil. There's an energy; there's a power there. So then you have to dissect that. Is it the subject matter? Is it the size? Is it the color? Is it the frame? Is it the room? The color of the walls? There were so many things happening that, even though I couldn't put my finger on it, I returned from the visit to Washington feeling that I needed to think this through.

FG: Did you have to teach yourself how to do color work? Was it rather intuitive or was it a process of learning what color might do in photographing musical performance?

DS: I've been photographing consciously since 1969, and I have never really photographed in color other than taking snapshots, family pictures. But I've also been a photography teacher and a gallerist for over thirty years. I've had access to some of the greatest photographers of the twentieth century, including most notably Eliot Porter. My wife, Janet Russek, was Eliot's assistant, and we had a very close relationship with him. I consider Eliot the father of color photography, and I had many opportunities to talk with him and hear his philosophies about color photography. So, though I had never worked in color, I wasn't totally ignorant of it. I was aware of it. Ansel Adams was known to say things like, "The most beautiful photograph is a black-and-white photograph in which you feel the color." Eliot thought that was ridiculous. He used color as I use tone. He was a master of subtlety in the way he worked with color, and the way he used color was the same way that I worked.

FG: Tell me a little bit more about the resulting pictures and what you're seeing that you like or that surprises you or that you feel is a good complement to the earlier black-and-white work.

DS: The black-and-white work is what I felt about hip hop when I started the project. It was what I felt I wanted my work to do, what I wanted it to say in terms of showing a positive image and getting a feel for the music. I feel those images have some of that angsty stuff and some of the speed, the movement, and the action. But here's the thing that I'm not certain about, but I think it's probably true: I think the color work actually shows it and says it all better. And in a way the color work is more accurate, and I'm not talking about in a documentary sense. Also, after making larger prints, bigger than I've ever made, I look at them and go, "This is what it looks like, and this is what it feels like." I can't say that there's more or less of me in it, but the color work seems to ring truer regarding the experience of being at the concert. Because of its size and color, it does get a lot more attention, whereas the black-and-white work seems to be truer to me internally.

FG: Because color is exuberant. It's noisy. It's raucous.

DS: Right. I believe it's going to bring the positive attention to the genre that I'm hoping for my work and show that hip hop is not only a serious and viable art form, but it's filled with joy and dedication and as much seriousness as other art forms. And it's not someone with a gun or knife in their hand. It's a very joyous experience.

FG: One last question around this idea of color. Could you comment on a specific photograph or two from the recent past that you feel best exemplifies the noise and raucousness that you like in this work?

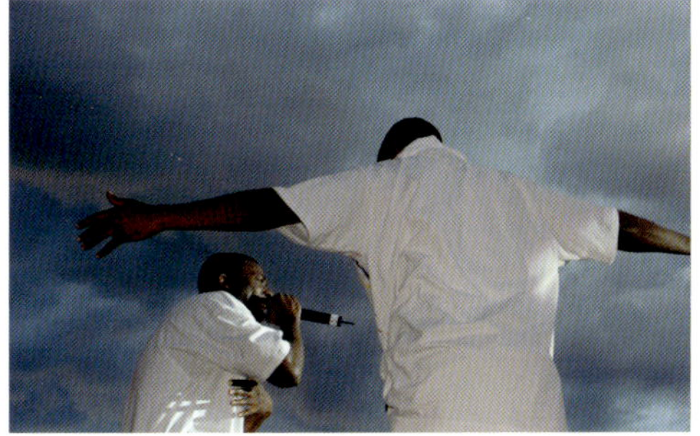

GZA (left) AND RZA (right), WU TANG CLAN, 2007

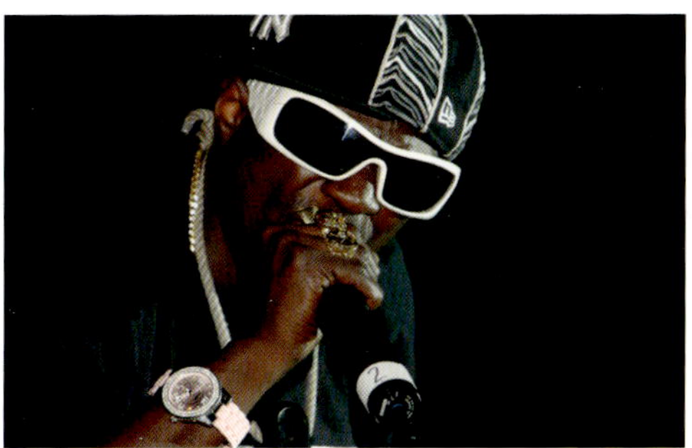

FLAVOR FLAV, PUBLIC ENEMY, 2007

DS: I have a couple favorite photographs. First, let me say that it's almost a joke here in New Mexico, but so many people write about why there are so many photographers in New Mexico. Everybody talks about the light and the clarity of the air at this altitude. I know that I'll look funny saying this, but there was an outdoor concert with the Wu Tang Clan here in Santa Fe several years ago. It was one of the earliest concerts that I shot in color, and I have to say that the light is so beautiful and so soft. And it's not just the photographs I love; it's the palette. At that same concert Public Enemy also performed, and I made a few images of Flavor Flav and Chuck D. These are images from that show that are especially dear to me. I can't believe I'm saying this, but a lot of it has to do with New Mexico and the light. Another image that I really like is of a young artist named Yelawolf. I shot it from backstage looking out, and it's basically this small figure against a field of red. It's almost like a Rothko red to me. Here I am, having just finished saying, "If you can't make it good ..." but that photograph really speaks to me. Again, it's the color that makes the picture work.

FG: Could you talk about how the series as a whole compares to other photographic projects in which you've been engaged. In some respects the hip-hop work might seem like a departure. Do you think of it in that way? Or does it relate squarely with your larger photographic career?

DS: In terms of subject matter, it's a departure, but I think every new project is a departure. But it's not a departure at all in terms of me and my relationship to photography. I've never been a photographer like Henri Cartier-Bresson who carries my camera around with me all the time. I've never been that kind of photographer. My work has always come from my personal experience. And it's never been driven by an assignment or a job. I can't be told what to photograph. One of the first major projects I did was photographing Miami Beach and the elderly Jewish community there. That whole book was about my grandfather and my relationship to my grandfather and the fact that it brought me to learning about old age and senior citizens and Judaism and immigration. It took me to areas that I never expected, but the bottom line is that it started because of my relationship with my grandfather. And when he passed away I accelerated the work because he made me aware of so many things going on for people his age. Then there's the Bisti project. I was very attracted to photographing the Bisti Badlands here in New Mexico. I didn't know anything about coal mining or conservation or outright environmental destruction. I started photographing there because I thought these formations were interesting. I didn't know where I was. I didn't know I was on the Navajo Reservation or anything about the BLM. So, again, the project brought me to many important issues. Regarding the I Ching book that I did with Janet I've been using the I Ching since I was sixteen years old. The second time I met Janet I gave her a copy and I taught her how to use it. The fact that we did a book on the I Ching is really about my relationship with Janet, and that whole project is really a visual diary. It's almost like a visual companion to our thirtieth anniversary. I mean that whole book is about our life together. But, of course, it's also about the I Ching. So my work needs to have that personal connection. For the most part, before I start photographing anything I already have an emotional attachment to the subject matter.

FG: So would you say that this particular series is about your relationship with your son?

DS: I have to say that. It started that way, and in a way continues to be that. And he's one of the few people I have my serious conversations about the work with. For the last twelve years he's been my main source for determining who to photograph. I try primarily to photograph people whom I consider positive artists, meaning artists who have a positive message for the youth of today. If someone's coming to Albuquerque, it was always Zac who I called. I think at this point I probably know more than he does. But certainly, for the beginning of the work, the first five or six years, Zac was my main decision maker about whom I should photograph. The work is very much about the relationship between a father and his son. Zac primarily, but also some of Zac's friends whom I'm still very close with. I can proudly say I'm close with most of them still. And they visit me. I visit them. They're the ones who want to see what I'm doing. They want to see the work, and in some cases they have seen more of the work than anyone else. Anyway, most things that I've ever done with my photography have come out of a direct, personal, emotional connection. And I have to say, when someone asks me to take a picture for them I always screw it up. Someone may ask, "Could you go and take a picture of my house?" I'm terrible at that. I can't ever succeed when I'm photographing for someone else.

ACKNOWLEDGMENTS

I am proud to have made these photographs. From my first concert, the people I've met, concertgoers, venue managers, promoters, tour personnel, music executives, security, and the many artists I have photographed—I have found them all to be highly serious about their music, intelligent, and clear about the role of hip-hop music and culture in today's contemporary society. I have also found that most of the artists are acutely aware of their position as role models to the youth of today, and they take that role and use that platform both ethically and with all seriousness in helping to bring about social responsibility and change while giving voice to the ills and inconsistencies in our contemporary society.

Many people have helped me produce this body of work. My mentors, Zac Scheinbaum and a number of his friends—Michael Rea, Adam Koroghlian, Sam Mauldin, Dylan Currie, Eric Wulc—to name a few, and to their first hip-hop dance and music teacher, Mark Fisher, who introduced them to break dancing and the early roots and history of hip-hop music and culture that was first fertilized in the South Bronx. Robert Dean of the *Santa Fe New Mexican* and Julia Goldberg, formerly from the *Santa Fe Reporter,* assisted me with press credentials early on to help me gain access to shows. Thomas and his Toozany crew from Albuquerque and the Sunshine Theater and staff who welcomed me and made this work possible in so many ways. There is no doubt that without their help and support along the way I could not have made these photographs. Tom Sarig, former record executive, made numerous introductions for me, and Damian (Domino) Siguenza from the Hieroglyphics crew assisted me in gaining access to all the Hiero artists, who welcomed me in Oakland and to their many shows over the years. To Bukue One for his friendship and support, and to Kattie Schad and DJ Johnny Juice for their help as well. Three former students from the College of Santa Fe—Robby Terry, August Thurmer, and Ryan Flannery—assisted me in the first exhibition of this work and the production of a video about my process. I also acknowledge Ryan for offering me a title for this work—*Portraits of an Urban Hymn*.

I have never been interested in "just" picture books. Thanks to my photographic mentor, the late Beaumont Newhall, and the work of his wife, the late Nancy Newhall, for building my appreciation and for having created volumes where text and images work together in ways that allow each to stand on its own but together both are elevated. My appreciation for their works continues to grow daily. My deepest thanks are to the authors of this volume—Frank H. Goodyear III, Brian Hardgroove, Gay Theresa Johnson, and Michael Eric Dyson. Their words and scholarship helped make this volume into the book I had envisioned from the very beginning. My wish was to produce a book that would contribute to the understanding of hip-hop music and culture in a positive way. So much misinformation and negativity in the media has been inked. My photographs can give a glimpse into the look and feel of the music and musicians, but it is their inspired words that give substance to the subject and I hope will aid in the understanding of the genesis of this musical genre and cultural phenomenon.

My thanks also go out to Joanna Hurley of Hurley Media, who helped place this work; to Mary Wachs, who perceptively edited the words; and to David Skolkin for his genius with the book design and his continued friendship, and to all my new acquaintances at Damiani Publishers for believing in this work.

Finally, to all the artists who generously allowed me to photograph and tolerated my presence on their stage.

ABOUT THE CONTRIBUTORS

David Scheinbaum is professor emeritus, College of Santa Fe, and former director of photography/artist in residence at the Santa Fe University of Art and Design. With his wife, photographer Janet Russek, he operates Scheinbaum & Russek Ltd., private fine-art photography dealers and consultants in Santa Fe, New Mexico. Scheinbaum has exhibited internationally and is represented in many museum collections. His previous books include *Bisti* (1985); *Miami Beach: Photographs of an American Dream* (1990); *Ghost Ranch: Land of Light* (with Janet Russek,1997); *Images in the Heavens, Patterns on the Earth: The I Ching* (with Janet Russek, 2005); and *Stone: A Substantial Witness* (2006).

Michael Eric Dyson is a writer, scholar, and ordained Baptist minister. Hailed by *Ebony* as one of the hundred most influential black Americans, he is the author of sixteen books, including *Know What I Mean? Reflections on Hip Hop* (2010); *Holler If You Hear Me: Searching for Tupac Shakur* (2006); *Is Bill Cosby Right?* (2005); *Why I Love Black Women* (2004); and *Between God and Gangsta Rap* (1997).

Frank H. Goodyear III is co-director of Bowdoin College Museum of Art and a former curator of photographs at the Smithsonian's National Portrait Gallery. He has written extensively about the history of photography. His books include *Faces of the Frontier: Photographic Portraits from the American West, 1845–1924* (2009); *Zaida Ben-Yusuf: New York Portrait Photographers* (2008); and *Red Cloud: Photographs of a Lakota Chief* (2003).

Brian Hardgroove is a record producer, bassist, radio personality, and member of the legendary hip-hop group Public Enemy.

Gaye Theresa Johnson, PhD, is a mother, a partner, an activist, and an academic. She is associate professor of Black Studies with affiliations in the departments of History and Chicana/o Studies at the University of California at Santa Barbara. Her new book, Spaces of Conflict, Sounds of Solidarity: Music, Race, and Spatial Entitlement in Los Angeles (2013), is a history of civil rights and spatial struggles among black and brown freedom seekers and cultural workers in L.A. She is working on a radical history of women in hip hop.

Portraits of an Urban Hymn

HIP HOP

Photographs

DAVID SCHEINBAUM

Editor: Mary Wachs

Design: David Skolkin

DAMIANI

Damiani

via Zanardi, 376

40131 Bologna, Italy

t. +39 051 63 56 811

f. +39 051 63 47 188

info@damianieditore.com

www.damianieditore.com

Printed in May 2013 by Grafiche Damiani, Italy.

ISBN 978-88-6208-273-0

PAGE 1: SLUG, ATMOSPHERE, 2009

PAGE 2: FLAVOR FLAV, PUBLIC ENEMY, 2007